D0365053

Information and Investment

A Study in the Working of the
Competitive Economy

Information and Investment

A Study in the Working of the
Competitive Economy

G. B. RICHARDSON
Warden of Keble College, Oxford

with a new Foreword by David J. Teece,
a new introduction, and two new chapters

CLARENDON PRESS · OXFORD

1990

SETON HALL UNIVERSITY
McLAUGHLIN LIBRARY
SO. ORANGE, N. J.

Oxford University Press, Walton Street, Oxford OX2 6DP

Oxford New York Toronto
Delhi Bombay Calcutta Madras Karachi
Petaling Jaya Singapore Hong Kong Tokyo
Nairobi Dar es Salaam Cape Town
Melbourne Auckland

and associated companies in
Berlin Ibadan

Oxford is a trade mark of Oxford University Press

Published in the United States
by Oxford University Press, New York

© G. B. Richardson 1990

All rights reserved. No part of this publication may be reproduced,
stored in a retrieval system, or transmitted, in any form or by any means,
electronic, mechanical, photocopying, recording, or otherwise, without
the prior permission of Oxford University Press

This book is sold subject to the condition that it shall not, by way
of trade or otherwise, be lent, re-sold, hired out or otherwise circulated
without the publisher's prior consent in any form of binding or cover
other than that in which it is published and without a similar condition
including this condition being imposed on the subsequent purchaser

British Library Cataloguing in Publication Data
Richardson, G. B.
Information and investment : a study in the working of the
competitive economy / G. B. Richardson : with a new foreword by
Donald Teece, a new introduction, and two new chapters. —— 2nd ed.
p cm.
Includes bibliographical references and index.
1. Competition. 2. Investments. 3. Uncertainty. 4. Equilibrium
(Economics) 5. Prices. 6. Capitalism. I. Title
HD41.R5 1990   332.6'01——dc20   90–7882
ISBN 0–19–828728–3

Library of Congress Cataloging in Publication Data
Data available
ISBN 0–19–828728–3

Typeset by Latimer Trend & Co Limited,
Plymouth, Devon

Printed and bound in Great Britain by
Biddles Ltd, Guildford and King's Lynn

FOREWORD
TO THE SECOND EDITION
by David J. Teece

FOR an author, the republication of any book is usually a time for celebration, for it is an endorsement by readers that the treatise is of enduring value. Such is the case with the republication of George Richardson's *Information and Investment: A Study in the Working of the Competitive Economy*. The enduring virtues of Richardson's treatise, it seems to me, stem in part from the fact that three decades ago it tackled some fundamental intellectual issues in economic science; in particular, how efficient co-ordination occurs in a market economy, and why it cannot occur in the competitive model presented in most textbooks. Economists generally impute the co-ordination function to the price mechanism; they are usually remarkably silent on the mechanics of how this actually takes place. Artificial mechanisms, such as Walrasian *tâtonnement*, have been invented to solve the theoretical problem. Such mechanisms, however satisfying in terms of their theoretical elegance, are at odds with what actually takes place and do not work at all well, especially once irreversible investments enter the picture. Richardson struggles with how co-ordination can be effectuated in such instances. His treatment is iconoclastic and insightful.

In exploring the limitations of the perfectly competitive model, Richardson helped to lay the groundwork for subsequent work on the economics of internal organization, particularly vertical integration.[1] A related literature on organizing for innovation and strategic alliances[2] also benefited from Richard-

---

[1] See O. E. Williamson, *Markets and Hierarchies* (New York, 1975); and O. E. Williamson, *The Economic Institutions of Capitalism* (New York, 1985), Ch. 6.

[2] See D. J. Teece, 'Economics of Scope and the Scope of Enterprise', *Journal of Economic Behavior and Organization*, Vol. 1, No. 3 (1980), pp. 223–47; and D. J. Teece, 'Profiting from Technological Innovation', *Research Policy*, Vol. 15, No. 6 (1986), pp. 286–305.

son's analysis of the need to co-ordinate complementary investments, and the inadequacy of national planning as a mechanism
to accomplish this task efficiently.

It is one thing to explain how a book, now over three decades
old, has influenced subsequent work. But that alone often is not
enough to justify reading it—except perhaps for students of the
history of economic thought. George Richardson has much to
offer which is still worth reading, as I will now attempt to
explain through a selective review. *Information and Investment*
is particularly relevant as Eastern European economies contem-
plate the adoption of market systems, and as the exemplary
performance of the Japanese economy triggers a deeper assessment of how economic structure affects performance. Traditional textbook treatments of market economies provide no blueprint of the institutional or market arrangements necessary for
efficient resource allocation. Richardson's work provides some
helpful insights.

Richardson is interested in the informational requirements
for competitive equilibrium. To generate equilibrium, economic theory assumes that the belief structures of consumers
and producers are given; but in Richardson's world this begs the
question, as typically no account is offered of the information
upon which beliefs are built. Nor is there any proof offered that
the necessary information would, under the conditions which
define the model, be available. Richardson points out that this
casts serious doubt on whether a general equilibrium of prices
and quantities, even if attained, would in fact persist. Far less
does it entitle one to claim that, under perfect competition,
prices and outputs would actually tend to their equilibrium
values. We have here Edgeworth's confession that, although
economists can describe the equilibrium position of a hypo-
thetically perfectly competitive economy, we are almost completely unable to describe the path to equilibrium. As Richardson points out, 'It is difficult to see what but an act of faith can
enable us to believe that equilibrium would in fact be reached in
perfect competition.' Unfortunately, this is as true today as
when Richardson was writing.[1] And, as has been observed

---

[1] The fact that there is considerable order and stability in the real world
should not, as Richardson points out, give us faith that the perfectly competitive
model in fact applies. 'Presumably it is the existence of a considerable measure

elsewhere,[1] this leads to a kind of sterility in the economic theory of markets which can lead to false policy and managerial prescriptions. In short, the framework of perfectly competitive markets, stripped of institutional detail, is hardly the stuff we want to teach our students if we expect them to be well equipped for managerial or policy decision-making.[2] That is the message Richardson appears to convey.

Many of these points had been made previously by Alfred Marshall.[3] Richardson's distinctive contribution is to look at the long run and to the adjustment of an industry's capital stock. In standard as well as advanced treatments of the perfectly competitive model, no explanation is given of how entrepreneurs can obtain the information on which their expectations, and therefore the investment plans required for equilibrium, would have to be based. Existing treatments, Richardson claims, fail to show how the necessary information basis for such activities can be presumed to exist.[4]

of order and stability in the real economic world around us that engenders faith that equilibrium can in fact be realized, but here it is most important to realize that the conditions of the real world are not those of perfect competition and that, if they were, it might no longer be possible for this order to be produced' (p. 12).

[1] See D. J. Teece and S. Winter, 'The Limits of Neoclassical Theory in Management Education', *American Economic Review*, Vol. 74, No. 2 (May 1984), pp. 116–21.

[2] Lest anyone consider this to be a vacant concern, readers could be reminded of major third-party antitrust litigation in the United States during the 1970s and 1980s. The so-called *Long Beach* cases, which alleged monoposonization of crude oil prices on the Western United States rested in part on the allegation that departures of crude oil posted prices from computed estimates of equilibrium values was evidence of monoposonization. Setting aside for the moment whether estimates of equilibrium prices were in fact computed correctly, it is indeed remarkable that plaintiffs would believe that a court of law would have such faith in the economic theory of perfect competition to award liability and damages on such a highly stylized view of real-world market behaviour.

[3] As Richardson points out (p. 15), Marshall (*Principles of Economics*, London, 1961, 9th ed.) stressed that 'every plain and simple doctrine as to the relations between cost of production, demand and value is necessarily false; and the greater the appearance of lucidity which is given to it by skilful exposition, the more mischievous it is'.

[4] '. . . modern theory about the attainment of equilibrium can, for the most part, properly be called mechanical; in general, it merely presumes the existence of functional relationships between different variables in the system and then

Richardson's analysis is unquestionably still relevant, but what light does he shed on the theory of economic adjustment? He begins in Chapter II by pointing out that the profitability of investment projects depends on the implementation of others. He terms investments 'complementary' when the profitability of one is increased by the carrying out of the other. Investments are 'competitive' when the profitability of one of them will be reduced by the implementation of another. And price movements, by themselves, do not form an adequate system of signalling for either competitive or complementary investments. Indeed, Richardson argues that some form of market imperfection is essential to the process of economic adjustment. He suggests that, in practice, the closest approximation to the so-called equilibrium associated with perfect competition 'is likely to be reached by arrangements in which both competition and deliberate co-ordination—whether public or private—play some part' (p. 45). In this, Richardson was ahead of his time in helping to make the case that co-operation, even among competitors, can invigorate competition.[1]

How then do firms get to know about the *competitive* investment plans of others? This is the topic of Chapter III. One way is through what Richardson calls 'implicit collusion'. Each producer persists in his particular activities, provided others can be presumed to do likewise. This might maintain a pre-existing equilibrium, but it would never produce one in the first place. In reality, first-mover advantages, which could depend on the ignorance of competitors (p. 57), assist in the adjustment of supply to demand; the presence of a temporary monopoly on information might be another. Still a third factor is the limi-

---

proceeds to work out the consequences. The considerable technical virtuosity in many of the demonstrations of this kind, and the scientific character with which the mathematical apparatus used may appear to invest them, should not hide from us the fact that they nevertheless offer no adequate answer to the key problem with which we are concerned, that of the way in which it would be possible, under the conditions of perfect competition, for the equilibrium configuration actually to be brought about' (p. 24).

[1] T. M. Jorde and D. J. Teece, 'Innovation, Cooperation, and Antitrust', *High Technology Law Journal*, Vol. 4, No. 1 (Spring 1989), pp. 1–113.

tations on firm capabilities; not all firms are in a position to expand, even if by some objective test it might appear desirable to do so.

Needless to say, many of these factors are inconsistent with perfect competition. (The gathering of market intelligence is obviously a critical factor, but it hardly, in any real sense, creates an 'imperfection' in the market.) Indeed, such activities enable markets to work. In this regard, Richardson points out, restrictive practices, often viewed suspiciously by the antitrust authorities, particularly if they are horizontal, are likely to be necessary to make a competitive market work.

Chapter IV examines the co-ordination of *complementary* investments. If the penalties on unilateral investments are heavy, no one will invest on the presumption that others will follow. Moreover, because of 'imperfections in technical information'—such as the fact that consumers are unable to accurately estimate their own future demand—firms are reluctant to enter into contractual arrangements. This uncertainty can be strengthened by lack of confidence on the part of one or both sides of the contract that the other will in fact be able to live up to its terms. In these arguments, Richardson anticipated and fuelled the vertical-integration literature spawned by Williamson's pioneering essays on this topic. Indeed, Richardson saw vertical integration as an important device for gaining the requisite control, particularly if markets are not well developed. In less-developed countries 'more deliberate planning' may be needed. Richardson also recognizes that the information problem exists in a centrally planned economy (pp. 86–7).

Half-way through the book, Richardson switches attention to two other requirements for the effective operation of a competitive system: efficient selection and market discipline (the need for rents to be temporary). Richardson thus sees an efficient competitive system as requiring that investments be both secure (to encourage them) and vulnerable (to weed out the inefficient). Price-fixing agreements accomplish neither, at least *prima facie*. 'Deliberate co-ordination' (p. 137) helps the former.

In the third part of the book, Richardson examines ways in which businessmen seek to increase the information at their disposal, and in particular how firms adapt their investment programmes to new information and changing circumstances. Once the businessman commits himself to a particular investment programme, 'the boundless sea of possibility which had lain before him is replaced by certain particular lanes along which he will, for a time, be obliged to proceed' (p. 151). Adaptability can be maintained through cash reserves and through investing in general-purpose rather than special-purpose machinery.

The final chapter assesses the viability of consolidation and public ownership. Imperfections in knowledge, according to Richardson, both initiate the movement to consolidation and halt its progress (p. 209). Richardson's balanced approach to this seems to anticipate both the need to displace markets with internal organization—in this sense his treatment is Coasean, though without apparent awareness of Coase's famous 1937 article on the nature of the firm.[1] But it also anticipates subsequent disenchantment with the conglomerate form for almost exactly the same reasons advanced by Dosi, Teece, and Winter[2]—the bounded rationality of managers (p. 210). Decentralization is thus virtuous. Planned co-ordination of investment activities may be necessary in some instances and not in others. 'We can hope to find which arrangements are optimal only by taking account continuously of different circumstances and by weighing up different requirements' (p. 222).

Information and Investment thus anticipates what is now a very large literature on transaction costs and the economics of internal organization and the treatise is still relevant to economic theorists as well as to men of affairs—be they managers or policy-makers. There are rich rewards here for those whose minds are not already shuttered by conventional theorizing about market economies. Read on.

                                                              D.J.T.

[1] See R. Coase, 'The Nature of the Firm', *Economica*, Vol. 4 (1937), pp. 386–405.
[2] G. Dosi, D. J. Teece, and S. Winter, 'Toward a Theory of Corporate Coherence: Preliminary Remarks', University of California at Berkeley, 1990.

CONTENTS

PREFACE

THE ideas which I endeavour to present in this book took root in my mind at an early stage of my study of economics. Even as an undergraduate, I felt a certain uneasiness as a result of realizing that, although economists were confident that they could identify equilibrium positions of the economic system, they appeared unable to offer wholly convincing accounts of how these positions might in practice be attained. Sometimes these accounts were impressionistic, referring in rather general terms to the 'forces' set up by the divergence of demand and supply; sometimes they took the form of mechanistic models based on highly unplausible assumptions about business behaviour. As I became more accustomed to the methods and procedures of economic theory, these doubts, for a time, were forgotten, but they came to life again when I went on to study the way in which business expectations were dealt with in our formal analysis.

It is easy to see that any satisfactory explanation of the attainment of equilibrium positions has to be grounded on some theory of the formation of entrepreneurial expectations. If economic adjustments are to be brought about by the investment decisions of particular entrepreneurs, then we should be able to show how these entrepreneurs come to have the information and incentives appropriate to the decisions required of them; the attainment of equilibrium is a process in time consisting of actions taken on the basis of beliefs about future conditions. Much of economic theory attempts to dispense with the need for a theory of the formation of expectations by simply postulating the existence of 'perfect knowledge'. This, of course, is merely an evasion, quite apart from the fact that the concept of 'perfect knowledge', particularly when attributed to members of an interdependent group, is usually given little, if any, definite meaning. An alternative approach is to concentrate on expectations of prices, and to assume that these are made by some simple projection of current or past values. An hypothesis of this kind, however, despite any partial validity, can be shown to be an inadequate substitute for a working theory of expectations.

The conventional ways in which we introduce expectations into economic theory seem to me to have this crucial deficiency; they ignore the fact that expectations are based on information, and that the availability to entrepreneurs of the required information is, in part, dependent upon the nature of the market structure or system of relationships within which they operate. The particular part of the required information so dependent is that which relates to actions of others in the economy, whether individually or in mass; this I have chosen to call market information. In the earlier chapters of the book, therefore, I have endeavoured to decide upon the kind of information which entrepreneurs would need and to assess how different market forms would affect the supply of it. This discussion, I should hope, may cast some light on two aspects of economic adjustment. The first of these concerns the rôle played by market imperfections; the second relates to the conditions under which deliberate co-ordination, or planning has to supplement or replace purely decentralized activity.

In the final part of the book I endeavour to draw out some of the implications of the fact that the information on which expectations have to be based is both incomplete and dispersed among many different minds. It is surely not enough to recognize that business expectations are uncertain; if we are to understand the working of an economic system, it is necessary to take account of the fact that expectations about particular economic circumstances may be capable of formation only by a limited number of people and that these expectations may be divergent.

The arguments which I advance are essentially theoretical, in that their purpose is to suggest particular categories of thought which may be of assistance in the analysis of the working of a modern competitive economy. No new facts about actual economic affairs are presented, and those facts which are adduced are of a general, and very familiar kind. Nevertheless, I have constantly borne in mind that the function of theoretical construction is to help us to understand the world which we live in, and I have been at pains to bring this construction into closer touch with the broad realities of which we are all aware. The elaboration of an appropriate conceptual framework, however, is no more than a first step in the exploration of actuality and should require progressive revision as our knowledge and experience grows.

My indebtedness to other writers is too considerable and too diffused for me to be able to list those whose ideas I have taken over. Mr. D. K. Stout and Mr. N. H. Leyland were kind enough to read large parts of my manuscript and to make most useful comments. I am particularly grateful to Professor J. R. Hicks, who read the whole book in both its present, and in an earlier, form; he gave me very valuable advice, but my debt to him extends beyond this to all the help and encouragement which he has so generously given me since my undergraduate days. For the views I put forward, and, more particularly, for the errors and confusions they embody, I take full responsibility. I am obliged to the Rockefeller Foundation for enabling me to have a year in America free from teaching obligations and to indulge in stimulating conversation with colleagues at Harvard and at the University of California at Berkeley. Finally, I wish to thank my wife for undertaking the unrewarding task of typing, and re-typing, much of the manuscript.

Oxford

May, 1960   G.B.R.

INTRODUCTION
TO THE SECOND EDITION

Information and Investment was published thirty years ago, the ideas behind it having developed in my mind over a period of several years before then. I had persuaded myself that I had something new and important to say, my aim being to present an account of how a free enterprise economy worked under realistic assumptions about the knowledge available to those within it. I believed that I had exposed radical flaws in the accepted model of how competition allocated resources and put something in its place that was both logically coherent and in accordance with the plain facts of economic life. I had wanted to call the book *The Economics of Imperfect Knowledge*, as it represented a sustained attempt to explain the processes of resource allocation as based on the actions of producers and consumers, whose knowledge of the relevant circumstances is necessarily limited and uncertain. The publisher, however, would not accept this title and, reluctantly, I chose *Information and Investment* instead. As the book was, as a result, often catalogued under the heading of the Stock Exchange, this was a mistake.

In any event, and to my disappointment, the book made little impact. Its arguments were not rejected, but simply ignored. I learned, the hard way, that it is difficult to get a hearing for new ideas, the more so when asking for the abandonment of old ideas long established, in constant use, and apparently fundamental to a large part of accepted doctrine. Gradually, however, greater interest developed in what I had to say, partly as a result of more explicit treatment within economics of the notion of information and partly through attention being drawn to my work by a few economists, most notably Professor Loasby. Oxford University Press had by then started to receive requests to reprint *Information and Investment*, which had been unobtainable for many years, by which time I had given up economics to become chief executive of that publishing house. Only after I had retired from OUP were the decisions taken to reprint the book and to invite me to write a new introduction.

During the thirty years that have elapsed since the writing of the book I have been engaged in 'applied economics' of one kind or another. For half the period, while continuing to do academic work, I acted as consultant to a number of business concerns and held public appointments which brought me into close contact with manufacturing industry. Half-way through the period I abandoned my academic career to become head of an international publishing concern. But although I came to be interested in business as a result of my work on *Information and Investment*, I was stimulated to write the book itself not by my experience of the realities of industrial organization, which was at that time slight, but by doubts about the logical coherence of the theory that I had been taught and was then teaching. Given perfect competition in the market for a good, so the theory went, the price and output of that good would tend to equilibrium levels with price equal to marginal and unit costs of production. And this was often explained, in the textbooks, by means of demand and supply curves, the intersection of which represented, rather compellingly, the equilibrium price–output combination. The point was made, of course, that things did not always happen this way in the real world, but then that world, alas, was not perfectly competitive.

Already as a student I was struck by the fact that the textbooks offered only impressionistic accounts of how equilibrium would be reached, and I tried, but failed, to make these more rigorous. I learned later than my failure was not very surprising. When Mr. J. R. Hicks (as he then was) became my tutor in my final undergraduate year, he used to ask me to read not, as was usual, the latest journal articles, but the writings of those responsible for the development of whatever part of the subject was to be dealt with in my weekly essay. So I read Walras and Edgeworth, Menger and Marshall. And from doing so it became apparent that the founders of formal equilibrium theory were well aware of the difficulties of explaining the path to equilibrium, difficulties that were subsequently pushed rather more into the background. It was several years later that I convinced myself that, with the market structure postulated, a tendency to equilibrium was not only undemonstrable, but could be proved not to exist.

On the face of it, one might have expected those who developed the theory to ask themselves whether difficulty in identifying a plausible path or process to equilibrium was not attributable to the nature of the market structure—perfect competition—that was being assumed, and to ask themselves further what alternative market structure might be consistent with decision-taking such as could produce the efficient adaptation of supply to demand. Perhaps they were influenced by the consideration that the real world was reasonably competitive and did show a reasonable degree of allocative order, thus implying that the invisible hand must work in one way or another. And the fact that monopoly and the restraint of trade could sometimes impede the proper adjustment of supply to demand would have led many to think that with more competition the real world would work even better and with perfect competition best of all.

Looking back on it all, one can surely be astonished by the boldness of the idea that the working of free markets could be represented in a model created by *a priori* reasoning from elementary assumptions about human behaviour. The parallel with Newtonian mechanics, with the principle of self-interest standing for gravitational force, is of course obvious. Walras himself is quite explicit when he remarks, 'The law of supply and demand regulates all these exchanges of commodities just as the law of universal gravitation regulates the movements of all celestial bodies. Thus the system of the economic universe reveals itself, at last, in all its grandeur and complexity; a system at once vast and simple, which, for sheer beauty, resembles the astronomic universe.'[1] But the claims of perfect competition theory exceed, in an important respect, even those of Newtonian mechanics, in that it purports to provide both a first approximation of the working of free markets and an ideal or yardstick by which to judge their efficiency. The model, of course, came in

[1] L. Walras, *Elements of Pure Economics*, trans. and ed. W. Jaffé (London, 1954), p. 374.

with the 'marginal revolution' of the latter part of the nineteenth century, when economists came to believe, in Hicks's words, that 'It was possible . . . to construct a "vision" of economic life out of the theory of exchange.'[1] Schumpeter considered Walras, as far as pure theory was concerned, to be 'the greatest of all economists' and claimed that his system 'is the only work by an economist which will stand comparison with the achievements of theoretical physics'.[2] Certainly, one can admire the grandeur of the conception, even if one does not share Walras's belief that during the twentieth century mathematical economics would come to 'rank with the mathematical sciences of astronomy and mechanics'.[3] And, as I argue in this book, one can also appreciate the central importance of the general equilibrium configuration in the theory of optimal resource allocation. But one may also ask oneself whether, in the endeavour to penetrate the secrets of what used to be called 'the natural economic order', to understand how free economies can actually work, a greater degree of caution and humility would have been misplaced.

H. G. Wells once said that economics was a branch of ecology, and, however unsatisfactory this may be as classification, the statement does help to remind us that natural order is to be found not only in economic life. I suspect that we are now more conscious than formerly of the complexity and subtlety of natural ecosystems, partly as a result of having done things which offered immediate advantage without realizing the indirect effects that would result in the long run. We would now be more inclined than formerly, for example, to assume that features of an ecosystem which we do not understand might nevertheless have some positive purpose. And I doubt if we would construct by deduction from a few premises simple models with which both to represent and to judge the efficiency of actual systems. We would rather try patiently to find out how actual systems in fact work.

Professor Kornai has made a similar point in his article 'The Health of Nations: Reflections on the Analogy between the

---

[1] J. R. Hicks, 'The Scope and Status of Welfare Economics', *Oxford Economic Papers*, Vol. 27 (1975), p. 322.

[2] Joseph A. Schumpeter, *History of Economic Analysis* (???????, 19   ), p. 827.

[3] Walras, *Elements of Pure Economics*, p. 48.

Medical Sciences and Economics'.[4] No one would dream of deducing from a few elementary assumptions a model of how the body works or should work. 'The human body is such as it is,' writes Kornai, 'and we have to set out from this fact and not from some phantasm of perfection.' 'The human organism', as he puts it, 'is a marvellous machine but it is far from perfect.' And something of the same can be said of the natural economic order. But, just as the body can be sick, the economy can malfunction. Economists then, like doctors, must offer help conscious of the limits of their knowledge, cautiously and with circumspection.

I do not believe that it makes more sense to offer a blueprint for a perfect economic organization than it does to prescribe the ideal form for the state. But it would seem likely on the face of it that in any effective organization both competition and co-operation would feature, as they in fact feature in all the working human and animal societies known to us. *Information and Investment* is in fact largely devoted to explaining the indispensable roles of both forms of behaviour, but the perfect competition model represents competition alone as promoting optimal allocation, and co-operation between firms appears by implication as dysfunctional.

By far the greater part of *Information and Investment* is constructive, in that it is given up to an attempt to build a theory able to explain how resource allocation in a free economy actually comes about. It was perhaps, therefore, unfortunate that the first two chapters were concerned exclusively with refuting the claims of the perfect competition model. Perhaps the reader was put off by the laboriousness of the criticism of something he did not in any case take very seriously. But I had thought that, without very thorough and painstaking considera-tion, the reader would be unlikely to be persuaded to give up a theory that had held, over the mind of the profession for almost a century, such a strong grip. Indeed, with the development of mathematical economics, this grip may even have become stronger. Writing in 1984, Professor Hahn was able to say of the Arrow–Debreu revision of general equilibrium theory, which

---

[4] *Kyklos*, Vol. 36 (1983), pp. 191–212.

assumes a perfectly competitive market structure, that it was a
'bench mark. By this I mean that it serves a function similar to
that which an ideal and perfectly healthy body might serve a
clinical diagnostician when he looks at an actual body.'[1] And any
doubt that a perfectly competitive market structure is still seen
as an ideal is dispelled by a further quotation from the same
author: 'When the claim is made—and the claim is as old as
Adam Smith—that a myriad of self-seeking agents left to
themselves will lead to a coherent and efficient distribution of
economic resources, Arrow and Debreu show what the world
would have to look like if the claim is to be true.'[2]

My first task in *Information and Investment* was to refute
argument of this kind, and, in the course of doing so, draw
attention to the way in which market structure affects the
availability of information to those who take decisions and
thereby determines the possibility and the mode of economic
adjustment. The rest of the book, and by far the greater part of
it, is about how competitive economies actually work. First, I
deal with the co-ordination of competitive investments, where
the crucial role of so-called imperfections is displayed. After
then considering how complementary investments are matched,
I turn to the way in which different processes of adjustment
affect the efficiency of production, particularly as regards the
employment of optimal techniques. Our standard theoretical
apparatus leads us to try to judge efficiency in this sense by
considering supposed equilibrium situations, but it seems to me
that the process of adjustment is much more relevant. I then go
on to consider what modifications must be made to the analysis
previously presented in consequence of admitting that economic adjustment is not a question of producing a fixed list of
goods in the right proportions, but in producing also the right
kinds of goods—in filling up uncharted economic space.

The remainder of the book is devoted to four main topics. I
consider the selective and disciplinary functions of competition,

---

[1] F. H. Hahn, *Equilibrium and Microeconomics* (Oxford, 1984), p. 308.

[2] F. H. Hahn, *Economica*, Vol. XL, pp. 322–30. For an excellent discussion of
Professor Hahn's views (and my own) see Brian J. Loasby, *The Mind and
Method of the Economist*, Ch. 8. I find myself very much in sympathy with
Professor Loasby's approach and conclusions.

how the process, that is to say, permits the differential expansion of the more efficient enterprises and prevents a misallocation of resources through the deliberate restriction of supply. I discuss how uncertainty affects business behaviour by requiring entrepreneurs to adopt flexible processes and plans, and, finally, I try to think through how the strategies and arrangements that exist to deal with imperfect information affect the correspondence between private profitability and public benefit. This leads me into a discussion of the capital market and of the merits of risk reduction through the consolidation of investments. In the text I refer to those by whose ideas I was influenced, but for the most part throughout all this analysis I felt rather on my own. What I had to say has been generally ignored, perhaps because it was not worth saying, but perhaps because the issues discussed, although intrinsically important, have been themselves neglected or rather put out of focus by the competitive equilibrium analysis that has for so long shaped our perceptions.

It remains to ponder, thirty years on, whether the issues to which I devoted myself in writing *Information and Investment* are of any practical import. My concern at the time was with understanding rather than recommendation, with analysis rather than policy. Certainly the theory of equilibrium under perfectly competitive conditions is not very familiar to businessmen or administrators, most of whom would think the model so unrealistic, at least in so far as manufacturing is concerned, that they would hardly care whether or not it was logically coherent. I was myself writing as a professional economist for my colleagues, but in the back of my mind was the belief, which subsequent experience has confirmed, that my argument was relevant to the ways in which we seek to modify or regulate free enterprise economies and to the ways in which the price mechanism might be brought into operation within economies previously centrally planned.[1]

Both the perfect competition model and the notion of centrally planned allocation are constructions depending on *a priori*

---

[1] The latter issue concerned me rather more in my textbook *Economic Theory* (London, 1964).

reasoning from simple assumptions; both are plausible only because they evade the key question of the information on which decisions are based, and both carry with them the implication that resources could be allocated more efficiently than they are in practice. The discrepancy between perfect markets and those in the real world has led some to advocate vigorous antitrust policies and others to urge that 'monopoly capitalism' be abandoned in favour of state ownership and control. Unqualified belief in the effectiveness of markets, when purged of all imperfection, and unqualified belief in the power of central planning, though they may seem diametrically opposite, have much in common; they are founded on faith, they have radical practical implications, and they are uninfluenced by any careful consideration of how in fact the world goes round.

In my article 'The Organization of Industry', written in 1972 and reprinted in this volume, I discuss the complex patterns of co-operation, affiliation, and agreement that are found in free economies. When writing *Information and Investment* I was not fully aware of these, but the theory I put forward seems to me to explain how they come about and how they may further efficient economic adaptation. Without such a theory, which takes information explicitly into account, these phenomena appear as either irrelevant or injurious to the working of the economy. I am far from thinking that inter-firm agreement or co-operation may not impair rather than promote the public interest, but in order to decide the matter in any particular situation one needs to have a theoretical framework that accepts the uncertainty and dispersal of knowledge, rather than a model in which conditions that make possible the availability of necessary information feature as undesirable imperfections. The arguments I put forward in this connexion found favour with neither the political right, for whom the maximization of competition was dogma, nor the left, who preferred a conspiracy theory of inter-firm co-operation and sought a radical change in the *status quo*. They seemed to me to be quite useful, however, for the work I had to do on the British Monopolies Commission, where it was accepted that judgement could be made only on the basis of the circumstances of the case. In any event, the doctrine that all restraint of trade is undesirable *per se*, is perhaps no longer espoused unquestionably, even in the United States, where it has for so long held sway. The success of the Japanese economy, in which inter-firm co-operation. is widespread, may have persuaded some observers that stringent antitrust enforcement cannot at any rate be an indispensable condition for efficiency.[1]

Despite what I said earlier about the impossibility of drawing a blueprint of how a free economy should work, the socialist countries of Eastern Europe are nevertheless finding themselves obliged radically to rethink how their economies should be organized, the aim being to move closer towards the market system. And of course it may not be easy to design and create institutions that developed gradually and spontaneously under capitalism, were abolished in socialist countries several decades ago, and are now unfamiliar to the great majority of their populations. Although these issues were by no means to the forefront of my mind when writing *Information and Investment*, nevertheless the ideas in the book are relevant to them and certainly of more use in this connexion than the theory of perfect and imperfect markets which would be picked up from our standard textbooks. The second article reprinted in this volume, 'Planning versus Competition', does little more than touch on some of the issues but, as it represents an extension of the argument of the book, it seemed appropriate to pull it in. Economic theory has in the past from time to time received useful stimulus from important economic happenings, so we can hope that the momentous events in Eastern Europe will generate fresh and constructive interest in the matters which exercised my mind over thirty years ago.

Information and Investment was written partly while on sabbatical leave at the University of Berkeley, California. I look back on this very enjoyable period with gratitude for the kindness with which my wife and I were received. It is perhaps not unfitting that Professor David Teece of that great university

---

[1] See T. Jordan and D. J. Teece, *Competition and Cooperation: Striking the Right Balance* (repr. in *California Management Review*, Calif., 1989).

should have written a new preface to this book, relating it better than I could have done to subsequent literature. I am most grateful to him for so very generously agreeing to do so.

Keble College, Oxford 1990

PART I

THE THEORY OF PERFECT COMPETITION.

I

THE TENDENCY TO EQUILIBRIUM

1. IT is natural that the theory of perfect competition should be the starting point of our inquiry, as it represents the most celebrated attempt to reduce the working of the competitive economy to essentials. Its importance is twofold. As an instrument of analysis, it has held, for some time, a central position in positive economic theory; indeed, as a result of the ease with which it lends itself to mathematical formulation, this position may even, in recent decades, have become consolidated.[1] In addition, the prices and outputs associated with perfect competition, in its supposed equilibrium state, have a normative significance, in that they are consistent—subject to certain reservations—with the optimum conditions of production and exchange which were enunciated by Pareto; perfect competition can therefore be represented as an ideal with which actual competitive organization may be compared. The conditions which define it, as everyone knows, are rarely, if ever, characteristic of the real world, but it can be argued that this divergence represents no more than the normal degree of abstraction associated with general theoretical models. In this and the following chapter, I shall advocate the setting aside of the concept of perfect competition, both as an explanatory device and as an ideal, my aim being to demonstrate that, even as a hypothetical system, it has one quite fundamental flaw, the exposure of which will point the way in which constructive revision can most properly be made.

It may be helpful to assert the central principle of my argument baldly and dogmatically in advance, even although its significance will become clear only as the discussion proceeds. 'The general equilibrium of production and exchange', I shall

[1] Vide G. Stigler, 'Perfect Competition, Historically Contemplated', *Journal of Political Economy*, February, 1957. 'Today the concept of perfect competition is being used more widely by the profession in its theoretical work than at any time in the past. The vitality of the concept is strongly spoken for by this triumph.'

contend, cannot properly be regarded as a configuration towards which a hypothetical perfectly competitive economy would gravitate or at which it would remain at rest. In support of this, it will be pointed out that entrepreneurs could rationally decide upon the activities required of them only if possessed of a certain minimum amount of relevant information. The degree to which this information is available to them can be shown to depend, moreover, on the nature of the market or economic system within which they are presumed to operate. Perfect competition, I shall affirm, represents a system in which entrepreneurs would be unable to obtain the minimum necessary information; for this reason, it cannot serve as a model of the working of actual competitive economies.

But this is to anticipate. Let us first examine the claim on which the key importance of the perfect competition model must rest, the claim that it enables us to relate the objective conditions associated with an economic system to the pattern of activities which they would ultimately cause the system's individual members to adopt. Provided there exist, that is to say, the hypothetical conditions of market structure which define the model, prices and outputs are supposed to tend towards equilibrium values which are in principle deducible from certain initial determinants, as represented by the preferences of individuals, the endowment and original distribution of resources and the state of technique. We thus seem to be afforded an explanatory hypothesis of great scope and power, which, by bringing so great a variety of phenomena under its sway, gives to economic theory a unique position among the social sciences. In order to be able to scrutinize this claim, it will be convenient to consider first the meaning of the concept of economic equilibrium as such, and then, having done so, to focus attention on the general equilibrium of production and exchange which is specifically associated with perfectly competitive conditions.

2. The function of the equilibrium concept in economics is to enable us to say what particular courses of action will be chosen in response to certain postulated conditions. The association between these may take a weak or a strong form, according to whether we wish to prove that the system will remain in equilibrium or will actually tend towards it. We may be content to demonstrate, in other words, that if the course appropriate to the determining conditions had already been chosen, it would be persisted in, provided these conditions remained unchanged; but it is clearly of much greater importance to establish that, whatever the initial situation, the appropriate activities would actually come to be adopted. In seeking to identify equilibrium activities, use is made of the normal analytic method, which supposes the problem to be solved and then examines what this implies; we argue, that is to say, that if a certain course of action is to be undertaken and persisted in, it will necessarily be compatible, first, with the particular constraints imposed by the assumed environment, and, secondly, with the objectives of the agents in question.[1]

We can begin by considering the applicability of this method to the case of a single individual. It is obvious at the outset that no *direct* connexion can exist between objective conditions and purposive activity; the immediate relationship is between *beliefs* about relevant conditions and *planned* activities which it may or may not prove possible to implement. Only those activities will be planned, it is assumed, which are compatible both with the agent's objectives and with the opportunities he believes to exist. It can then be shown that, in certain

---

[1] In the simplest case, the determining conditions would be represented by a state of affairs which remained the same over time, so that the equilibrium course of action would correspond to continued repetition of the same activities. (The consumer, for example, with a fixed income and unchanging preferences, and faced with choice between goods at unchanging prices, would, in equilibrium, distribute his income in the same way during each time period.) But it is possible to conceive of the determining conditions as a set of circumstances which alter systematically over time, in which case the equilibrium course of action would correspond to a changing pattern of activities. We can still define this equilibrium course as that which will be persisted in so long as the determining conditions unfold over time in the specified way. (The consumer might correctly predict the time pattern of his future income and plan a particular time pattern of expenditure in response to it; if, in carrying out this plan, he found no reason to change it—assuming of course that the time pattern of his income and the other determinants did not change—then it would correspond to the equilibrium course of action.)

circumstances, only one particular set of activities will meet these requirements. The simplest way of proceeding from here to the establishment of relationships between objective conditions (as opposed to beliefs) and fulfilled actions (as opposed to plans) is to assume that the agent's beliefs are correct, which will be the case, most commonly, if he has adequate information. In our ordinary theory of consumers' behaviour, for example, the determinants of equilibrium are the prices of the goods available, together with the income and the preference system of the consumer in question. We, the model builders, postulate a person with certain objectives and opportunities from which we deduce the pattern of expenditure which would be best for him; by then assuming that he is fully acquainted with the determinants of this expenditure pattern, we can represent him as choosing it himself. In this way, a model of individual behaviour can be derived from a theorem about the logic of choice. The informational requirements, in this case, are simply that the agent have knowledge of the determinants of the equilibrium as laid down by the model builder; if they are met, then the equilibrium activities will immediately be undertaken and persisted in so long as the determinants remain unchanged. For all simple models constructed in this way, the informational requirements are of this kind, but they cease to hold good, I shall later argue, when we pass from the equilibrium of an individual to that of an interrelated group.[1]

All models of individual equilibrium are not of this simple kind. Though full information is a sufficient condition for attaining the equilibrium, it is not necessary. All that is required is, first, that the man should believe a particular course of action to be optimal and, secondly, that the process of carrying it out

[1] A more exhaustive discussion of the meaning of equilibrium would recognize that the activities undertaken in response to given determining conditions would depend on the time allowed for adjustment to take place. It is possible, following Marshall, to distinguish, for example, between short- and long-period equilibrium according to whether there has been time to carry out major adjustments such as alteration in the quantity of fixed equipment. Distinctions of this kind, though of great practical utility, are not directly relevant to the central argument of this chapter. The equilibrium relationship which I have in mind throughout is that between the determining conditions and the activities which would be undertaken once all adjustments were made.

should provide no information which is inconsistent with, or would cause him to doubt, his belief. By and large, however, economists have concentrated on the case where equilibrium is secured because beliefs are actually correct, though attention has also been given to hypothetical constructions in which the execution of a plan formed on the basis of inadequate information brings new evidence to light, so that full information, and therefore equilibrium also, are obtained gradually by a process of trial and error. What concerns us here, is to note that in no case can we identify equilibrium activities without reference both to objective conditions and to states of belief, the correctness of which will depend on the information presumed available. This holds true regardless of whether we are concerned with the existence of an equilibrium relationship in either the strong or the weak form; whether we assert, that is to say, that certain activities will actually be adopted, or merely that, once adopted, they will be persisted in. Economic activity being purposive and forward looking, the beliefs on which it is based must of necessity be taken into implicit or explicit account.

Our aim in identifying the equilibrium of a group, as in the case of an individual, is again to relate given objective conditions to the pattern of activities which members of the group will come to adopt in response to them. It would be possible to define equilibrium in such a way that the group as a whole could be said to be in equilibrium even although its component members were not; it could be taken to imply the attainment and maintenance of particular values for aggregates, such as the levels of output for different commodities, irrespective of whether the activities of individual producers and consumers were constantly changing. Marshall, notably, conceived the equilibrium of an industry as being maintained in the long run by the simultaneous and offsetting rise and fall of different firms, just as the size of a forest could be kept constant by the decline of some trees and the growth of others. Nevertheless, the majority of writers, and particularly in their more formal analysis, make the attainment of group equilibrium depend on the attainment of equilibrium by all component members. This requires, as we have seen, first, that everyone believes his projected activities to be optimal, and, secondly, that their implementation can be carried out according to plan, so that there appears to be no reason for changing them. This latter condition would be met, we noted, provided each person had adequate information about the external conditions on which the planned activities were based. In our discussion of individual equilibrium, these external conditions (income, prices, etc.) were merely taken as given; they were represented as fixed opportunities and restrictions and subjected to no further analysis. Now that our concern has shifted to the equilibrium of a related group, however, it is important to distinguish between two different kinds of external conditions with which each individual member will be confronted and with which their activities will have to be compatible. On the one hand, there are those aspects of external reality, such as the available technical production opportunities, which are represented as the ultimate determinants of the equilibrium; on the other, there are the activities of other members of the system. The feasibility of a particular producer's plan, for example, will depend on its consistency both with technical production possibilities and with the plans of customers, competitors and suppliers. Now this fact has a very important bearing on what we have called the informational requirements for equilibrium. In dealing with an individual in isolation, we could say that the knowledge he required in order to move to the equilibrium position was simply that of the ultimate determinants of this position as laid down by the model builder. In turning to the analysis of a related group this ceases to be true; there is clearly no presumption that the general equilibrium of production and exchange would be reached provided that all the members of the system had full information about its ultimate determinants. We have, therefore, to inquire as to precisely what kind of information must be presumed in order that they should set out on courses of action such that equilibrium will ultimately be attained. This question, which, despite its crucial importance, has received insufficient systematic attention from economists,[1] will concern us very fully in the chapters to come.

[1] For a notable exception, see F. A. Hayek, 'Economics and knowledge', *Economica*, 1937.

At this stage we shall merely note once again that, whether our concern is with either an individual or a related group, the attainment or maintenance of equilibrium must depend on the possession of appropriate information by the people concerned.

3. With these considerations in mind, let us now examine the celebrated attempt to identify a general equilibrium of production and exchange under perfectly competitive conditions. Perfect competition is defined in terms of the existence of many buyers and sellers of each homogeneous commodity and by the absence of any artificial restraints upon their activities—a condition sometimes referred to as perfect mobility. Most writers also recognize that these buyers and sellers must have certain necessary information, but this requirement is usually left obscure, and its relationship with the other conditions of the model is not examined. Given perfectly competitive conditions an equilibrium pattern of economic activities is identified and made to depend on external conditions represented by the preferences of individuals, the endowment and original distribution of resources, and the state of technique. It will be convenient to begin by giving an brief objective description of these activities and of their relationship to these external conditions; having done so, the question of their relationship to the beliefs and intentions of those who undertake them can then be taken up.

The equilibrium configuration has two kinds of special properties, the first relating to the situation in which each individual unit finds itself, the second to relationships between the aggregate levels of the activities in which they are engaged. Every consumer has an expenditure equal to his income and a pattern of consumption such that his marginal rate of substitution between any two goods is equal to the ratio of their prices, which are the same for everybody. Each producer is taken to be producing as efficiently as possible, given the state of technique, and the price paid to any of the factors of production is equal to the value of its marginal product in that use. These conditions suggest optimality, the others, consistency. The aggregate current production of each commodity is neither more nor less than is used either by other firms or in final consumption.

(I avoid saying simply that supply and demand are equal, for this would involve a reference to plans and expectations which are not to be introduced at this stage.) All scarce resources are likewise fully employed, and the expenditure of any individual is equal to the income derived from the sale of the resources at his disposal, as determined by the distribution of skill and property originally assumed.[1]

These then are the relations which characterize the perfectly competitive economy in what is believed to be its equilibrium state. But, as has been observed, equilibrium is not secured merely by the existence of a particular set of economic activities in themselves, but by their coexistence with a particular set of beliefs. Therefore we have to discover what beliefs must be associated with the configuration we have described in order that it can be regarded as self-perpetuating. One of its properties consisted of the correspondence of marginal rates of substitution to relative prices, so that consumers were each objectively in an optimum position, provided their incomes and the prices of commodities were regarded as fixed and given. They would themselves believe their situation to be optimal, and therefore have no wish to change it, provided we endow them with certain information and beliefs. It would be sufficient to assume that they were fully acquainted with their own preferences and with the prices of all goods, and that they expected that neither these preferences and prices, nor their income, would change in the future. Producers will also wish to persist in the activities the configuration allotted to them, if they know all the production possibilities, if they know all product and factor prices and expect them to remain the same, and finally, if there is some reason for preventing them expanding the current scale of their operations. (The significance of this important third and final condition, will be developed in due course.) Similar conditions of belief will ensure that the suppliers of productive resources are also content with the rôle they have been allotted.

[1] This account of the conditions of equilibrium is of course loose and inadequate; but, for our particular purposes, there is no point in taking up space with a full elaboration. We shall ignore questions as to the 'existence' and 'stability' of equilibria, at least in the particular sense in which these terms feature in current theoretical discussions.

The second set of properties of the equilibrium configuration, those concerned with the consistency of the various component activities, now ensure that the plans of consumers and producers can be successfully carried out and the beliefs or expectations which formed their basis will be proved correct. We are now entitled to say that, in every particular market, demand equals supply, in the sense that the amount which buyers plan to buy equals the amount which sellers plan to sell. It seems therefore that the conditions of belief required for equilibrium have been established; they consist in the possession of information about preferences and production functions and in the belief as to the permanence of existing prices, although it is necessary to add, somewhat untidily, that each producer must feel unwilling or unable to raise the level of his output.

But here we must pause to consider, rather more carefully, what the analysis so far does and does not establish. It shows that a particular economic configuration, if associated with a particular set of beliefs, can be regarded as self-perpetuating, so long as the ultimate determining conditions remain unchanged.[1] No explanation was given, however, of how these beliefs could come to be established, no account was offered of the information upon which, if rationally held, they would have to be based, and no proof was given that this information would, under the conditions which define the model, be available. The analysis cannot therefore be regarded as offering sufficient grounds for the conclusion that, if once the general equilibrium were attained, it would persist.

Far less, we shall see, does it entitle us to claim that, under perfectly competitive conditions prices and outputs would actually tend to their equilibrium values.

4. There has been a general recognition that the problem of identifying an equilibrium in perfect competition does not end

---

[1] The beliefs referred to are sufficient but not necessary, as it is possible to conceive of others which would perform the same function. Suppose, for example, that each producer expected the prices of his own inputs and outputs to remain unchanged, but was totally ignorant of production functions and relevant future prices elsewhere. It could reasonably be maintained that he would then continue what he was doing rather than take the chance that random combinations of other factors would give a larger profit.

with finding solutions to the set of simultaneous equations which was believed to define it, and the need to offer some explanation of the way in which the configuration could be reached in practice has been given varying degrees of attention. I shall endeavour to provide nothing but a brief and cursory survey of some of the forms which these explanations have taken. None of them, it seems to me, is fully adequate, and I shall argue later that this inadequacy is inevitable, in that the conditions which define the system of perfect competition are not such as would permit the economic adjustments required. The reasons to be offered in support of this assertion, however, will not be set out fully until we reach the following chapter.

It is very frequently observed that, although we can describe the equilibrium position of a hypothetical perfectly competitive economy, we are unable to given an account of the path by which it is reached. According to Edgeworth, for example, '. . . we have no general dynamical theory determining the path of the economic system from any point assigned at random to a position of equilibrium. We know only the statical properties of the position' (*Papers*, vol. ii, p. 311). But this way of stating the problem is perhaps misleading in that it may suggest two implications, neither of which can be accepted. It may be taken to suggest our ability to prove, first, that if equilibrium were once reached it would persist, provided the ultimate determinants remained unchanged, and, secondly, that the economy must necessarily tend to equilibrium even although we cannot give an account of the precise route that it will take. It became apparent in the above discussion, however, that the equilibrium activities would be persisted in only so long as everyone expected equilibrium prices to continue; the traditional analysis then expounded, moreover, gave no reason for believing that this would be the case or that the information on which these expectations could rationally be grounded would in fact be available. It may be argued that these difficulties would not arise if the equilibrium configuration had been in existence for some time, for in this case everyone might be presumed to have grounds for expecting that current prices, having persisted so long in the past, would persist also in the future; such in fact are the circumstances postulated by economists in the fiction of the 'stationary state'.[1] By associating the notion of equilibrium with this imaginary state of affairs, recognition is at least given to the need to explain the grounds on which particular price expectations would be held, although, as a solution to our problem, the expedient has little else to commend it. While it may be justifiable to assert that prices would have their equilibrium values in the future if only they have had them for some considerable time in the past, we are left with the question of why this latter condition can be assumed to be fulfilled; the concept of the stationary state, therefore, merely diverts us from what is the really important task, that of identifying the conditions under which entrepreneurs could in fact normally obtain the information on which to base rational price expectations. Professor Hicks would seem to be justified, on more than one ground, in what he calls his 'firm belief that the stationary state is, in the end, nothing but an evasion' (*Value and Capital*, 2nd ed., p. 117). In any case, it is a demonstration of the possibility of reaching equilibrium, rather than merely maintaining it, which we most urgently require; it is surely in the analysis of the direction in which, at any particular time, the economy may be moving, rather than the positions at which it may be at rest, that the equilibrium concept is to be of use. But it is difficult to see what but an act of faith can enable us to believe that equilibrium would in fact be reached in perfect competition even although we cannot say how this might come about. It may indeed be possible to show that any other possible configuration would involve such inconsistencies as would necessarily bring about change, but, unless we have some reason for ruling out a state of perpetual change, this does not justify the belief that the

---

[1] This has been described by Professor Hicks as follows: 'The stationary state is that special case of a dynamic system where tastes, technique, and resources remain constant through time. We can reasonably assume that experience of these constant conditions will lead entrepreneurs to expect their continuance; so that it is not necessary to distinguish between price expectations and current prices, for they are all the same. We can assume, too, that entrepreneurs did expect in the past that today's prices would be what they now turn out to be; so that the supplies of commodities are fully adjusted to their prices. Then it can be shown that the price system established in such a stationary state is substantially identical with that static price system whose properties we already know' (*Value and Capital*, 2nd ed., p. 117).

economy would eventually gravitate towards the equilibrium position. Presumably it is the existence of a considerable measure of order and stability in the real economic world around us that engenders faith that equilibrium can in fact be realized, but here it is most important to remember that the conditions of the real world are not those of perfect competition and that, if they were, it might no longer be possible for this order to be produced.

5. In certain respects, the founders of modern equilibrium analysis were more keenly aware of the problem of the attainment of equilibrium than have been most of the economists who subsequently developed their work. Walras himself, the very originator of general equilibrium analysis, was certainly aware of it and offered, as a hypothetical solution, what Professor Hutchison has termed 'the brief dynamic fantasia of the tâtonnements'.[1] The supposed operation of this process is not always perfectly clear, but it is easy to see the function which it was supposed to perform. In discussing the equilibrium of exchange only, as contrasted with that involving production, Walras suggests that equilibrium could be brought about by means of the successive announcement of provisional prices; if the demand and offer called forth by the announcement of a price do not balance, then fresh prices would be proposed until those which secured equilibrium were hit upon. Now it can be shown that if transactions do in fact take place at the provisional prices, then this could not but affect the nature of the equilibrium reached, which would no longer be deducible from the original determinants; whether Walras was aware of this difficulty, it is not easy to say. In turning to the full equilibrium of production and exchange he suggests an arrangement which would be free from this objection. The contracts entered into during the time when the provisional prices are being '*criés au hazard*' are to be imagined as nominal and capable of revision; only when the prices proposed call forth equilibrium values of supply and demand are they to be carried out.

[1] The process of tâtonnement is described by Walras in his *Elements of Pure Economics* (translated and edited by W. Jaffé, London, 1954). See pp. 169–72, 243–54, and 284–95.

According to Professor Patinkin, Walras' theory of tâtonnement would seem to be one of his most imaginative and
valuable contributions to economic analysis'. This indeed is to
rate its claims very high, for although it shows that Walras
was very much aware of the problem of the actual attainment
of equilibrium, and contrived, in Professor Hutchison's words,
'noisy and rather obscure dynamics' to deal with it, there is
no doubt that the solution offered is exceedingly fanciful. It
represents, as Edgeworth pointed out, 'a way, rather than the
way by which economic equilibrium is reached'. It does
certainly meet the requirement that those in the economy
should have sufficient reasons for expecting that they will be
able to buy and sell in the future at particular prices, but it
demands the existence of a very special kind of agency to
operate the system of tâtonnement, such as is not normally
postulated as part of the system of perfect competition. Much
the same can be said of the hypothetical procedure of recontracting, suggested by Edgeworth, which proceeds on very
similar lines; it is of value in that it stresses the need for the
individual members of the system to obtain information on
which to base feasible plans, but nevertheless fails to provide
a genuinely acceptable account of how, without the presumption of certain fictitious devices, the need is to be met.

Walras advances another explanation, relevant to the working
of actual competitive economies, of how the equations defining
the general equilibrium would in practice be solved. Let us
assume that equilibrium is disturbed by an increase in the
demand for a certain product; provided then that this causes
—as will normally be the case—a movement of price in the
same direction, there will be an incentive to increase supply and
to reduce demand so as to eliminate the original disequilibrium.
This of course is the form of almost all explanations of equilibrating adjustment, and it would be wrong to underestimate the
care and thoroughness which Walras devoted to its exposition;
nevertheless, it appears on reflection to be less than fully adequate. A rise in the price of a good, other prices remaining
the same, will create what may be conveniently called a
'general profit potential'; it opens up an opportunity for
particular entrepreneurs to increase the production of the

commodity and sell it at a profit. But, as we shall have occasion to recognize more fully later, the existence of such a general profit potential cannot automatically be assumed to create particular profit opportunities for individual entrepreneurs. Before any particular entrepreneur is prepared to invest in the production of the commodity, he will have to be assured that the volume of supply planned by competing producers, who are also aware of the opportunity, will not be so large as to overstock the market, thus converting the expectation of profit into the realization of loss. But how, in a perfect market, where all producers are free to move in response to the profit opportunity, is that assurance to be afforded him? And yet without this assurance, entrepreneurs would not invest, and supply would not be expanded; a general profit potential, which is known to all, and equally exploitable by all, is, for this reason, available to no one in particular. Thus summarily expressed, this objection may not appear to be worthy of much weight; in the following chapter, however, I shall endeavour to present it in fuller and more convincing form.

6. Meanwhile it will be instructive to turn to Marshall, whose account of the movement to equilibrium is presented within a context very different to that of his renowned French contemporary. We are not entitled to expect from Marshall an account of how, in a system of perfect competition, general equilibrium would be attained, if only for the reason that such a system is not presumed by his analysis. Competition is presumed to be 'free', in a loosely-defined way, but there is at no time any suggestion that it is 'pure' or 'perfect' in the technical sense. I doubt if it is legitimate for us to consider that Marshall avoided these terms merely because of a desire to keep the analytical skeleton of his argument well in the background or to give the effect of realism by presenting the economy with all its imperfections on its head.[1] He, far more

---

[1] 'Just as Walras, more than any other of the leaders, was bent on scraping off everything he did not consider essential to his theoretical schema, so Marshall, following the English tradition, was bent on salvaging every bit of real life he could possibly leave in. As regards the case in hand, we find that he did not attempt to beat out the logic of competition to its thinnest leaf.' (J. A. Schumpeter, *History of Economic Analysis*, p. 974.)

than either Walras or Edgeworth, was deeply concerned with the problems of adjustment and of time, and his treatment of them is much more profound. What can be argued is that, because of the perhaps deliberate imprecision with which he defines the conditions of competition, it is exceedingly difficult to conclude, from the analysis of the *Principles*, whether the attainment of equilibrium depends on the existence of certain imperfections or whether it would proceed all the more easily without them.

Marshall, to a much greater extent than Walras, was at pains to stress that, in a world of constant change, general theory becomes much more difficult to apply, to such an extent indeed that 'every plain and simple doctrine as to the relations between cost of production, demand and value is necessarily false; and the greater the appearance of lucidity which is given to it by skilful exposition, the more mischievous it is.' As is well known, he chose to break up the complex problem of equilibrium into several parts and to consider it chiefly with reference to a single industry rather than to the economy as a whole. As regards market prices, the supply of the commodity is taken to be that which is 'on hand', or at all events, 'in sight'. The determination of normal prices is examined first in the short period during which the 'existing stock of plant' is given, then in the long period which affords time to vary this stock, and finally within a secular period long enough to permit changes in technique and other fundamental determinants. It is to the third of these periods, concerned with the adjustment of the industry's capital stock, that I propose to confine my examination. The analysis of it which Marshall provided is important, not only for its own sake, but because it was based on a conceptual apparatus which later came to be applied, or misapplied, in many accounts of the attainment of equilibrium.

This apparatus is represented by the schedules of demand and supply, towards the intersection of which price is presumed to gravitate. The demand curve is ultimately derivable from the income and preferences of consumers, and in that this is so, should strictly be regarded as representing the locus of all these combinations of price, and quantity bought, for which consumers would be in equilibrium. Provided we can assume, however, that consumers can quickly and easily adjust the pattern of their consumption so as to be in equilibrium at current prices, then it is legitimate to represent the function as relating a given price to the amount that consumers would be immediately willing to buy at that price, on the assumption, of course, that they did not expect it to be about to alter. It can be regarded, that is to say, as *ex ante* in character, in that it expresses total plans to buy as a function of the current level of price. In seeking to interpret the long-run supply curve, much more caution is required. The information which it embodies, according to the principle of its construction, is the relationship of different volumes of total output not to any price, whether actual or expected, but to the 'expenses of production' of the commodity concerned. It represents the long-run unit cost curve of the representative firm, as the dependent variable, and the total volume of the industry's output as the independent variable.[1] Costs may rise with the volume of the industry's output if it is necessary to offer higher prices in order to withdraw factors from other uses, or they may fall because of external economies of various kinds.

Now although the original significance of this function is that which we have attributed to it, we may also interpret it as representing the locus of all combinations of price and total output which meet a particular equilibrium condition—that which consists in the equality of the receipts of firms to their costs of production, taken to include normal profits. Were the process of long-run adjustment to be carried through, that is to say, the total volume of the product of an industry, and its unit price, must correspond to some point on the supply schedule. We may be tempted, therefore, following an analogy with the demand curve, to further modify our interpretation of the function by representing it in an *ex ante* form, as relating expected price to planned supply. Encouragement to do this

---

[1] As we noted earlier, Marshall, with characteristic scrupulousness, recognizes that the industry can be in equilibrium although the individual firms composing it are not. In introducing his concept of the representative firm, he presumably wishes to acknowledge this fact, while at the same time abstracting from it in his analysis of price determination. Thus, to quote Professor Robertson, '. . . The state of the industry is the same as it *would* be *if* the industry consisted entirely of firms of this kind.' (*Lectures on Economic Principles*, Vol. I, p. 119.)

may appear to be offered by Marshall himself, when he remarks that 'In every case the (normal supply) price is that the expectation of which is sufficient and only just sufficient to make it worth while for people to set themselves to produce that aggregate amount . . .'.[1] There can be no doubt, however, that such a step is wholly illegitimate; the Marshallian long-run supply curve, at least if perfect competition is being assumed, cannot properly be given an *ex ante* interpretation.

It is clearly an elementary, if much neglected truth, that the supply planned in response to the expectation of a particular price will depend on the number of people by whom the expectation is held. This is a consideration frequently concealed from us by the habit of referring to expectations impersonally or in the passive voice, by postulating, for example, that such and such a price 'is expected'. It may be retorted that the usage is quite harmless, in that it can be taken simply to imply that the expectation is quite general, being held unanimously by all entrepreneurs; yet if this interpretation is accepted (and no obvious alternative is available), then some very curious consequences can be shown to follow. Let us assume that there exists a particular level of normal profits which is just sufficient to induce any entrepreneur to invest in any particular direction and that this level obtains throughout all the economy. Let us further assume that 'it is expected' that the price of one commodity will be higher in the future than it has been in the past, the expectation being held unanimously by all entrepreneurs. Now if this price exceeds the unit cost of production, as based on whatever prices of the relevant inputs are also expected by all, abnormal profits will be offered, and there will be an incentive for all to plan investment in this direction; everyone, in perfectly competitive conditions, being completely free to do so, an indefinitely great volume of supply will therefore be planned, although of course the plans cannot be carried out. If, on the other hand, the expected price fails to exceed the expected costs, no output will be planned. Under no

[1] Professor Robertson also, in his very careful discussion of the supply curve, says that 'we can define the long-period supply price of an output x as "the price the expectation of obtaining which for the whole output x will just suffice eventually to evoke that output"'. *Lectures on Economic Principles*, Vol. I, p. 123.

circumstances, therefore, would a finite output be planned, far less the particular output corresponding to the expected price on the supply schedule.

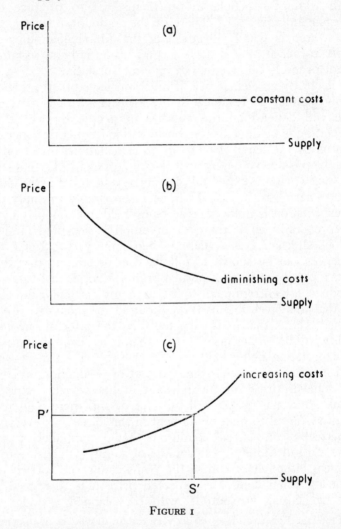

FIGURE 1

These unwelcome results, it should be stressed, are independent of the shape postulated for the supply curve. If the supply of factors is perfectly elastic in the long run, and if there are no economies or diseconomies external to the firm, costs will be constant for all levels of output and the supply curve will be horizontal, as in Fig. 1 (a). In this case the *ex ante* interpretation is clearly inapplicable, as the function associates one price with an indefinitely wide range of total output levels; the general expectation of this price by entrepreneurs cannot therefore be assumed to call forth any particular level of planned supply. In the case of diminishing costs to the industry,[1] and therefore of a downward sloping supply curve (Fig. 1 (b), the inapplicability of an *ex ante* interpretation is immediately apparent, as it would oblige us to accept that the lower the price expected by entrepreneurs the greater would be the volume of planned supply.

The situation might at first appear to be changed by the assumption of inelastic factor supply and therefore of a rising supply curve, for, in this case, each possible value of price will be associated, as in Fig. 1 (c), with only one value of supply. In fact, however, the *ex ante* interpretation is no more valid than before. Let us assume that the 'expected price' is P'. In the absence of any further specification, we must take this to imply that an indefinite number of people expect (presumably with confidence) this particular price. If they are to be conceived of as making any supply plans at all, we must credit them with some expectations about future factor prices, which would also presumably be unanimous and certain. Now the supply function which we are considering implies, according to the principle of its construction, a different level of factor prices for each possible value of product supply. For the supply S', for example, the level of factor prices, say f', is presumed to be such as would make the unit costs of production equal to P'; and the same relation holds for any point on the curve. It is clear, therefore, that if entrepreneurs expect the price P' and at the same time expect the level of factor prices to be less than f', abnormal profits would be envisaged; on the assumption that profits elsewhere were normal, therefore, an indefinitely large supply would be

---

[1] If competitive equilibrium is to be ensured, such diminishing costs must arise from external economies and not from increasing returns to individual firms. This matter is discussed more fully in the next chapter.

planned. Any attempt to implement these plans, needless to say, would, by raising factor prices above f', demonstrate the falsity of the expectations on which they were based. Where the level of factor prices is expected to be greater than f', no profit opportunity would be envisaged and no supply planned. If the level of factor prices expected by entrepreneurs happened to be f', and therefore that appropriate to the supply S', the expected profits would be normal. This however gives no reason for believing that the total supply planned should in fact be S', for it would now be a matter of indifference to entrepreneurs whether they invested in this or in other directions. We must conclude therefore that there is no level of expected factor prices which, in conjunction with P', would give a value for planned supply which is not either zero or indefinitely large—far less give the precise value S' on the supply function.

7. To some extent, these awkward consequences can be avoided by the introduction of a very special assumption. We might conceive that no two entrepreneurs were alike, each of them having different degrees of comparative advantage in different lines of production. In this case, the general expectation of a particular product price, coupled with expectations regarding the prices of the associated inputs, might induce only a finite volume of supply, in that it would offer abnormal profits to some but not to others. One might even imagine that these differences were taken into account in the construction of the supply function, so that one could say that, if a certain product price were expected, and if factor prices were at the same time expected to have the values presumed by the function, then the appropriate supply would be planned. But it must be conceded that this attempt to salvage the *ex ante* interpretation of the supply curve is scarcely satisfactory. The special kind of differentiation of entrepreneurial capacity which is required is not generally laid down as an assumption necessary to ensure the working of perfect competition. In addition, there would seem to be no particular reason why entrepreneurs should come to form the particular factor price expectations which are necessary to bring forth the scheduled supply.

8. It would seem necessary to conclude, therefore, that a long-run supply curve, constructed as relating total output to the unit cost of producing it, cannot be interpreted as expressing 'planned supply' as a function of 'expected price'. The importance of this will, I hope, emerge in later discussion; meanwhile it is worth while to note how the long-run supply curve differs in this respect, not only from the demand curve, but also from the supply functions which are employed in the analysis of market, and of short-run equilibrium. In his discussion of the temporary equilibrium of demand and supply,[1] as it occurs on 'market day in a local corn exchange', Marshall postulates a schedule of supply which is genuinely *ex ante* in character, representing the amount of the commodity which 'holders will be willing to supply' at various levels of price. Current price, in this case, is the independent variable and plans to sell the dependent variable; the stocks of corn being *ex hypothesi* fixed in amount, and the sellers having made different calculations about 'the present and future conditions of the market', the values of planned supply will be finite and different for every price offered. A similar interpretation can be given to a supply curve of a particular kind of labour, provided we assume that it is to apply to a fixed number of workers 'already in existence and trained for their work'.[2]

The short-period supply curve for the product of a particular industry can be drawn up, as was the long-period curve, to relate volumes of output to the cost of producing them; in this case, however, it is the marginal cost of production from an existing fixed volume of equipment rather than the unit costs of the representative firm which would appear as the dependent variable. Subject to various qualifications, however, this schedule does lend itself to an *ex ante* interpretation, the reason for this being, of course, that certain factors are presumed to limit the possible sources of supply. If we postulate, in this case, the quite general expectation of a particular price, there is no reason to believe that the volume of supply planned would be either zero or indefinitely large, as only those entrepreneurs with equipment already in existence will be in a position to mount the increase in supply which appears profitable.

[1] A. Marshall, *Principles of Economics*, 8th Ed., p. 333.   [2] Ibid., p. 142.

The supply actually planned, and in fact also realized, will be that which is scheduled, provided certain important conditions are fulfilled. It is necessary, in the first place, that the estimated factor prices on which they base their plans are those which are assumed to determine the values of marginal cost given by the supply curve. In addition, if the price expected falls below the prime costs of production, no output will generally be planned; at this point, that is to say, the supply curve can no longer be interpreted in the *ex ante* sense. Indeed, as Marshall was careful to point out, this may become so in practice (if not in perfectly competitive conditions) even before the price equal to prime costs is reached, for the fear of 'spoiling the market' might prevent firms from being willing to produce for prices which, though in excess of prime costs, were nevertheless substantially lower than their total costs per unit output.

9. I have thought it important to set out these differences between the supply functions employed by Marshall, in the belief that their neglect has vitiated certain accounts of the attainment of equilibrium which were later based upon them. But before taking up this matter, we must endeavour to complete our discussion of the equilibrating adjustment as described by Marshall himself. This description, it must be admitted, is couched in rather general terms. For any given total volume of output, the price which would be established, we are to presume, is that given by the schedule of demand; but this price might fail to correspond, at any particular time, to the normal supply price (or unit costs) given for this output by the long-run supply function. 'When therefore,' according to Marshall, 'the amount produced (in a unit of time) is such that the demand price is greater than the supply price, then sellers receive more than is sufficient to make it worth their while to bring goods to market to that amount; and there is at work an active force tending to increase the amount brought forward for sale. On the other hand, when the amount produced is such that the demand price is less than the supply price, sellers receive less than is sufficient to make it worth their while to bring goods to market on that scale; so that those who were just on the margin of doubt as to whether to go on producing are decided not to do so, and there is an active force at work tending to diminish the amount brought forward for sale. When the demand price is equal to the supply price, the amount produced has no tendency either to be increased or to be diminished; it is in equilibrium' (ibid., p. 345).

Now, in so far as it goes, this account is unexceptionable; but one has to realize what it does not, as well as what it does, tell us. We have already observed that, if entrepreneurs are to be prepared to invest, they will require some assurance that the volume of demand, at the normal supply price, would be greater than the volume of supply which is being planned by other competitive producers. It is not clear, from Marshall's account, why we can safely assume that this will in fact be the case; and there is no suggestion, moreover, that the presence or absence of this kind of assurance will depend (as I shall later contend) on the precise nature of the market structure assumed. Marshall, as we observed, does not assume a perfect market; although 'there is much free competition', yet at the same time individual firms have their own 'special markets'. In all this there is characteristically much careful imprecision; and it might be argued that the imperfections recognized by Marshall were introduced as a means of giving flesh and blood to a conceptual framework, rather than as elements which, as I hope to show, are essential to the working of the system. His readers may therefore be left with the same impression, as they would obtain, much more indisputably, from the writings of Walras, namely that the system works in spite of certain 'imperfections' and not, to some degree, because of them.

10. The problems of the existence and stability of equilibrium under perfectly competitive conditions have received, during the last half century, since Marshall and Walras, sustained and elaborate attention. Economists have analysed, for example, the way in which a tendency to equilibrium might depend on the particular shapes of the demand and supply schedules or on relationships between different markets. Notwithstanding this work, however, I feel convinced that one of the essential elements of any adequate account of the attainment of equilibrium has not been provided; for the most part, indeed, the need for it has been ignored. No explanation has been given of how, in the conditions which define the perfectly competitive model, entrepreneurs could obtain the information on which their expectations, and therefore the investment plans required for equilibrium, would have to be based. Existing theory does not meet the full requirements of the principle of 'methodological individualism'; although it does, admittedly, assume that equilibrium is reached as a result of the actions of individual persons or enterprises, it fails to show how the necessary informational basis for such action can be presumed to exist. In this sense, therefore, modern theory about the attainment of equilibrium can, for the most part, properly be called mechanical; in general, it merely presumes the existence of functional relationships between different variables in the system and then proceeds to work out the consequences. The considerable technical virtuosity of many of the demonstrations of this kind, and the scientific character with which the mathematical apparatus used may appear to invest them, should not hide from us the fact that they nevertheless offer no adequate answer to the key problem with which we are concerned, that of the way in which it would be possible, under the conditions of perfect competition, for the equilibrium configuration actually to be brought about.

Ordinary accounts of the path to equilibrium almost always begin by postulating functions which relate demand and supply to levels of current price. In some of them, it is assumed that, should the current price deviate from that given by the intersection of the schedules, then it will either rise or fall towards this intersection at a rate proportional to the difference between the scheduled values of demand and supply corresponding to it. In others, it is assumed that the amount supplied tends towards its equilibrium value at a rate which depends on the difference between the demand and supply prices corresponding, on each of the two schedules, to the supply actually being produced. According to Professor R. G. D. Allen, these two different sets of assumptions correspond respectively to the Walrasian and the Marshallian accounts of the path to equilibrium. With certain postulated shapes for the demand and supply functions, both approaches indicate a movement to equilibrium; for others, one of the hypotheses may indicate movement towards equilibrium while the other implies departure from it.[1] The detailed character of these demonstrations need not concern us here, but we have to recognize that their validity is relative to the assumptions on which they are based. The fundamental premise underlying them is that there exist causal relationships, of the kind postulated, between demand, supply and price; unless it can be shown that this premise is justified, the existence of tendencies, either towards or away from equilibrium, has not been demonstrated. All that has been done is to indicate the implications of the particular causal relationships which were initially assumed.

11. It is also possible to construct models which, by virtue of the introduction of expectations and time-lags, offer, superficially at any rate, a less mechanical appearance. In period analysis of this kind, planned supply is represented as depending on 'expected price', which is in turn made a function of the price of the previous period or of some combination of past prices. The prototype of this kind of analysis is the cobweb theorem which, despite its inclusion in elementary textbooks, is in fact as intricate and treacherous as its name suggests. It can be interpreted as showing that, provided the shapes of the demand and supply functions meet certain requirements, equilibrium would be reached ultimately, if only indirectly, as a result of output decisions taken on the basis of current prices only. The general form of the demonstration is well known. We postulate a demand function which indicates the amount which would be bought at current prices, and a supply function which relates these prices to the supplies which would be planned in the current period and forthcoming in the next. It is assumed throughout that no stocks of the commodity can be held. Starting from an initial position of equilibrium at P_1, the demand curve is presumed to shift from D_1 to D_2

---

[1] The reader can obtain a fuller account of these demonstrations in Professor Allen's book (*Mathematical Economics*, R. G. D. Allen, p. 21).

(Fig. 2). As the supply available during the current period is the fixed quantity previously produced, the price of the product is presumed to rise immediately to its temporary equilibrium position at P_2. Producers, expecting that this price will remain unchanged, plan to increase output to the scheduled volume S_2, so that, in the succeeding period, when this amount comes to be marketed, the price will fall to P_3.

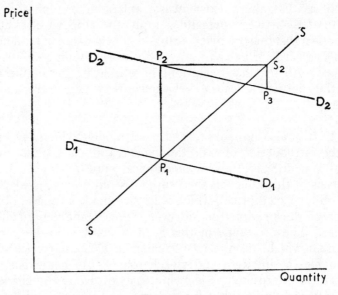

FIGURE 2

Producers, once more expecting that this price will remain unchanged, take supply decisions accordingly, and thus the process continues on its erratic course. Provided that demand is more elastic than supply (which need not of course be the case), it can be shown that price and output will gradually tend towards the magnitudes given by the intersection of the curves.

Now the internal logic of this theory may pass undisputed, however unreasonable the way in which it presumes that expectations are formed. But its validity as a demonstration of a possible way in which equilibrium might be reached depends on the interpretation which can be placed on the demand and supply schedules employed in it. The values of price and output which correspond to the intersection of the two schedules do certainly represent an equilibrium in a quite limited sense, in that at this point *ex hypothesi* the amount that buyers are prepared to buy equals the amount that producers are willing to sell. But they correspond to true long-run equilibrium values, as determined by preferences, resources and production functions, only if the demand and supply schedules employed have a particular significance. The demand schedule must represent the locus of those combinations of prices and amounts purchased for which all consumers would be in equilibrium, with the relative prices of commodities equal to their marginal rates of substitution. This is an interpretation which the *ex ante* demand schedule, relating price to the willingness to buy, can reasonably be given, on the assumption that all consumers are able to proceed without delay to the equilibrium adjustment. At the same time, the supply schedule must represent unit costs of production, for the firm, as a function of the total volume of output, for otherwise the equilibrium would not be determined by the cost conditions implied by the production functions, etc., initially assumed. In the cobweb theorem, however, the schedule is interpreted as relating the price current in one period to the supply forthcoming in the next. But what is the justification for this identification? I have already endeavoured to prove that the schedule cannot be taken to relate expected price to planned supply. It is therefore by no means obvious why the establishment of a particular price in one period should result, in the succeeding period, in the particular volume of output scheduled on the long-run supply function. Simply to presume this, is to take for granted a process of adjustment scarcely less difficult to account for than the tendency to equilibrium which the theorem sets out to explain. We must conclude, therefore, that the cobweb theorem, whatever its legitimate alternative uses, cannot be regarded as showing a possible way by which equilibrium might be reached; it offers no reason for believing that, if entrepreneurs were to base their investment decisions on the current values of product prices, then supply would, under certain circumstances, gradually, if circuitously, adjust itself to demand.

I have thought it necessary to offer this most cursory survey of some of the accounts of the movement to equilibrium in order to convince the reader that there is, in fact, a genuine gap in our theoretical presentation of the working of the competitive economy. The theory of the maintenance or the attainment of equilibrium under perfectly competitive conditions fails to account for the process of adjustment in terms of investment decisions by individual entrepreneurs, who have expectations which they could reasonably be presumed to form, on the basis of information which can reasonably be presumed to be available. The following chapter will be devoted to a further examination of this gap, and to an attempt to explain why it has not been filled.

II

THE AVAILABILITY OF MARKET
INFORMATION

1. It must be admitted, if the analysis of the previous chapter
is correct, that there is a crucial deficiency in the traditional
model of the competitive economy, the nature of which must
now be more carefully examined. Any adequate theory of
economic adjustment, whether it be in terms of the maintenance
or the attainment of an equilibrium position, must represent
entrepreneurs as taking investment decisions on the basis of
expectations about the relevent future circumstances. This
indeed would probably be widely admitted; what commonly
fails to be recognized, however, is that the possibility of forming
reliable expectations is not independent of the particular
market conditions which define the model employed. In saying
that expectations or beliefs are reliable, I imply that they are
grounded on adequate information or evidence. It is the
availability to entrepreneurs of this information which, I now
wish to demonstrate, is a function of the nature of the particular
form of economic organization or system within which they are
presumed to operate. If the defining conditions of our model
are such as to preclude this availability, as I believe to be the
case with perfect competition, then we cannot hope to obtain a
proper understanding of the process of economic adjustment
or of the factors which will influence its success or failure.

It will be important to distinguish between two different
sets of conditions upon which the profitability or even the
feasibility of investment programmes will depend. I shall
denote as '*market conditions*' the projected activities of others
in the system—such as customers, competitors or suppliers—
by which the profitability of the investment, directly, or indirectly,
is influenced. All other conditions, which do not consist of
plans and actions by other people—such as the production
possibilities created by the existing state of technology—will
be called '*technical*'. It will also prove convenient to talk of

'*market information*' and of '*technical information*' according
to whichever conditions are concerned.[1] The importance of
this distinction, from our point of view, lies in the fact that it
corresponds to a difference in the way in which the two kinds
of information can become available. The extent to which an
entrepreneur can obtain market information can be shown to
depend on the nature of the prevailing economic organization,
in a way in which his access to technical information does not.
It is perfectly legitimate, quite independently of whatever
economic system or market structure we presume is in force,
to postulate that entrepreneurs are acquainted with a certain
'state of the arts', or 'given production functions'. In doing so,
it is true, we may endow entrepreneurs with fuller and more
precise information than in actuality they are likely to possess;
our model may, in consequence, be less useful, but it will not
thereby be made subject to internal contradiction. If however
we assume, directly or by implication, that an entrepreneur
possesses some necessary minimum information about, for
example, the total output of a commodity which is likely to be
produced by his competitors, then we are obliged to take care
that the conditions of the model are such that this information
could conceivably be acquired by him.

2. Let us for a moment recall the variety of ways in which
the profitability of one particular investment project will depend
on the implementation of others. It is of the essence of the
private enterprise economy that although its individual members
are independent (in the sense that they are free from central
direction) yet their activities are nevertheless interrelated. We
say producers are in a competitive relationship where consumers regard the commodities which they offer as, in greater

---

[1] In an earlier article, 'Equilibrium, Expectations and Information',
(*Economic Journal*, Vol. LXIX, June, 1959), I referred to 'primary' and
'secondary' information, rather than to 'technical' and 'market' information.
The terms now chosen may be more likely to remind the reader of the nature
of the distinction which I believe it is important to make. It must be admitted,
however, that the notion of market conditions, as employed here, is wider
than that of ordinary usage; it has to be taken to refer not only to the plans
of consumers, but also to the plans of other producers who may invest in
directions which are competitive with or complementary to the project being
considered.

or lesser degree, effective substitutes; in this case the profitability of investment by one of them will be reduced by the implementation of the investment plans of others. Investments may be termed complementary, or mutually supporting, on the other hand, where the profitability of one is increased by the carrying out of the other; this would be the case, for example, where the increased availability of one product increases the demand for another, or where the output of one firm provides a raw material or intermediate product for the manufacture of another. A further and very important form of interdependence derives from the fact that any form of production generates income, and therefore demand for other goods; but the issues arising from this kind of complementarity lie outside the scope of this study.

It follows from the nature of these relationships—which will be considered more fully in later chapters—that any single investment will in general be profitable only provided, first, that the volume of competitive investment does not exceed a critical limit set by the demand available, and, secondly, that the volume of complementary investment reaches some minimum level.

With these considerations in mind, let us now turn to examine, once again, the theory of perfect competition. We may begin by noting that the theory would cease to be applicable if firms were to enjoy increasing returns to scale, for in this case, as everyone knows, it would be unreasonable to assume that industries were always composed of a large number of individual firms. It would seem necessary to assume, therefore, that returns to scale are either constant or decreasing; these alternative possibilities will be considered in turn.

Since the publication of Sraffa's celebrated article,[1] it has been widely recognized that the assumption of constant costs creates difficulties for the perfect competition model. The general view has been that, while the equilibrium prices and outputs for each commodity were determinate, the size of individual firms was not. It has been held, however, that this

[1] 'The Laws of Return under Competitive Conditions,' P. Sraffa, *Economic Journal*, 1926.

indeterminacy was of slight importance, since, under the assumption of constant costs, it did not matter from the point of view of productive efficiency, whether firms were large or small.[1] Doubts have been entertained, however, about the viability of a system of perfect competition under these conditions, for although there *could* be many firms in each industry, there would be no guarantee—without some restraint on the size of each firm—that this would be the case. I now wish to argue that the absence of such restraints creates difficulties for perfect competition which are of a different and more far-reaching character than has been presumed.

It is evident that an entrepreneur could rationally undertake an investment decision only if he had some minimum information about what entrepreneurs would or would not do, if he were assured that competitive investment would not exceed, and complementary investment would not fall short of, certain critical levels. It would be unreasonable to expect that his information on this score would ever be quite complete or that it would ever be wholly lacking; business men may operate in twilight but not in utter darkness. How then is access to the information to be provided? This could obviously be done, for example, if all the members of the related group were to plan their activities in concert and agree in advance about what they would unfailingly do, or if, renouncing their independence, they were to put themselves under the orders of some higher authority, which, by itself taking all the related decisions, would require no market information in the sense that I have defined it. The practicability of any complete solution along these lines need not concern us at this point; arrangements of this kind can be set aside as clearly incompatible with free, far less perfect, competition. And yet, without such measures of concert, how can we suppose individual producers to become informed about each other's prospective actions?

[1] Vide *Linear Programming and Economic Analysis*, by R. Dorfman, P. A. Samuelson, and R. M. Solow, p. 348. '. . . Walras maintains the assumption of constant returns to scale. In fact the assumption is a vital one if he is to be able to talk about the outputs of various commodities without worrying about the allocation of output among firms.' And, in a footnote, 'If all firms in an industry have the same production coefficients, the allocation of output among firms is indeterminate, but unimportant.'

The special difficulties in the way of obtaining the necessary market information can be shown up most starkly if we consider the case of an entrepreneur, working under perfectly competitive conditions, who wishes to assess how much investment, in the article he is planning to produce, will be undertaken by other people. Let us assume that he is aware that the total demand for the product will rise by a certain amount. He has no reason to believe, we shall further assume, that this awareness is his particular monopoly; there may be one or more of his competitors who are equally ready to respond to the profit opportunity which has opened up. Each of these, moreover, under the assumption of constant costs, is able to plan an increase in supply of indefinitely large proportions. Now in this situation, even if only one other competitor became simultaneously aware of the profit opportunity, it would seem to be impossible for our particular entrepreneur to form a reliable expectation of what the volume of competitive supply, and therefore the article's future price, would be. He would be unable to take an investment decision without some information about the expansion plans of his potential rival, who would himself be faced with precisely the same difficulty. Given that there is to be no collusion between them, and that they are both equally ready and willing to invest, their interdependence seems to place an insurmountable barrier in the way of obtaining the information necessary for an investment decision. The damage done by the constant costs assumption would therefore appear to be somewhat different from that generally supposed. It is not only that the size of the individual firm becomes indeterminate, or that the persistence of large numbers of competing firms is no longer assured; it is rather that the whole mechanism of adjustment breaks down.

It remains to inquire, however, whether the inaccessibility to entrepreneurs of the necessary market information, and therefore the breakdown of the mechanism of adjustment, is peculiar to conditions of constant returns to scale. Let us now assume that the unit costs of production for each firm will ultimately rise with the volume of its output, putting aside for the moment the difficulty of finding any reason, under perfectly competitive conditions, why this should be so. Will it now be possible for entrepreneurs to obtain the information necessary for rational investment decisions? Let us again consider an entrepreneur who learns that the demand for a particular product has risen by a certain amount and who has no reason to believe that an indefinite number of other producers, actual or potential, do not share this awareness. Each of these, under the assumption of decreasing returns to scale, can plan an increase of supply of finite size only; given that there is perfect mobility, however, they are all free and able to plan to expand by this amount. Here again, therefore, the maximum potential volume of competitive supply is unlimited, not because of the possibility of indefinite expansion by each individual firm, but of the indefinitely large number of firms which might expand. No entrepreneur is able to formulate his investment plans on the basis of information about those of his competitors, because they likewise first require information about his, and other, relevant plans. The circularity which rules out, in this case, the possibility of informed investment decisions is the inevitable consequence of the particular system of arrangements which were initially postulated. It is clearly independent of any assumptions as to scale economies—or diseconomies—for the individual firm, but would arise wherever there were many independent producers all aware of a profit opportunity and able simultaneously to respond to it. Here we have an example, if albeit an extreme one, of the way in which the nature of the economic organization, or relationship between entrepreneurs, affects their access to market information.

An analogy may help to reinforce the point. The opportunities open to an entrepreneur in a perfectly competitive market might be compared to an unusual kind of lottery. Entry, let us suppose, is invited on the following basis. If subscriptions amount, by a certain date, to say £1 million, they will simply be returned in full; should they amount to less than this, they will be returned together with a share of a certain prize money; but should they exceed £1 million, they will be returned subject to a deduction depending on the excess. Now evidently, unless it were possible to make some assumptions about factors which independently restrict how many people would enter the lottery, and what stakes they might make, it would scarcely be possible for anyone to form a rational estimate of the chances of success. In the analogue of the competitive market there would be no basis for a rational investment decision; here also the possibility of making profits or losses depends on the total commitment of resources, while it is by no means obvious that any way of obtaining information about this is available.

This difficulty has frequently been noticed but is presumably regarded as no more than a tiresome logical catch. Yet this reaction is curious in view of the attention which has been given to oligopoly and the so-called indeterminacy inherent in it. If there are only a few firms, then A, in formulating its output policy, must consider B's reaction to it, which may itself depend on what B thinks that A will do in return; this being so, it has been recognized that, without making additional special assumptions, we cannot say what A will do. The existence of many sellers does indeed eliminate this particular obstacle to the rational formation of investment plans; there is no need for one entrepreneur to expect that the policies of his competitors will be significantly affected by what he himself may decide to do. But this by no means implies that we can assume that their policies will be predictable by him, or that he is somehow freed from the need to obtain some information about them. Unless we can show that such information will somehow be available, then we are obliged to continue to regard the actions of any one entrepreneur as indeterminate, even although he may be a member of a large group. Presumably the conviction that perfect competition eliminates this kind of uncertainty is based on the fact that the entrepreneur cannot, in such conditions, affect the price at which he sells, which therefore acts as a 'given' parameter in his decision-making; but this fails to recognize that the price which is relevant to his investment decisions is that which is expected in the future, and that this price is certainly not 'given' in the sense of being known in advance.

4. It is possible that the reader, while accepting the above analysis, may still be prepared to attach to it only the most limited significance, on the grounds that, in order to demonstrate the inability of entrepreneurs to obtain the necessary market information, very special assumptions had to be made. The trouble arose, it could be argued, because the entrepreneur was unable to rule out the possibility that an indefinitely large volume of competitive investment might not be undertaken simultaneously with his own decision to produce the good in question. Were the times at which competing entrepreneurs became aware of the profit opportunity, or the speeds at which they were able to respond to it, only fractionally different, then this problem would disappear, each firm being able to invest successively in the knowledge that no other investment decisions were being taken at the same time elsewhere. The postulation of such fractional differences in awareness or in responsiveness, it could also be pointed out, need not be inconsistent with the conditions of perfect competition.

On a little reflection, however, it becomes apparent that the difficulty is not so easily disposed of. Entrepreneurs, even if they could disregard the possibility of investment decisions being taken simultaneously with their own, would have to have some knowledge of the additional volume of competitive supply already planned. But there is no special machinery, in the perfect competition model, to ensure that investment programmes are made known to all concerned at the time of their inception rather than at the time when, by culminating in an additional flow of goods on the market, they affect prices. It might be possible to save the model by postulating the existence of this sort of machinery, by assuming, that is, that each investment decision was announced, immediately on having been made, to all other producers.[1] Were this the case, then prospective producers would all be reliably informed about the volume of competitive supply forthcoming, and, provided demand conditions were also known, the movement

---

[1] Producers, where they are not too numerous, may sometimes be able to obtain information about competitive investment plans directly in this way. A manufacturer, although he may be secretive about his costs and production methods, has a positive incentive to inform others of the fact that he will invest. From announcements in the trade journals and elsewhere, therefore, it may be possible to make some estimate of the volume of competitive supply being currently projected. One should note, however, that it would not be sufficient merely to circulate a report to all entrepreneurs about the provisional intentions of everyone in the industry, for these intentions might

to equilibrium would take place. By having to postulate a system of announcing all investment decisions, however, we effectively admit that price movements, by themselves, do not form an adequate system of signalling. We complement perfect competition, moreover, with an apparatus the existence of which is not presumed in the defining conditions of the model. The introduction of these additional assumptions, essentially represents, as did the 'tâtonnement' of Walras, or the 're-contracting' of Edgeworth, an evasion of the central problem of the working of a decentralized system; by enabling us simply to presume the possession of certain information, it diverts attention from a study of the conditions which would in practice determine its availability.

These remarks, however, should not be taken to imply that the adaptation of supply may not come about by successive investment decisions, or that differences in the responsiveness of entrepreneurs may not be a condition which permits the formation of reliable estimates of the volume of competitive supply already planned. I shall in fact explore, in the following chapter, possibilities of this kind. It will become apparent however, that, in order to ensure successful adaptation, the awareness and responsiveness of different potential producers have to be assumed to be more than fractionally different. What I wish to stress here is, first, that there is no reason for believing that these differences will necessarily, under all circumstances, be of the size and kind required, and, secondly, that their existence is very doubtfully consistent with the conditions which define the perfect competition model. According to these conditions, resources are fully mobile; all entrepreneurs are able to borrow funds freely and to apply resources wherever they please. Such a situation would be difficult to reconcile with the staggered responses which, it appeared, might be necessary for informed investment decisions and successful adjustment; for, if, within any particular period, one entrepreneur is presumed to be able

then be revised on the basis of the information received. The subsequent circulation of information about these revised intentions would, in general, merely give rise to further revisions.

In this and the following chapter I have concentrated on the possibilities of obtaining market information in the absence of any system of announcing firm investment plans.

to invest, whereas others are not, there would have to be restraints, either temporary or permanent, on the activities of the latter, restraints which, as we shall have occasion to observe more fully later, are associated with the existence of market imperfections of one kind or another.

The initial deficiency, therefore, of the traditional model of competition is that it ignores the fact that decentralized systems can work only provided their constituent members can obtain the minimum necessary information, and that a principal objective of our analysis should be to explain how this is made possible.[1] Expectations, it may be admitted, are sometimes brought into the model, albeit reluctantly, but there is no recognition that their rational formation requires a basis of information, the availability of which, where it relates to market conditions, is not independent of the market structure assumed.

5. One further question remains, to which our attention will be devoted for the rest of the chapter. If the theory of perfect competition is thus defective, how are we to account for its original adoption and for the firm hold which it has continued to exercise over the thinking of theoretical economists? If, as I have suggested, but have yet to prove, some market imperfections may be essential to the process of successful economic adjustment, how did they come to be wholly banished from the standard model of the competitive system?

The broad rationale of the private enterprise system was of course appreciated long before the development of modern equilibrium analysis. It was realized that, if the demand for

---

[1] For a recognition that there is deficiency in our competition theory, see Tjalling C. Koopmans, *Three Essays on the State of Economic Science*, p. 146–7. 'To my knowledge no formal model of resource allocation through competitive markets has been developed, which recognises ignorance about all decision makers' future actions, preferences or states of technological information as the main source of uncertainty confronting each individual decision-maker and which at the same time acknowledges the fact that forward markets on which anticipations and intentions could be tested and adjusted do not exist in sufficient variety and with a sufficient span of foresight to make presently developed theory regarding the efficiency of competitive markets applicable. If this judgment is correct, our economic knowledge has not yet been carried to the point where it sheds much light on the core problem of the economic organisation of society; the problem of how to face and deal with uncertainty.'

an article increased, the profit opportunities created would permit private self-interest unwittingly to further the public good, subject of course to qualifications which were paid a varying degree of attention. It was realized also that if the total supply of the article were in single hands, then the terms of sale could be influenced to the benefit of the seller, but to the general disadvantage; and it could also be shown that both ignorance and the artificial restriction of enterprise could hamper the invisible hand. These ideas, in the latter half of the nineteenth century, were expounded with a new degree of logical rigour and precision, and were fitted together so as to form a hypothetical system purporting to represent the workings of the economy reduced to essentials. If artificial restrictions and ignorance were impediments, they should be wholly expelled from the model; monopoly being an evil, it seemed proper to assume a multiplicity of atomistic units and the absence of any collusion between them, in order that the terms of any exchange could safely be withdrawn from individual control. Competition was thus made 'perfect'; such a system was not represented, at least by reputable economists, as accurately describing the actual state of free enterprise, from which all elements of restriction, ignorance and monopoly had not been purged. But it undoubtedly stood, for many people, as an ideal or model form of organization—strictly speaking only a logical as opposed to an ethical ideal, although this distinction was not always sharply made. It does not seem to have been recognized that the fact that 'imperfections', in some forms and degree of strength, are clearly an obstacle to adjustment, does not entitle one to conclude that it would be best if 'imperfections' were absent altogether. Yet the pedagogic convenience of perfect competition, and its suitability as a base for extensive formal and mathematical elaboration, gave the system a central place in theoretical discussion, and the many qualifications with which, say, Marshall, would have hedged the concept fell into the background. In the 1930's, it is true, theories of imperfect competition were developed and given prominence, yet even they did not break away from the older analysis in so far as our central issue is concerned. The comparative neglect of the informational aspects of economic systems may perhaps be explicable in terms of two sorts of confusion. The first we might term a confusion of perspective, to denote the failure to distinguish clearly enough between the point of vision of the model-builder himself and that of his creatures within the model. For the creator there is no problem of knowledge, for the objective facts about the system appear as postulated data from which could be deduced (or so it was believed) the equilibrium configuration. Was it always appreciated that information about these 'determinants', that 'perfect knowledge', in this sense, would have been of no use to the members of the system even if they could ever have been assumed to possess it? To put the matter somewhat differently, was it realized that the problem of knowledge for a member of a group was not the same as that of an isolated agent working in a passive medium? The question is not so much whether these contentions would have been explicitly denied, but whether anything approaching full weight was given to them in the construction of theoretical foundations.

6. The second reason why hypothetical economic systems may have been conceived as they were, is one familiar to all students of the social sciences. It was inevitable that methods of analysis which had originally proved so triumphantly successful in mechanics, and later over the whole field of the physical sciences, should have been carried over into the study of social phenomena, and that the reputability of procedures adopted in this latter field should be gauged by their resemblance to those applied in the former. 'Scientism', the term sometimes employed to denote this attitude, has a long history and it is certainly at least as prevalent today as it was in the eighteenth and nineteenth centuries. Economics has undoubtedly gained much in terms of analytical rigour since, let us say, Adam Smith, and this may, in part, be attributable to procedures taken from the physical sciences; but it has also suffered through neglecting aspects of economic activity which have no counterpart in this other sphere. Thus an equilibrium was regarded as 'determined', as if almost directly, by real, objective factors such as production possibilities, preferences and the like. States of belief or knowledge, which had of course no place among the conditions of equilibrium in, say, mechanics, were also denied at least a prominent rôle in economics. It is true that present day 'communication theory' has found for the informational aspects of social systems a respectable parallel in the properties of electrical circuits. Real benefit may result from the study of such correspondences, but possibly also real harm; for if we are led to study the informational aspects of social systems only in terms of a rigid conceptual framework borrowed from physics, we shall certainly obtain a distorted picture. Prices, for example, and particularly the current values of prices, assume from this point of view an undeserved prominence, because it is in terms of them that a quasi-physical signalling mechanism can be elaborated and given mathematical expression.[1]

---

[1] This is perhaps too dogmatic. The notion of information does enter into accounts of certain physical systems; thermometers may conveniently be said to 'observe' and 'record' temperature, and thermostats, on the basis of this information, to control the level of an operation. It is true that in such physical systems we have responses to the current level of stimuli, whereas human action is chiefly based on expectations as to future states. But even this division can be bridged in principle, for expectations are themselves based on past and present events. If the principle on which they are so based could be clearly determined and set out, there would be no objection to representing purposive or teleological action in terms of a sequence of causes and effects. It may well be convenient and illuminating therefore to describe some kinds of human and social activity in terminology borrowed from physical systems, and particularly from those of a self-regulating kind.

I have therefore no methodological axe to grind. But it seems, simply as a matter of practical convenience, that a satisfactory explanation of economic activity cannot be given wholly, or even chiefly, in terms of the concepts appropriate to the description of physical systems; for we have to take explicit account of factors for which no convincing physical analogues are available, factors such as differences or uncertainty of opinions, or the spontaneous or deliberate development of institutions which facilitate communication. The appropriate methodological position is surely one of tolerance and eclecticism, of choosing the approach and terminology which seems to suit the subject in hand, of indiscriminate plundering of concepts from other fields whenever they seem illuminating. If, out of loyalty to a rigid methodology, or more likely because of habit or prevailing fashion, we endeavour to squeeze a knowledge of economic activity into a conceptual straight jacket borrowed from mechanics, we are likely, as a result, to ignore, distort or play down those inconvenient aspects of reality which do not easily fit. This is undoubtedly happening in much modern economic analysis; communication in the economy is represented almost exclusively in terms of a signalling system of current prices simply because actual prices and quantities lend themselves easily to mathematical expression and to analogies with electrical circuits. If expectations are introduced they are very often

7. We have yet to consider one final, but important attraction of the received theory of the competitive equilibrium. It was apparent from the beginning that the configuration which had been identified merely as the equilibrium position of a hypothetical system had also, and as it were incidentally, optimal properties. Its exponents, as did the Lord in the beginning, created it and saw that it was good. More recently, a precise sense has been given to the word optimal, as used in this connexion, by demonstrating that, in a purely competitive equilibrium, no one could be made better off except at someone else's expense. Needless to say, this statement has straight away to be hedged with all manner of qualification; even if realizable (which would imply, for example, the absence of significant economies of scale), perfect competition would be compatible with influences, such as external economies, which upset the correspondence with the so-called Pareto optimum—which is, of course, itself no unqualified ideal. Much attention has been devoted to this topic and there would be no point in attempting to summarize here the

assumed certain, and almost always unanimous, in order that we can again give the kind of explanation we have previously decided (or unconsciously assumed) to be respectable. As a result we form a false vision of economic processes.

One should not forget that the concepts we employ in describing physical processes were themselves frequently borrowed from the field of human thought and action—the notions of information, sensing and control have obviously this provenance. But this may also be so in less likely cases, and it is interesting to note that John Locke questioned 'whether the mind doth not receive its idea of active power clearer from reflection on its own operations than it doth from any external sensation' (*Essay Concerning Human Understanding*, Bk. II., Ch. 21.4). There is, however, no need to give any field of experience priority, for the same kind of notion may arise in more than one. Here again we may quote this undogmatic philosopher: 'Power also is another of those simple ideas which we receive from sensation and reflection. For observing in ourselves that we do and can think, and that we can at pleasure move several parts of our bodies which were at rest, the effects also that natural bodies are able to produce in one another occurring every moment to our senses, we both these ways get the idea of power' (op. cit. Bk. II., Ch., 7.8). These epistemological issues are, however, not our direct concern. But reflection upon them should caution us against regarding the procedures and concepts of any one science as having any general, ideal appropriateness. Having explained the properties of physical systems in terms borrowed from human activity, there seems little justification in then attempting to explain human activity in terms of the physical systems we happen so far to have developed.

voluminous literature.[1] We shall be concerned not with the qualifications but with the content of what has been called the 'fundamental theorem' which 'contains everything of significance and provides the backbone of modern welfare economics'. The theorem, that is, that 'Every competitive equilibrium is a Pareto optimum; and every Pareto optimum is a competitive equilibrium'.[2]

The Pareto optimum is conceived in terms of the categories of centrally planned allocation on the basis of full knowledge. Available resources and the possibilities of transforming them are 'given'; so also are the consumers' preference orderings which form the basis of the objective to be realized. From these data a special configuration, or rather an infinite set of them, can be found, each of which has certain properties, the most familiar of which being the equality, for all consumers and all producing units, of the marginal rate of substitution (or trans-formation) between any two goods. In addition, however, the configuration meets other obviously necessary requirements; the levels of production and consumption postulated are all compatible with the data about production functions and resources available.

In our discussion of the equilibrium of an atomistic, decentra-lized economy, we observed how a very similar procedure was followed, although ostensibly for a wholly different purpose. In this case we postulated private ownership of all resources and the existence of entrepreneurs to allocate them; neverthe-less the problem was similarly posed in terms of given resources, together with production and preference functions, and here also a configuration was sought which met, in effect, the same requirements. The marginal rates of substitution and trans-formation between any two commodities were made equal to the ratio of their prices, and therefore to each other, in order that consumers and producers were in the best position open to them. Resources used were also made compatible with the conditions of their availability. Only one further condition was

---

[1] The essence of this theory is set out in an article by Professor Hicks, 'The Foundations of Welfare Economics', *Economic Journal*, 1939.

[2] *Linear Programming and Economic Analysis*, by Dorfman, Samuelson and Solow, pp. 409–10.

assumed to be met and this served to determine a single configuration rather than an infinite set of them. On the basis of the prices which the system could be said to imply, the value of the expenditure of any individual was made equal to his income, as derived from the sale or hire of the productive services assumed, in terms of the original distribution of skills and property, to be at its command. This condition could equally well have been introduced, however, in the determination of an optimum, had we wished to identify one particular configuration from among a class. So far, therefore, identical reasoning has been employed in order to discover ostensibly two quite separate states, the one a Pareto optimum, the other the situation to which a purely competitive economy would gravitate or at any rate remain at rest. It is not, in fact, until conditions of belief are introduced, that the analysis, which might otherwise have been devoted merely to the determination of a particular optimum, appears to be concerned with equilibrium. In order to have an optimum, any individual has to be as well off as he can be made, subject to the condition that no one be made worse off—and this condition the configuration directly fulfils. In order to have an equilibrium, each individual has to be as well off as he believes he can make himself and he must be able to carry out his plans without his beliefs being contradicted by his experience. This situation can be realized simply by postulating the universal belief that goods will always be bought and sold at the existing (equilibrium) prices; the activities which make up the configuration then appear as planned and intended and their compatibility, both with each other and with objective technical conditions, is assured by the consistency conditions which the configuration has to meet.

Thus presented, the identity of the competitive equilibrium with a Pareto optimum appears artificially contrived, with expectations of a special kind being the *deus ex machina* which, at the last moment performs the miracle. It is to the credit of Walras and others to have discovered the configuration which combined certain optimal characteristics with important internal consistencies, but in then representing it as the equilibrium state of a particular hypothetical system, many corners were unjustifiably cut. Particular expectations were simply conjured up to meet a need, without regard to how, or even whether, they could have been formed. All that had genuinely been demonstrated was the logical possibility of a hypothetical economic arrangement with certain harmonious properties, or simply of a kind of 'optimum'; but perhaps Walras, like Columbus, mistook the proper nature of his own discovery.

The theory of perfect competition, I would therefore suggest, offers us, under the guise of an equilibrium position, a particular configuration to which the organization of production and exchange could conform, a configuration moreover which has important normative characteristics. But the theory provides us, neither with a satisfactory account of how this state of affairs might come about, nor with a blue-print of the institutional or market arrangements which would best promote it. The so-called equilibrium could be brought into being, in principle, by the allocative decisions of a central planning authority; its realization, in practice, however, as a result of the inevitable limitations in the knowledge of any such authority, could never be more than approximate. In addition, as I shall later argue, it could also be produced, at least in principle, without central planning, as a result of the investment decisions of independent entrepreneurs operating within a competitive, but not a perfectly competitive, framework. The closest approximation to the configuration obtainable in practice, however, is likely to be reached by arrangements in which both competition and deliberate co-ordination—whether public or private—play some part.

But this is to anticipate the content of the following chapters, the nature of which it now remains briefly to indicate. The second part of the book will be concerned with how entrepreneurs can be supplied with the information which will enable them to take the investment decisions required by a rational allocation of resources. The first of its chapters will deal with the availability to the entrepreneur of information about the activities of his competitors, the second with information about those engaged in complementary investment activity. In each case, the object will be to determine the conditions under which the supply of the necessary information would or would not be adequate without the introduction of explicit measures of co-ordination designed to provide it. The chapter then following, on the assortment of production, will consider the complications which are introduced by recognizing the desirability of commodities being produced in appropriate variety as well as in appropriate proportions. Finally, in this second part of the book, we shall investigate the process of competition more closely, bearing in mind the need for some machinery to ensure that the authority to take investment decisions will pass to those who are proved most able to take them.

PART II

INFORMATION AND ADJUSTMENT

III

THE CO-ORDINATION OF COMPETITIVE INVESTMENTS

1. IF the analysis in the previous chapters is correct, there exists a serious deficiency in the accepted theory of the working of a competitive economy, a deficiency represented by the absence of any satisfactory explanation of how the members of the system could obtain sufficient information on which to base investment decisions. In order to endeavour to fill this gap, we shall have to inquire how information might come to be available, notwithstanding the special difficulties created by the diffusion of the power of decision among autonomous yet related units. This will oblige us to determine both the minimum amount of information which entrepreneurs would need to have and the different conditions which would, or would not, permit access to it.

The profitability of any one investment project, it was observed, would be dependent on the volume both of competitive and of complementary investment undertaken by others. I shall concentrate now on the former relationship and postpone discussion of the problems raised by complementarity to the next chapter. The analysis will be further restricted to decisions to invest in fixed equipment; decisions of a more short-run character, about, for example, the appropriate volume of goods which should be produced from this equipment, or which should be held in stock, will receive only very incidental consideration. This choice of subject matter can be justified on the grounds that it is particularly in relation to the long-run investment decisions that the problem of forming reliable expectations—which is our central concern—will be most acute; it must be admitted, however, that, in a more complete analysis, the question of short-run predictions, and of the information required for them, would have to be given systematic study. The treatment to be offered here will be very far from exhaustive, and the conclusions to which it points will, in some cases, be somewhat tentative. It may be fair to say, however, in extenuation, that the issues to be dealt with, though important, have received very little attention elsewhere.

2. Let us then consider an entrepreneur who expects the demand for a particular product to rise and to remain, for some considerable time, at this higher level. He will recognize that there has been created, as a result, a 'general profit potential', in the sense that the additional investment of resources in this direction would, up to a certain point, afford profits to those who controlled them. But, if he is to believe that there exists, at the same time, a profit opportunity for him in particular, he will have to be assured that the volume of investment undertaken by his competitors will not be so great as to cause a substantial excess of supply over demand at any time during the economic life of the equipment which he has to employ. If the existence of a general profit potential were to call forth an excessive supply response, then clearly it would result in losses rather than profits for all concerned.

In representing the future profitability of investment by a particular firm as depending solely on the balance between the total volumes of demand and supply for the commodity in question, important simplifications are of course involved. It is being assumed, in effect, that all firms will have the same production costs and will therefore make profits or losses according to whether the demand, at a price corresponding to these costs, is greater or less than the volume of supply. In fact, of course, the costs of different producers will not be the same, and the profits they can earn will vary accordingly. In addition, the magnitude of the losses imposed by any excessive volume of investment will depend on a variety of factors (such, for example, as the flexibility of production and the elasticity of demand) which will be introduced into the discussion only at a later stage.

It will further simplify matters if we assume that the process of investment, once it has reached a certain point, is irreversible and represents a firm commitment. Such investment commitments will give rise to an additional flow of output, but only after a certain interval of time, commonly called the gestation period, has elapsed. Let us first suppose that all entrepreneurs become immediately aware of all investment commitments as soon as they are made. In such a case, it would require only fractional differences in the times at which they learned of the general profit opportunity, or in the speed at which they could respond to it, in order that each of them could have the market information necessary for investment decisions. All entrepreneurs would know the exact extent of the competitive investment commitments already made; were they also assured that no one would misjudge the magnitude of the increased demand, they would have no reason to fear any future excess of supply. As a result of decisions taken successively by different firms, and without the need for deliberate co-ordination, production would gradually be increased to the appropriate higher level. Adjustment of this kind, however, would require the existence of machinery able to ensure that everyone was immediately made aware of the full extent of competitive investment commitments. Such machinery is not obviously a part of the private enterprise system; the larger the number of firms in each industry, and the less the co-operation between them, the more difficult is it to see how the required information could be obtained.

It therefore seems more reasonable to assume that entrepreneurs will generally learn of the investment commitments of others only after a certain period of time, which, for convenience, will be called the 'transmission interval'. The duration of this interval, it seems safe to presume, would not be greater than the gestation period, after which the extra flow of goods would have made themselves felt on the market, but could be shorter than this, where entrepreneurs were able to obtain evidence about the amount of construction under way. Provided only that it is greater than zero, the smooth process of adjustment described above can no longer be depended upon. An entrepreneur contemplating investment will be unable to estimate the volume of competitive production which may have been prepared during the period of time, just elapsed, equal to the transmission interval; nor will he be assured that other producers may not undertake future investment, which, lacking information about the volume of existing commitments, they may not realize to be excessive. Adequate market information, in other words, seems unobtainable, and the most obvious ways of obtaining it, such as collaboration between producers, is ruled out by the conditions of free competition which are being assumed.

And yet, in any actual private enterprise economy, successful adjustment does in fact take place, at least in some industries, for some of the time. The problem, therefore, is to explain how this can happen, and, in particular, how the required information is somehow made available. It will be instructive to consider first some lines of approach to the problem, which, although unsatisfactory, are not without interest. None of them take the dilemma, in which entrepreneurs might appear to find themselves, very seriously; they imply, that in forming expectations about the activities of competitors, general experience and a knowledge of business psychology can make up for the lack of any other firm evidence.

3. Some of the arguments along these lines will bear very little scrutiny. It cannot be maintained, for example, that an entrepreneur, knowing that no one has an adequate amount of market information, would be prepared to invest in the conviction that his competitors would be inhibited from doing so; he might equally well assume that they had themselves decided to invest on the presumption of his own inaction. Nor can one plausibly contend that it would be possible to predict the actions of competitors merely by considering what one would do, in like circumstances, oneself; for an essential factor in these circumstances is the lack of information on which rational decisions can be taken.

Another argument, somewhat similar to these, might be suggested by the undoubted fact that many business decisions are of an uncalculated, routine, or conventional form. Could not an entrepreneur predict the activities of his competitors merely from a knowledge of their habits? The implied premise, however, is that everyone else will behave in a habitual way in order that this one entrepreneur may take calculated decisions. It would be inconsistent to represent actions as the result both of routine response and of informed calculation, even although, on occasions, both these procedures might yield the same result. We would, of course, be logically entitled to regard all business decisions as being wholly routine or conventional, so that the need for information simply does not arise. This particular supposition, however unrealistic, is nevertheless implicit in many theoretical models of economic adjustment, the defects of which we pointed out in the previous chapter. Although some social systems, such as anthills, may operate without the need for rational, informed activity, it is perfectly clear that our own does not. But while it would be ridiculous to suppose that all business decisions were conventional and uninformed, it would be wrong to conclude that none of them are. In conditions of great uncertainty, individual persons, or firms, or banks, may do things not as a result of calculated decision, but simply because that is what they did before, or what others did, or simply because it is 'the thing to do'. Conventionalism of this kind has been more frequently recognized as playing a part in the furtherance of political order; its rôle in the production of unplanned economic order may also be significant.

There is, however, one way in which investment plans could be co-ordinated as a result of decisions which could not be regarded strictly either as informed or as habitual. The theoretical possibilities of this kind can be illustrated by reconsidering one of the questions which were taken up in Chapter I. An attempt was then made to determine the conditions which would permit the general equilibrium of perfect competition, once reached, to be maintained. Each member of the system, it was decided, would persist in the activities already adopted provided he could expect all prices not to change. Now it would be rational to hold this expectation, provided there was reason to believe that the activities of everyone else in the system would not be altered, for, were this the case, demand and supply conditions would remain the same throughout the whole economy. Each person would persist in his particular activities, therefore, and equilibrium would be preserved, provided he was assured that everyone else would do likewise. In the absence of any means by which producers might become informed about each other's plans, however, there might seem to be no very obvious way in which such an assurance could be obtained; nevertheless, in the special circumstances which we have presumed, one could legitimately expect the *status quo* to be preserved. Let us suppose that each entrepreneur expects technical conditions, in the form both of production techniques and consumer preferences, to remain unaltered and that he knows profits to be everywhere normal. And let us suppose further that each entrepreneur is aware that all others hold these same beliefs. Under these conditions, albeit fanciful, everyone has an incentive not to change what he is doing, having realized, first, that each individually was powerless to improve his lot, and secondly that, if all kept their course, at least no one would be worse off. Equilibrium would in this case be preserved as a result of what we may term 'implicit collusion'.

It would be difficult to find an account of this notion more concise and striking than that given by Hume. In a discussion about the respect for property he has this to say '. . . When this common sense of interest is mutually expressed, and is known to both, it produces a suitable resolution and behaviour. And this may properly enough be called a convention or agreement betwixt us, though without the interposition of a promise; since the actions of each of us have a reference to those of the other, and are performed upon the supposition that something is to be performed on the other part. Two men who pull the oars of a boat, do it by an agreement or convention, though they have never given promises to each other' (*A Treatise of Human Nature*, Book III, Part II, Section II).

Although implicit collusion can be conceived as maintaining the perfectly competitive equilibrium, it is difficult to see how it could enable it to be produced. If a number of people, for example, were each asked to write down a particular number, in the endeavour to make their combined sum equal to 100, then, in the absence of explicit collusion, they would have only an infinitesimal chance of success. But if they did miraculously happen to choose an appropriate set, and knew that they had done so, it would be reasonable to expect that they would then write down the same numbers if invited to play the identical game on further occasions.

But even if the whole movement to general equilibrium could never be accounted for in terms of implicit collusion, certain more limited adjustments might proceed on this basis. If it could be assumed that increased production of a particular commodity could come only from those competitors already in the field, further entry being ruled out, then an increase in supply, appropriate to a rise in demand, could be the result of uncoordinated investment decisions taken on the assumption that each firm would maintain just that share of the total market which it had enjoyed in the past. Each competitor would have to be convinced that the others had properly estimated the amount by which demand had increased and that they would themselves act according to the convention which he himself proposed to follow. Procedures of this kind, however, although they might be followed under special circumstances, can hardly be regarded as the principal way in which economic adjustment is successfully carried out. Implicit understandings of this kind are likely to be highly fragile and might usually be expected, in the absence of any special sanction, either to break down, or to be replaced by arrangements of a more formal and binding character.

4. There remains one further solution of this general kind which deserves our attention. Could not an entrepreneur form a reliable estimate of the volume of competitive investment, not from any insight into the psychology or habits of other producers, but merely from his experience of what had happened in the past. Might he not have observed, simply as a matter of historical fact, that whenever he is in a position to respond to an increase in demand he can do so safely and with profit, confident that the volume of competitive supply will not be excessive? It would be absurd to deny that this would indeed be possible, but in recognizing this, we should regard the problem with which we began merely as being referred back, rather than brought in any degree nearer to solution. It is still necessary to explain why the entrepreneur's experience should have been as it was, and why, therefore, he can always assume that there will be some safe limit to the volume of competitive supply that will be planned in response to any future rise in demand. Clearly if there were no limits to the number of people who were aware of the increased demand, and who were able to increase supply in response to it, then the reasoning which we have just considered would inevitably lead entrepreneurs to initiate an excessive volume of investment; the reasoning would prove justified only if there were some forces which operated as a check on the ability to act upon it. There must be some genuine grounds for expecting, in other words, that the amount of competitive investment which might have been undertaken, but which had not yet made itself felt, was within definitely safe limits. But it is precisely this expectation that the conditions of perfect competition, if taken to imply the full mobility of resources, seem unable to justify.

It does in fact seem to be the case that entrepreneurs would have access to the market information they require only if there existed a variety of restraints, of differing degrees of strength and durability, to which their freedom of action would frequently be subject. These restraints feature, in our accepted analysis, as imperfections or frictions which clog the competitive system; in fact, as I hope to show, they play an important, and indeed an essential rôle in its successful operation. The difficulty which we have been discussing arose, it will be remembered, because of the length of time—the transmission interval —which would elapse before decisions to commit resources in a particular direction became generally known; competitive investments initiated during this interval would affect the profitability of any project being contemplated, but information about their likely extent would not be available. Now this difficulty would be removed, or at any rate reduced in importance, if there were factors at work which set an upper limit to the volume of competitive investment commitments which could possibly be undertaken during any particular period of time. If an entrepreneur could presume, for example, that the maximum possible volume of investment commitments which could have been made during the transmission period, by actual or potential competitors, was small, relative to the increase in demand, then he could be assured that, in the near future in any event, a market would be found for his output. The danger would remain that too much competitive investment might be undertaken in the future, but its seriousness would be limited by the fact that, given sufficient checks on the rate at which commitments could be made, the unprofitability of further investment would become apparent before the volume of excess supply had become very great. It may appear, at first glance, that, having explicitly assumed that entrepreneurs could not have information about other investment commitments until the transmission period had elapsed, I am now maintaining that they could do so. But any contradiction is apparent rather than real; it may be impossible to estimate the actual volume of such commitments, but possible nevertheless to deduce an upper limit by which they would be bounded.

5. We have now to consider whether there are factors, in actual competitive economies, which might be presumed to fix a ceiling to the rate at which investment commitments could be made. The response of supply to an increase in demand could be checked, we may say, for three different reasons. Entrepreneurs might not all be aware of the general profit opportunity which had been created; they might not all be able to undertake the necessary investment except after a substantial delay, or they might be prevented from selling the goods desired, even if they could produce them. Each of these possibilities must now be considered in turn.

It may seem paradoxical to regard ignorance, in its rôle as a restraint on investment, as actually furthering, in certain circumstances, the successful adaptation of supply to demand. And yet it is clear that an entrepreneur may undertake a certain project chiefly on the grounds that only he, and possibly a very few other producers, are aware of the impending increase in demand. Ignorance, by checking the response of some, may be a necessary condition for any response by others; an unequal distribution of knowledge of final demand, therefore, may actually promote successful adjustment. A general profit opportunity, which is both known to everyone, and equally capable of being exploited by everyone, is, in an important sense, a profit opportunity for no one in particular; it will create the incentive to invest only provided some people are less able to discern it, or to respond to it, than others. That this may seem paradoxical results from a scarcely conscious habit of carrying over, into the study of the production of economic order by a group, notions appropriate only to an isolated planner; it results, that is to say, from the confusion of two different perspectives, that of the participant and that of the onlooker. Any limits on the knowledge or freedom of an individual can be represented as imperfections when considering him in isolation, but they need not impair, and may indeed facilitate, the working of the whole system in which he plays a particular part.

In certain circumstances, the fact that certain producers have a temporary monopoly of information about a general profit opportunity may be important in securing its successful exploitation. The incentive to invest could be created, not only by prior knowledge of an increased demand for an old product, but also by belief in the possibility of successfully marketing a new one; profits may be earned, in other words, both by foresight and by innovation. But when, as must frequently be the case, the existence of a profitable opportunity becomes known to many people at about the same time, then other factors will have to be relied upon to produce an appropriate volume of total investment.

An entrepreneur's ability to set some limit to the maximum possible competitive supply chiefly depends on the existence in the economy of elements of continuity and stability, on the force of the dictum with which Marshall prefaced his *Principles*; *natura non facit saltum*. There are forces at work which narrow individual freedom of action, either in the production, or in the sale of goods which are expected to be in demand. Let us first confine ourselves to those restrictions which operate on the supply potential of a particular commodity, by assuming that once produced it could as easily be sold by one firm as by another.

6. It should be relatively easy to set a lower limit to any estimate of the volume of competitive supply to be expected in the future, merely from evidence about the amount of capacity already in existence or under construction; bygones may be bygones in economics, but not in the sense that future actions are untrammelled by those of the past; at no time is there a *tabula rasa*, and earlier decisions will have momentum, even although it will weaken with the passing of time. The upper limit with which the volume of future competitive supply is associated will depend on the number of firms which could increase their capacity within the relevant period of time and on the extent to which each of them could do so. The management of any particular firm, even if they are convinced of the profitability of investing resources in a particular direction, will frequently be unable to do so to the extent that they would wish. The funds at their own immediate disposal will be limited and they will be unable or unwilling to add to them indefinitely from outside sources. Money may be raised on the security of assets to an extent determined by the value which general opinion puts upon them, but, beyond that, a firm will have to look towards wealth-owners who have sufficient information about the proposed nature of its activities or who put faith in its reputation. Given the inevitable fragmentation or dispersion of the knowledge available to society, the number of such people or institutions will be limited, as will be the degree to which they are prepared to invest in this or any other single concern. A firm will therefore generally find that funds for new investment can be obtained, beyond a certain point, only at increasing cost and with the danger of a loss of control by the original owners to outside interests.

Limits to expansion, at any particular time, may be set also by the organizational changes required, for large changes require men of unusual ability who are not always available; some business men maintain that a firm has to settle down and 'digest' large expansions before it can successfully carry out others. 'Managerial diseconomies' may indeed be more plausibly associated with the rate of growth of a company's operations, rather than, as is more usual, with their existing scale.

There is then a variety of factors which limit the supply potential of the individual firm, in the sense not of the size to which it might ultimately attain but of the maximum increase in capacity and output which it could efficiently realize in a limited time. Some of these factors, it may be noted, are inconsistent with the letter of perfect competition, others with its spirit. The impossibility of borrowing unlimited sums at the same rate of interest is a crucial check, which is usually referred to as an 'imperfection' of the capital market and incompatible with the state of perfect competition. And managerial difficulties, though sometimes conjured up to save the atomistic character of competition, are in fact hard to envisage in a hypothetical world where price and output decisions can be taken, as it were mechanically, on the basis of current prices and costs.

An entrepreneur contemplating investment in a particular line, therefore, knows that there would be a limit to the increase in supply which any individual competitor, if he so wished, could produce within any given time. But would there be any limit to the number of firms, whether already established in the industry or not, which could invest? Other things being equal, firms already in the industry have obvious advantages over potential entrants. They enjoy substantial 'economies of experience'; they have a nucleus of skilled people and of equipment around which growth can more easily and rapidly take place. Certain outsiders will be better placed, however, than others; firms who have previously manufactured a product requiring similar experience, skills and equipment will have an obvious advantage over firms in wholly different lines, and a firm which is established anywhere will be a more serious potential entrant than one not yet in being. Even those firms already engaged in manufacture of the product will not all be equally well placed for rapid expansion. Some may have large reserves while others may not; others may only recently have undertaken a large expansion while others were already on the point of doing so. Where it is difficult to increase capacity except by large discrete stages, that firm may be more likely to expand which needs in any case to replace its equipment.

There is, therefore, good ground for believing that there will generally be substantial differences in the period of time which would have to elapse before different firms would be prepared to invest in response to a recognized profit opportunity. Inertia, as well as momentum, has its counterpart in the economic world. Whether the inevitable staggering of investment commitments would be sufficient to provide an entrepreneur with the assurance of a safe upper limit to the volume of competitive supply is something that would clearly depend on the circumstances of each case. Successful adaptation, it would appear, will be promoted by differences in the rates at which firms can respond and therefore by differences in the circumstances in which they find themselves.

Of crucial importance also will be the duration of the transmission interval. It may be possible, particularly if the number of firms is small, to obtain direct evidence—such as, for example, building in progress—of investment commitments having been made; but, in other cases, the transmission interval may be as long as it takes for increased supply to be produced and its effect registered on the market. Under certain circumstances some indication of the volume of investment initiated may be given with less delay through its effect on the factor, rather than the product market; the more specific the resources required for the manufacture of the product, and the smaller their elasticity of supply, the greater will be the likelihood that scarcities and bottlenecks will deter further expansion. Expansion in the capacity of some industry may be temporarily held up, that is to say, by delay in undertaking complementary investment elsewhere. More will be said about this kind of relationship in the succeeding chapter. What we should note now is that a limited supply of the factors required for the construction of capacity in a particular industry may prevent an excessive volume of capacity being created and thereby remove a deterrent to investment; this kind of check, however, cannot always be relied upon, for the quantity of resources required for an increase in the capacity of one particular industry, provided that they are purchased also by many others, may be small in relation to the global supply available.

On the strength of these considerations, it would seem that, given circumstances which favour a staggered response of supply to demand, an entrepreneur may sometimes be able to set a tolerable limit to the amount of excess production which may inadvertently be planned, even although he cannot rule out the possibility of such an excess entirely. His expectation of profit will be subject, in every case, to a degree of uncertainty, which, even if it does not deter investment altogether, will influence the nature of the programme adopted, in ways which will have to be considered later in more detail. We should note now, however, that the effect on profit expectations of possible divergencies between demand and capacity will vary very widely according to circumstances. The gravity of any loss resulting from excessive capacity will depend, for example, on the elasticity of demand for the product, on the practicability of accumulating stocks, and on the extent to which it is possible to reduce costs when reducing output.

Agriculture may be taken as an example of an industry in which the conditions for successful adjustments are highly unfavourable. The decision whether to increase the output of a particular crop is one which, in the nature of things, has to be taken by producers at much the same time. Given their large number, and in the absence of any collusion between them, the transmission interval will be as long as the gestation period for the particular crop in question—rarely shorter, that is to say, than a year. Demand will frequently be inelastic, supply may be inflexible and storage may be possible only at great cost. Quite apart, therefore, from the additional disturbance introduced by the weather, there would be every reason to expect a very inefficient adaptation of supply to changes in demand; planned co-ordination, in some form or other, may therefore be introduced where it appears practicable.

7. It has been assumed so far, throughout the whole discussion, that all sellers, actual or potential, have equally good access to the market for their goods; under these conditions, entrepreneurs appeared able to obtain information about the likely volume of competitive investment only by virtue of the fact that firms would experience different degrees of difficulty and delay in increasing production; the chances of successful adaptation, therefore, seemed rather slender. In the real world, however, circumstances are frequently more favourable, chiefly because of the limited ability or willingness of buyers to transfer their custom from one seller to another. Our previous assumption that the level of a producer's sales would depend exclusively on the current price and quality of his goods, is valid for only some of the markets of actual competitive economies; throughout many others, and especially in those concerned with manufactured articles, there exists a pattern of commercial connexion which is reasonably stable over short periods, to be ruptured only by strong or sustained pressures. This factor, which serves so as partially to insulate the market of one producer from that of actual or potential rivals, was explicitly recognized by Marshall; he remarked that '. . . When we are considering an individual producer, we must couple his supply curve—not with the general demand curve for his commodity in a wide market, but—with the particular demand curve of his own special market. And this particular demand curve will generally be very steep: perhaps as steep as his own supply curve is likely to be, even when an increased output will give him an important increase of external economies' (*Principles*, p. 458 n.).[1]

Let us first consider the motives for such connexion and then the forms it may take. On the side of the producer the motives are strong and obvious. We have stressed the fact that investment may be undertaken only if a reasonably secure demand can be expected, and this will be more likely if the loyalty of customers makes sales less vulnerable to competitive encroachment. A firm will wish its sales to be not only predictable, but stable also, for even if custom ebbs and flows in a foreseeable way, regularity in output will probably be impossible, so that if overheads are important, capital cost per unit of output will rise. In general a producer will be more eager to guarantee his sales than his purchases, especially if his fixed equipment leaves more scope for variation on the input, as compared with the output, side. He will be unwilling to commit himself in advance to any factor purchases unless the corresponding product sales can first be guaranteed, but this, if

---

[1] Cf. also: 'Everyone buys, and nearly every producer sells, to some extent in a "general" market, in which he is on about the same footing with others around him. But nearly everyone has also some "particular" markets; that is some people or groups of people with whom he is in somewhat close touch; mutual knowledge and trust lead him to approach them and them to approach him in preference to strangers. A producer, a wholesale dealer or a shopkeeper, who has built up a strong connection among purchasers of his goods, has a valuable property. He does not generally expect to get better prices . . . but he expects to sell more easily to them . . .' (Marshall, *Industry and Trade*, p. 182).

sales are to final consumers, may be very difficult to do. The pattern of a consumer's purchases is much more flexible than a producer's output plan and, as his tastes may change, or because new improved goods may later be available, he will be unwilling to purchase very far ahead of requirements. Most of the cards are therefore in the buyers' hands, but not all. Sellers will be able in times of shortage, to give preferential treatment to particular buyers, and they may use this power to induce loyalty from their customers in normal times. It would seem likely, nevertheless, that, as a general rule, the motives for forming market connexions are stronger on the side of the sellers. This disparity, and therefore the comparative weakness of the bonds of market connexion, arises ultimately from the impossibility of predicting accurately what future preferences and productive opportunities will be. Further discussion will be devoted, in the succeeding chapter, to the way in which inevitable uncertainties of this kind reduce the practicability, or desirability, of arrangements designed to increase market information.[1]

8. Let us now turn briefly to the various forms which market connexion may assume. These may range from mere conservatism at one extreme to formal contracts or rigidly exclusive arrangements at the other; all of them may be regarded as the antithesis of competition (if this is taken to imply the willingness of customers to transfer their purchases in response to price and quality changes, however small), but in fact they *need* not prevent the attainment of the objectives which competition is valued as serving, such as productive efficiency and the rational allocation of resources. The relationship between these objectives and market connexion is highly complex and will be deferred for later consideration; our present concern is with the way in which attachments, by providing entrepreneurs with the market information on which to base rational investment decisions, permit the successful adjustment of supply to demand. It is for this reason that we have preferred the term 'market connexion' to, let us say, 'degree of monopoly', which

---

[1] Vide the analysis by Professor Hicks of forward contracts and the causes of disequilibrium, *Value and Capital*, 2nd Ed., Chapter 10.

is more immediately associated with the ability to raise price and gain an abnormally high return. Certain forms of connexion do permit this kind of exploitation, but many others afford at most the opportunity to make only temporary gains at the expense of profitability in the long run.

Perhaps the most obvious way in which a producer may attempt to secure the loyalty of his customers is by offering a differentiated product which they prefer to any substitutes.[1] The protection this offers will be further buttressed if the product has an established reputation, for, prejudice and conservatism apart, buyers who lack skill or time to determine the properties of a complex commodity will be likely to buy those varieties which are bought by many others. Commodities may be differentiated, not only by the possession of particular attributes, but by the point in space at which they are available; transport costs are a very obvious and long recognized form of protection, even if somewhat less important now then they may have been in earlier times.

The particular form of market attachment known as 'goodwill', however, has probably received more attention from business men than it has from the majority of economists. Buyers may be unwilling to transfer their custom from a particular producer, even if momentarily tempted, provided they believe that loyalty to him affords them the best chance of good treatment over the long period. Goodwill of this kind can be promoted by offering rapid delivery, by providing good servicing facilities, and by the willingness to take on special, and not very lucrative, orders. It will be further strengthened if the seller refrains from charging the highest obtainable price in times of temporary scarcity. Many businesses appear to be influenced by factors of this kind; they prefer, in times of shortage, to keep their customers on waiting lists rather than to 'freeze them off' by raising prices so as to clear the market, and they may be willing to plan to work normally at less than full capacity in order that the demands of faithful clients can always rapidly be met. The scope for policies of this kind varies considerably according to circumstances and would seem to be

[1] This preference may of course be created, through advertisement, by the producer himself.

wider in transactions between firms themselves than where a supplier deals with a large number of customers on an almost anonymous basis.

The practice, in manufacturing business, of frequently keeping prices invariant to changes in demand has consequences which are rather directly relevant to our principal concern— the availability of adequate information. If demand and supply are continuously brought into equilibrium by a flexible price, little evidence is provided about the magnitude of the demand changes for which producers should plan. Waiting lists, or advance orders, provided they contain no duplication, are, however, a fairly good index of future sales. Whether the benefits of short-run price stability from the communication or information point of view are offset by impairment of allocative efficiency, is a matter we shall consider later.

The market attachment obtained by goodwill may be sought in a more rigid and formal way by a variety of contracts between buyers and sellers. These might, on occasions, firmly secure for a producer the exclusive custom of a buyer for the whole future period with which he is concerned, but only rarely would buyers find it in their interest to agree to such an arrangement. But producers may hope to secure contracts to guarantee planned utilization of their plants for at least some time ahead.

In the trade in raw materials, or 'commodities' in the narrow sense, the 'particular markets' afforded by product differentiation or by goodwill are generally absent; a similar function may be performed however, at least to some extent, by dealings in 'futures'. These may enable a person who expects to have a quantity of the commodity for sale at some future date to fix in advance the price at which the transaction will be carried out, or enable a prospective purchaser to obtain an agreed quantity at an agreed price on the particular date at which he wishes to do so. But it is characteristic of these arrangements that they offer protection only against the uncertainties of the period immediately ahead; they ensure, at a certain cost, that purchases or sales can be made, on predictable terms, at a date some few months removed, but do not give guaranteed markets beyond this. The device of futures trading may therefore provide an entrepreneur with sufficiently secure expectations to induce him to hold a particular commodity in store, or to undertake production from the equipment which he already possesses; they cannot give him the security on which to base an investment decision which will commit him to buy or sell a particular commodity over a period of years. Given our particular interest, which is in the supply of the market information on which long-run investment decisions could rationally be made, futures transactions are relevant only to a limited and subsidiary extent, quite apart from the fact that they are practicable only where commodities are of standardized and specifiable quality.

Producers may endeavour to increase the security of their individual markets not by direct linkage with customers but by agreements with their competitors. These may assume the limiting form of a cartel or of other formal market-sharing arrangements, or they may consist merely of a tacit understanding not to compete too strenuously. Each producer may, for example, plan merely to maintain his share of the total market, or at any rate to eschew the more aggressive policies, such as price competition, by which he might increase it.

All such arrangements will be facilitated if the number of close competitors is small and if entry is difficult. Given the fulfilment of both these conditions, successful adjustment of supply to demand could be achieved, as we previously recognized, by conventional responses on the part of entrepreneurs; for if each firm correctly anticipates the increase in total demand and automatically seeks merely to maintain his share of it, then the appropriate supply could be produced (though not necessarily in the most efficient way) by their uniform and simultaneous adjustment. Provided the number of producers were small, this conventional behaviour would be supported by a further sanction, for then each of them would know that, if by attempting to increase his share, excess supply were to result, the attendant losses would bear significantly on himself, rather than being distributed widely and thinly over many sellers. With excess supply thus penalized, the likelihood of deficient supply need not be increased; for if each producer expected his competitors not to increase their market share, he would then be the more willing to expand up to the limit of his. There are, of course, all manner of reasons why supply should not be able to adjust to demand precisely in this way, though we could regard such 'simultaneous adjustment', as well as the distinct 'successive adjustment' discussed earlier, as both representing 'pure forms' to which adjustment in practice may to a greater or lesser extent correspond.

The renunciation of price-cutting as a normal competitive weapon may also be intended, if only in part, to give greater security to each individual producer's market. Although tacit agreement to this end would be more likely with few sellers, it is possible also where there are many, especially if a quasi-moral inhibition attaches to the practice of price-cutting. But such arrangements are likely to be fragile unless they assume a more binding form, for at any particular time there will be firms whose interests are partially divergent from those of the group as a whole—because, for example, they are working below the average level of capacity utilization and hope that, if they cut price, demand will be reshuffled in their favour, even if competitors soon follow suit. Large numbers by themselves are scarcely a barrier to more formal and binding agreements, at least since the development of modern methods of communication, but variety of interests and ease of entry—with which large numbers are often associated—usually are.

9. This very summary discussion has had one end in view —to stress that these forms of market connexion, whatever the additional objectives for which they are designed, and whatever their indirect effects, do afford entrepreneurs a more secure market for their individual products. They serve, in other words, as a means of increasing the amount of market information in a decentralized economy, or, in other words, of increasing the predictability of the entrepreneurial environment. Whether the price paid for this, in terms of possible inefficiency and misallocation is too high, is a question of some difficulty which I must deliberately defer. By considering in succession the natural inertia or friction in the system and then those restraints which have been deliberately contrived, we were enabled to observe their essential homogeneity. The availability of market information was, I originally claimed, a function of the nature of the economic arrangements or system with which we are concerned; we must now recognize that the availability of one kind of such information—that related to competitive production—depends in particular on the existence of restraints which, in varying degree, reduce the freedom of action of individual entrepreneurs. There is without doubt an optimum strength for these restraints, as determined by their net effect in terms of the several objectives of a system of competition, but it is certainly not equal to zero. By assuming, overtly or tacitly, that it is zero, and therefore by neglecting the whole problem of information, the perfect competition model condemns itself not only to unrealism but to inadequacy even as a hypothetical system. It is no defence to appeal, moreover, to the analogy of mechanical statics which, though neglecting friction, can still identify the equilibrium position of a system of forces, for we cannot demonstrate that economic systems have such positions of rest without reference to expectations and information which could not be presumed to be available in the absence of restraints.

It can hardly be doubted, in this connexion, that thinking has been shaped by terminology. If the factors which I have referred to, by analogy as momentum, inertia, or friction, are categorized as 'imperfections', then it is natural to presume, if only by implication, that ideally their effect would be zero. If the deliberately contrived arrangements we discussed are termed 'monopolistic', then their possible use in exploitation comes most readily to mind. It is for this reason that it seemed convenient to refer to both these factors simply as 'restraints', for they increase the supply of market information by reducing the freedom of action of individual units in the system. Those who sedulously pursue hidden value implications will doubtless find them in this word also, but at least they will be neither wholly good or wholly bad. Restraints are no doubt bad, because freedom is good; but although customs, conventions, and the laws themselves restrict freedom, they nonetheless constitute at worst a very necessary evil.

It is also illegitimate to equate the optimum level of restraint to that which would be produced by natural circumstances in the absence of any arrangements deliberately contrived to this end. It is clear that the level of restraints most likely to permit successful adaptation will vary from one industry to another according to particular circumstances; one would expect it to be higher, for example, where production required a large amount of durable and highly specific fixed equipment. No essential economic distinction can be made between those restraints which are natural and those which are contrived; both produce the same sort of effects and both can do so to an insufficient or to an excessive degree. It is also important to avoid the conclusion that either differences between entrepreneurs in the awareness of, or the ability to respond to, profit opportunities, or the existence of market connexion in its several forms, will necessarily always enable the required information to be obtained and the desirable adjustments to be carried through. It is perfectly possible to conceive of conditions under which the adjustment of capacity, whether to an increase or a reduction in demand, would be best accomplished by central planning, whether by the government or by the industry itself. In choosing between the various alternatives with automatic market forces and central direction at either end of the spectrum, weight would have to be given to a variety of considerations, some of which have yet to be discussed in the chapters which follow.

It will no doubt have occurred to the reader, that when restrictive practices are at present under examination in Great Britain, whether within the courts or elsewhere, little stress is laid on the need for secure expectations and on the part which such practices might play in providing them. This might suggest that entrepreneurs can obtain all the market information they require without the need of contrived restraints on their freedom of action, or that the analysis which I have presented has falsely represented either the importance of such information or the conditions which determine its availability. But it is difficult not to conclude that lawyers and economists, and even business men themselves, may unconsciously focus on these aspects of restrictive practices which the traditional theoretical model of competition is capable of interpreting, while neglecting those aspects which it is not. It is indeed remarkable how much the arguments, if not the actions, even of practical men of affairs, are influenced by theoretical notions, usually of an elementary form. It has seemed to me, that in the great contemporary discussion of monopoly policy, the contribution of economic science has been, in the end, rather disappointing; an important reason for this, I am tempted to conclude, may be the inadequacy of the basic conceptual instruments with which we endeavour to analyse the process of economic adjustment in competitive conditions.[1]

[1] Since writing this book, my attention has been drawn, by Mr. J. B. Heath, to the significance of 'open price' agreements between manufacturers. The parties to such agreements do not commit themselves to follow a common price, but undertake to keep themselves fully informed about the prices which they are actually charging. The agreements may take a variety of possible forms, all of which—ostensibly, at any rate—imply merely the provision of information, rather than the existence of a restrictive covenant. May these be relied upon to supply all the market information which is required? It has to be admitted, I think, that they can not. Producers may wish to have some degree of assurance about the prices which will be charged by their competitors in the future, and this can be provided only by promises, and not merely by statements about present or past policies. Only if 'open price' agreements were to form the basis of tacit collusion, would they perform the same informational function as ordinary price agreements. Needless to say, this does not imply that ordinary price agreements should be considered the more desirable; their superiority from the informational point of view has to be weighed against their adverse effects on selection and market discipline. (See Chapter VII.)

Mr. Heath has also pointed out to me that tacit collusion may be practicable only where homogeneous products are being sold at published prices. Where goods are produced by order, each manufacturer privately submitting his own tender, the basis for such collusion is greatly weakened; individual price cutting, in times of slack demand, would be much less obvious. Formal agreements would be required if the effects of tacit collusion were to be produced.

The reader is referred to Mr. Heath's article on 'Some Economic Consequences of the Restrictive Practices Act', *Economic Journal*, Sept. 1960.

IV

THE CO-ORDINATION OF
COMPLEMENTARY INVESTMENTS

1. THIS chapter will be concerned, as was the previous one, with the general problem of how, in a competitive economy, a rational allocation of resources can result from the investment decisions of many independent entrepreneurs. But it will concentrate on the co-ordination of investments which are complementary to each other, in the sense that their combined profitability when undertaken simultaneously, exceeds the sum of the profits to be obtained from each of them, if undertaken by itself. As in the discussion of competitive investment decisions just completed, it will be necessary to inquire both as to the information which entrepreneurs will wish to have and as to the conditions which will permit access to it. It will be convenient, however, to ignore, for the time being, the fact that the adequacy of the information available, and therefore the success of the co-ordination which depends upon it, is a matter of degree; the effects on the efficiency of adjustment, of the inevitable incompleteness and uncertainty of this information, will be studied in the third part of the book. Once again, in order to simplify the analysis, the discussion will be confined to the limited problem of the proportions in which a 'fixed list' of goods will be produced, but the assumption will clearly have to be relaxed at a later stage, for it is probably in connexion with the qualitative assortment of production that the relationship of complementarity is of greatest importance.

Investments may be complementary either because the costs of one are reduced when the other is undertaken, or because the demand for the output of one of them rises with the increased availability of the output of the other. The nature of these two forms of complementarity will now be considered in turn.

The final production of any commodity is the result of an extensive complex of operations or investments taken both by the firm engaged in final manufacture and by those which supply it. Many of the operations taken within one firm are obviously complementary; it is recognized that the cost of obtaining additional output will be less if the level of several operations can be varied and not merely that of one of them. This of course is the principle lying behind Marshall's distinction between the behaviour of costs in the short run, when only the more easily variable factors can be adjusted, and in the long run, when the fixed equipment can be adjusted also.

But complementarities of this kind characterize the operations not only of the individual firm, the boundaries of which are, in any case, to some extent arbitrary. An entrepreneur will have to recognize that the profitability of his own investment will depend on the terms on which he can obtain inputs, and therefore indirectly on the volume of investment which has been, or will be, undertaken elsewhere. Thus the same kind of complementarity which exists between the application of different resources within the firm, exists also between the application of resources by different firms. In the former case, co-ordination, designed to ensure the best combination of complementary factors, is brought about directly by the entrepreneur in control; in the latter, it has to be achieved by different means the nature of which will presently be considered.

It is also possible for two or more firms to be in a complementary relationship without there being transactions between them. Several different producers may purchase the same raw material or intermediate product which, it could be supposed, was being made by one firm under conditions of increasing returns; if this were so, simultaneous investment by the supplying firm, and by its several customers, would reduce the costs of all of them. Thus investment by two or more firms might be competitive, from the point of view of the market for their products, and yet complementary, in so far as their costs were concerned. Here again this triangular relationship may exist both within and between firms; investment in the production of a standard chassis may be profitable only if there is investment in the two or more models, made by the firm, which incorporate it; and investment in steel capacity may be made profitable by, and itself make profitable, investment by several car manufacturers. The whole economy, one may presume, is united by bonds of this kind, the strength of which will vary widely according to circumstances.

Complementarity of the second kind can be said to exist when consumers' demand for the output from one investment varies inversely with the price, and therefore directly with the volume supplied, of the output from another. At least in advanced countries, complementarity of this kind, which arises from a close association between two or more goods in consumption patterns, is unlikely to be very strong; though examples of it can easily be found (knives and forks, petrol and cars, etc.), there seems no reason to attach to it any very great importance. In poorer societies, however, the goods on which consumers would choose to spend any additional income are likely to be much less substitutable for each other, so that a fall in the price of one of them will not generally call forth a large increase in demand so long as the prices of the others remain unchanged. Under these circumstances, there may be little incentive to invest in one direction unless investment takes place simultaneously in other complementary directions at the same time; and it is this fact which has suggested the doctrine of 'balanced growth', as discussed by Professor Nurkse and others.[1]

There is yet a further kind of complementarity by which almost all investments are related; it results from the fact that investment of any kind, by generating income, will increase the demand for other goods and services. As, however, the additional demand is likely to be distributed widely throughout the whole economy, no very close relationship between particular firms is likely to be created by complementarity in this form; the successful co-ordination of investments, from this point of view, would therefore depend very little on the factors of market structure and inter-firm relationships, which are our principal concern; it is the responsibility of government in its fiscal and monetary policies.

[1] See Chapter 1 of Professor Nurkse's *Problems of Capital Formation in Under-developed Countries*. Complementarity through costs is discussed in Professor Rosenstein-Rodan's article, 'Problems of Industrialisation of Eastern and South-Eastern Europe', *Economic Journal*, June–September, 1943.

2. The problem, with which this chapter will deal, is to explain how, in a competitive economy, producers may obtain information or assurances about the likely volume of complementary investment sufficiently reliable to persuade them to invest themselves. The entrepreneur would have to be confident, it was decided, that the volume of competitive investment was not likely to be excessive; his concern, as regards complementary investment, is that it should be adequate. In the former case, the inaction of others, in the latter, their positive action, is required. The 'restraints' or 'inertia', which afforded stability and predictability in relation to competitive production, are therefore of no assistance here. But those elements making for continuity, which were termed momentum, will enable a producer to set a likely lower limit to the level of complementary activity, as this will inevitably be associated with productive apparatus and arrangements which, because of their relative permanence, imply a commitment for the future. A level of complementary output which is somewhat higher than the current one will in fact be guaranteed; for it will generally be possible to use existing equipment more intensively so as to meet a limited increase in demand at short notice, though probably at higher cost. This short-run elasticity of production may provide an entrepreneur contemplating expansion with sufficient assurance about his supply of inputs. It might also give the producer of an intermediate product sufficient confidence that an increase in its production would be absorbed by the consuming firms merely as a result of a fall in its price and without a prior increase in their fixed capacity.

It does not, therefore, follow that complementarity between various lines of production will necessarily imply that investment in them will have to be simultaneous and co-ordinated. An appropriate pattern of investment might be built up by additions to capital undertaken successively by one firm and then another; and this kind of adjustment would be facilitated by a high short-run elasticity of production and by the absence of scale economies such as would oblige producers to add to their stock of capital in large discrete amounts.

I have so far proceeded on the assumption that the entrepreneur had no reason to expect any increase in complementary production, except to the extent that this could be obtained from more intense utilization of existing capacity. Frequently, however, this assumption would be unduly pessimistic, for competitive economies are by no means destitute of the means for ensuring co-ordination. Simultaneous investment in complementary directions may proceed merely on the basis of what has been described as implicit collusion. If we assume that the profitability of selling more of a final product is generally evident to those entrepreneurs both directly and indirectly concerned, then it may be reasonable to expect investment in both the industry manufacturing the product and in industries complementary to it. Firms in one industry might not be prepared to expand without the assurance of expansion in others, and conversely; yet even if no explicit assurance is available, there may be a very reasonable presumption that the necessary complementary investment will take place. A manufacturer of metal cans, anticipating an increase in the demand for canned fruit, might extend his productive capacity on the presumption that the canning industry would do likewise, even if he had no explicit assurance to this effect. And, of course, there is no reason why the one industry should not inform the other of its intentions. Yet there are fairly obvious limits to the efficiency of 'natural presumption', or 'implicit collusion', as a means by which the market information necessary for efficient adjustment can be obtained. It can be depended on only if certain relatively stringent conditions are fulfilled. Some entrepreneurs in each of the complementary industries must be aware of the profit opportunities which affect them all. They must also know that others in complementary industries share their expectation. In order that the general profit potential should be particularized into profit opportunities for individual firms in each industry, it is also necessary, as we concluded in the previous chapter, that conditions exist which make available the market information necessary for the efficient adjustment of competitive production. In addition, it must be generally recognized that these conditions do exist. Producers will have to be able to presume not only that complementary production will be increased, but that the increase will be sufficiently large, appropriately timed and available at a certain price.

Although producers may therefore be able, merely on the basis of implicit collusion, to expect an adequate increase in complementary production, it seems doubtful whether expectations so based could often be held with confidence. Whether they would be firm enough for those who held them to invest in capital equipment would depend on the magnitude of the gains which would result if the expectations were fulfilled and of the losses which would result if they were not. If the conditions were such as favoured the successive form of adjustment discussed above, then the likelihood of implicit collusion proving effective would be strong; for in this case the losses contingent on a failure of complementary investment to materialize would not be large. But if the penalties on unilateral advance were heavy, no one might be willing to act merely on the presumption that others would keep in step. The conditions of trust which represent the basis of implicit collusion are therefore more likely to exist precisely when the need for them is least, in circumstances, that is to say, where successive adjustment is likely to be feasible. If the relations of complementarity are strong, if fixed capital is important and the minimum efficient scale of investment is large, then implicit collusion will be an inadequate means of providing the market information required.

The phenomenon which we have been discussing would assume somewhat different forms according to whether the complementary group of firms were large or small. Were it large, the implicit collusion would be on what we might call an anonymous basis; each entrepreneur would presume not that this or that particular firm would undertake complementary investment but merely that the aggregate supply of complementary investment would be adequate. Such a presumption might simply be grounded on past experience, on the fact that whenever a profit opportunity developed which affected a group of industries, a sufficient supply of complementary production could usually be relied upon. But where implicit collusion relates to a small number of firms, the expectations held by each of them about the others' likely action would more probably be based on more specific evidence. Each member of the group would be aware that the others shared his view about the profit opportunity which had arisen and that they had the means to invest in response to it; even without any explicit guarantees, therefore, they might confidently presume that steps to produce the required complementary output would be taken. A mutual understanding of this nature would be of a somewhat more palpable character than the implicit collusion of the large number case, especially if further strengthened by experience of common action in the past, and by the bonds of confidence and loyalty which such experience may have created. It deserves, therefore, the name of tacit rather than implicit collusion, in order to mark the more manifest character of the engagement, although the relationship which we are considering should be regarded as a continuum rather than as existing in distinct varieties. And the relationship is in fact simply the 'market connexion' discussed in the previous chapter; in that context it performed a defensive function by making a particular market less easily invaded by competitors, whereas here it appears as a means by which it may be possible to arrange co-ordinated investment in two or more concerns.

Tacit collusion is more likely to be effective than implicit collusion, though it has similar weaknesses. Not only will explicit promises—and *a fortiori* legal contracts—provide a generally more secure expectation of action by others; they will also enable the character of the action to be more precisely determined. Collusion can succeed on a purely informal basis only if the particular performances required of the parties to it are clearly apparent to all of them; if they are not, then more express and deliberate arrangements have to be made. The full force of this familiar consideration will be better realized when we relax the assumption of a fixed list of goods, for then the integration of complementary investment requires not merely that firms should increase capacity, or even increase it by precisely so much, but that the products which they make should be related qualitatively in a special way. Tacit collusion, therefore, is likely to be resorted to only when more explicit forms of co-operation are artificially proscribed by governmental regulation or by the force of public opinion. Where the co-operation is designed to integrate complementary investment, as opposed to competitive investment, barriers of this kind are unlikely to be erected and explicit agreements will be the principal means by which market information is made available. This information, however, and therefore also the co-ordination of complementary investment, is unlikely ever to be complete, for there exist factors which limit both the willingness and the ability of firms to undertake binding commitments. Careful study of these factors will enable us to understand what determines the scope and efficacy of contractual agreements in the competitive economy; in addition, it will afford a partial explanation of the limitations which the attempt to co-ordinate related activities will necessarily experience, irrespective of the nature of the economic system presupposed. It is to this complex question that our attention must now turn.

3. Every business can be regarded as having to formulate, with greater or lesser precision, an investment programme consisting of a set of planned activities related through some process of production or transformation. It will be based on an assessment of the various technical and market conditions upon which the prices at which the firm will buy its inputs and sell its outputs will depend. As this assessment is likely to be in the form, not of certain knowledge, but of expectations of varying degrees of reliability, an entrepreneur will wish his programme to be as flexible or adaptable as possible, in order that it can be modified to take account of changing and unexpected circumstances.[1] But in the very nature of things, inflexibility will be, to a substantial extent, unavoidable; most processes of production, if they are to be efficient, have to be designed for more or less specific purposes; both the kinds and quantities of outputs and of inputs are more or less closely determined by the fixed equipment and personnel which have to be employed.

The entrepreneur's willingness to commit himself in advance to a particular transaction will depend, therefore, on a variety of considerations. If he contracts to purchase inputs, or sell outputs, at some future dates, then market uncertainty is, to that extent, substantially reduced; the flexibility of his programme, however, is likely to be reduced at the same time. Ideally, he would wish merely to have the secure option of

---

[1] The need for adaptability is considered more fully in Chapter VIII.

being able to buy or sell, at agreed prices, at specified future dates, whereas in practice, this assurance will generally be obtainable only in exchange for a reciprocal commitment on his side. Uncertainty may be reduced, but only at a sacrifice of the adaptability which is required to deal with such uncertainty as remains. In deciding whether to commit himself to future transactions, therefore, the entrepreneur will first have to weigh up the terms of the contract against the reduction in uncertainty which it affords him; in addition, he will have to assess the advantages of this increased certainty as set against the increased rigidity of his production programme.

It will be necessary, therefore, to form some estimate of the terms on which the planned transaction would be carried out in the absence of a contract, an estimate which can be conceived in terms of a range of possible prices associated with the probabilities of obtaining them. This general prospect can then be compared with that offered by a contract, which will usually consist in the expectation of selling or buying so much at a particular price. Were it not for default risk, this expectation would be perfectly secure, but even although it is not, the uncertainty of the transaction will generally be much reduced. The terms to be agreed, however, may offer the firm a less favourable price than that which he considered he would be most likely, but not certain, to get in the absence of a contract.

In addition, the contract may introduce an extra element of rigidity into the production programme, the importance of which will vary according to the circumstances in which the firm is placed. It may be that the entrepreneur is already more or less committed, by the rest of his programme, to carry out the transaction in some form or other. Should he, for example, have previously contracted to deliver so much of a particular output, then he will usually be obliged to purchase inputs of the appropriate quantity and kind. But quite apart from contractual obligations, his freedom of choice, in the immediate future, is likely to be very restricted, if only by the fact that certain work is already in progress and certain specific inputs have already been purchased; being thereby effectively committed to the sale of a certain volume of output, he has an incentive to secure the terms in advance. Fixed commitments, therefore, in so far as they merely complement others already made, do not add to the rigidity of the programme.

The longer the future period which is envisaged, the more flexible will the entrepreneur's investment programme become; both the quantities, and frequently also the kinds of outputs and inputs will become a matter for subsequent decision according to the circumstances which come to prevail. Contracts which extend into this more distant period, therefore, are likely to diminish the entrepreneur's ability to modify his plans in order to meet unexpected developments, without at the same time producing a very substantial reduction in uncertainty. The point will be reached where the greater predictability yielded by contracts does not justify the loss of flexibility which they involve. Attempts to secure a more perfect co-ordination of complementary activities by means of binding agreements between firms, will, therefore, encounter a barrier, the existence of which is the consequence of the inherent imperfectability of both technical and market information. Because of this, the efficiency of any economy, viewed as a system of communication, can never be made perfect; there is a resemblance in this respect to electrical networks, the efficiency of which for communication is limited by the irreducible element of random molecular motion known technically as 'noise'.

4. Irreducible uncertainty, as a factor in any conceivable economic system, owes its existence, in part, to incomplete information about preferences and production functions. In much of our economic theory, this incompleteness is ignored; preferences and the state of technique are taken as 'given' in the sense both of remaining constant and of being known to whoever is concerned. The legitimacy of this assumption depends, of course, on the purpose of the analysis; where our concern is chiefly with the logic of choice, it may be appropriate to take the relevant ends and means as given so as to be able to concentrate attention on the problem of rational resource allocation. But where the object is to study the working of a competitive economy, the question of the availability of information cannot thus be pushed aside. If certain preferences and production functions are to be postulated, then these should usually be regarded as objective conditions, information regarding which will be uncertain and dispersed among many minds. It may be useful, for some purposes, to endow consumers with complete preference orderings between commodities, even if we admit that these orderings are known only imperfectly to consumers themselves; and, similarly, it may be convenient to envisage the existing state of technical knowledge as fixing upper limits to the maximum output obtainable from a certain combination of resources, even although not all entrepreneurs are assumed to possess the information and skill required fully to realize these potentialities.

It is easy to see why any analysis, if it is to have much applicability to real conditions, will have to take account of the uncertainty of technical information. It is quite unrealistic to assume that consumers would be able to state in advance their preferences between any possible combinations of goods; they can be assumed to know, with any degree of certainty, only those among their possible preferences which relate to the commodities or activities of which they have had acquaintance. If we do decide to endow the consumer with an innate, stable, but partially known, system of preferences, then we must recognize that his actual choices may deviate from it, many of them being designed expressly to discover what these preferences, and the properties of commodities, truly are.[1] In fact, of course, innate preferences will themselves be subject to change, in ways never wholly predictable, and there will even be a desire for change and novelty as such. In any economy, therefore, final consumers have strong motives for preserving the flexibility of their consumption programmes and little

---

[1] Recent formulations of the theory of demand often attempt to side-step the question of the knowledge on which decisions are taken. This is done by assuming merely that consumers have a consistent pattern of response, expressed in terms of stable behaviour functions, to different price and income situations. This could be taken to imply that consumers' behaviour takes the form of stock reactions, rather than of informed choices. Alternatively, if this seems too unreasonable, it could be taken to imply that consumers have unlimited information, so that, so long as their ultimate preferences do not change, their choices would be consistent with them and with each other. This failure to take explicit account of the conditions of information greatly reduces the usefulness of all theories of economic action which are couched in behaviouristic terms.

incentive for committing themselves to purchases in advance. The producers of final output, therefore, being unable to guarantee sales in advance, are made reluctant to enter into related contracts.

This reluctance is likely to be strengthened by the entrepreneur's uncertainty about the particular factor combinations which, at some future date, it will prove most advantageous to adopt. The process of manufacturing is not to be represented as the equivalent of a chemical reaction in which substances combined in the correct proportions will yield unfailingly calculable products. There will frequently be present an element of trial and error, and if the entrepreneur is to be able to modify the process in the light of accumulated experience, or in response to new technological possibilities, he will wish to preserve the maximum possible freedom of manœuvre.

5. The inevitable imperfection of technical information will therefore limit the willingness of firms to enter into the contractual arrangements by which the supply of market information could be increased. Such engagements moreover, require adequate confidence on both sides. One entrepreneur may be willing to offer others long-term contracts, but they will be prepared to accept them only if convinced that he has the ability, as well as the will, to fulfil them. He may have information sufficient to convince himself that this will be the case, but others may not, and their willingness to make investments complementary with his will depend on the strength of his reputation or on his ability to offer compensation in the event of his failure to meet the undertaking. The co-ordination of complementary investments may be checked, therefore, not only as a result of the uncertainty of technical information, but also by the fact that this information is dispersed among many different units.

Long-term contracts to buy and sell certain quantities at certain prices are unlikely, in any case, to be more than a subsidiary means by which complementary investments can be co-ordinated. An entrepreneur may believe that only by gaining some degree of control over the firm responsible for some complementary investment will he be fully assured of it being undertaken; vertical integration may be carried out with this end in view. It may be very difficult, moreover, to arrange that the terms of a long-term contract are such as offer each of the parties a prospect of return which is in proportion to the risks which they are assuming. One manufacturer might be asked, for example, to supply another with a specialized component, the manufacture of which required heavy investment. If all went well, he would be assured of a market for his output for some years ahead, and at a price fixed by the terms of contract; but, however profitable the sale of the final product, he could not expect more than this return. If, on the other hand, the purchaser's enterprise fared very badly, then the contract would be likely to be broken and the supplier would suffer loss. In order to obtain a more equitable distribution of possible gains and losses, a form of co-operation more intimate than that of a simple contract would be sought; the two companies might form a subsidiary in which they both possessed some equity interest or might decide wholly to amalgamate.

6. It would seem to be apparent, therefore, from all this discussion, that there is no unique single way in which complementary investments come to be co-ordinated. Co-ordination may occur spontaneously without the intervention of measures expressly adopted to that end; under different circumstances, it may be brought about by means of agreements, of one kind or another, between independent firms; in other circumstances, it may require deliberate planning, such as is possible only when the different investments are under unified control. This perhaps is an untidy conclusion, but it corresponds to the state of affairs in actual competitive economies as we know them. Almost all investments are complementary, in some degree, with others, but the strength of the relationship varies greatly from case to case. In advanced economies, at any rate, strong complementarity is likely to be the result of the nature of the methods of production rather than of the way in which goods are linked in the expenditure patterns of consumers; it will characterize, that is to say, the relationship between investments in a particular product and investment in the related inputs. If the greater part of the total production of a certain material or component is used as an input for one particular commodity, then the degree of complementarity resulting is more likely to be acute, and it will be difficult for expansion to take place in the one industry without corresponding expansion in the other. The seriousness of the difficulty will depend, of course, on whether alternative markets could easily be found for the component, and on whether those who purchase it could turn to substitutes. It will be mitigated by any significant short-run flexibility in the supply of either the output or the input. Spontaneous co-ordination, as a result of investments taking place successively in two or more complementary directions, will be possible only where the absence of important scale economies permits this gradual and continuous form of adjustment.

For these reasons, it seems reasonable to expect that the measures necessary to achieve co-ordination of complementary activities would differ according to the degree of development of the country in which they are undertaken. In an advanced country, with a large manufacturing sector, the output of one industry—for example, the steel industry—is likely to have a large and varied number of outlets, so that there may be no acute complementarity between the investment decisions of any few particular units. In poorer countries, on the other hand, the manufacturing sector is likely to be small, so that any increase in output by, say, a steel producer, would have to be absorbed by a small and clearly identifiable number of user firms. In such a situation complementarity would be strong, and profitable investment by one producer might depend on simultaneous expansion by others. The price mechanism, in the ordinary sense, breaks down; the steel producer may not judge investment to be profitable on the assumption that the *status quo* will be preserved elsewhere. Nor may he feel justified in relying on projecting any trend in demand; such projections may be made with some confidence where the users of steel are numerours and diverse, but would be inapplicable in a situation in which the demand for the product depends on the investment decisions of a handful of firms themselves uncertain about the adequacy of complementary investment.

It is difficult to resist the conclusion, therefore, that in underdeveloped countries, the co-ordination of investments—at least in the manufacturing sector—may require more deliberate planning than is necessary in advanced economies. Unfortunately, of course, it is precisely in these countries that the administrative skill and experience required for such co-ordination is most likely to be absent. It might be argued against this conclusion that some of the present developed countries succeeded in industrializing without measures of this kind; but this objection ignores a crucial difference between the two situations. The need for planned co-ordination depends on the relation between the size of the market and the economies of scale; the underdeveloped countries of the present day have a small manufacturing sector at a time when technology offers scale economies much greater than those which were significant in the early stages of the industrial revolution.

Even in advanced countries, however, technological developments, where they tend to increase the degree of complementarity between different investment decisions, may have a profound effect on market structure. There exist between the firms in a modern competitive economy complex interrelationships of ownership and control, which are abstracted from in much of our more formal analysis; their justification derives, in part, from the need to co-ordinate complementarity activities. And the optimum size of the firm may be determined, not so much by the scale economies associated with any particular operation, but by the number of operations which require planned co-ordination. Nevertheless, as we have seen, all the forces do not work in the direction of integration. The inevitable imperfection of the entrepreneur's knowledge, both about technical conditions and about the prospects of other firms, checks his willingness both to make long-term binding commitments and to throw in his lot with that of others.

7. Finally, it is worth noting that not only competitive economies will fail to achieve a complete co-ordination of all related economic activities; the uncertainty and dispersion of information which create the barriers to such co-ordination would be found in any conceivable economy. It is true that an important source of uncertainty, under free enterprise, is the freedom given to consumers to spend their incomes as they please; this freedom could in principle be withdrawn in planned economies, although in practice it is unlikely to be withdrawn completely. And even if the central authority itself decided the objectives of production, it might still wish to give itself the freedom to change them as circumstances altered. Uncertainty which has its root in changing technological possibilities would undoubtedly inflict both planned and competitive systems alike.

The counterpart, in a planned economy, of entrepreneurial reluctance to make binding commitments, will be a policy of deliberately limiting the degree of integration provided for in the plan. Close complementarity between several investments is equivalent to a conductor of error; some degree of independence acts as insulation. The greater the extent to which the profitability or propriety of any one investment depends on others being implemented exactly according to plan, the wider will be the area over which the consequences of any particular failure will be felt. The absence of a sufficiently wide consensus about the profitability of simultaneous investment in related directions is also a check to concerted activity in both kinds of economy; in a planned system the combined investment can still proceed, provided the controlling authority issues the appropriate fiat. Whether this is a desirable outcome, however, depends of course on whether its assessment of the situation is correct. Opinions about the best allocation of resources are weighted in a competitive economy by the wealth and the credit which those holding them can command; in a planned system, by the position of those holding them in the hierarchical structure. But a fuller discussion of this difference must be postponed.

V

THE SCALE OF INVESTMENTS

1. AN attempt was made, in the preceding two chapters, to ascertain the conditions which would (or would not) permit entrepreneurs to obtain information and assurances sufficient to induce them to invest in response to an increase in demand. We were concerned, in particular, with whether the co-ordination of related investment decisions could come about automatically, or whether it would have to be furthered by arrangements deliberately contrived for this purpose. Throughout all this discussion, it was assumed that information either would or would not be adequate and that adjustment either would or would not take place. In both of these respects, however, it is important to recognize differences of degree; the process of adaptation may be more or less efficient, depending, in part, on the nature and amount of the information to which entrepreneurs have access. The deliberate co-ordination of entrepreneurs' activities may be necessary not so much to secure an increase in supply as to ensure that this increase is produced in the best possible way. In this chapter, attention will be confined to one particular way in which the information available to entrepreneurs, and therefore the process of adjustment, may affect the efficiency of production; we shall inquire whether certain modes of adjustment are consistent with the full exploitation of the economies provided by large-scale equipment. It will be more convenient to take up the other aspects of productive efficiency elsewhere. Chapter VII will deal with its dependence on the personal ability of those who control resources, which is itself a function of the prevailing economic system in what may be termed its selective aspect. The chapters which form the third part of the book are concerned with the ways in which methods of production, and investment programmes generally, are influenced by the inevitable uncertainty of entrepreneurial estimates.

I shall contend that it is possible to judge the efficiency of production in a competitive economy, and in particular the likelihood of full realization of scale economies, only by considering the actual processes by which supply may adjust to demand. In much of the discussion of this subject, the scale of investments is regarded as being determined by the particular equilibrium configurations with which different market structures can be associated. Thus the perfectly competitive equilibrium, for example, is characterized by the full utilization of such scale economies as exist. In order that competition should preserve its atomistic character, however, these economies have to be exhausted at rather small levels of output, beyond which costs must be presumed to rise. As such conditions would not generally be found in practice, the relevance of the analysis, for this reason alone, is much reduced. More fundamentally, however, there is no reason to expect that the hypothetical market conditions which define perfect competition would in fact ensure that production would be carried on by the most efficient means, for there is no reason to believe that the supposed equilibrium position would ever be reached. The link between market structure and the scale of investments is to be sought more in the particular modes of adjustment, than in the supposed equilibrium situations, with which the structure can be associated. Here, as elsewhere, much that is of importance has been denied adequate analysis as a result of the tyranny which the equilibrium concept has exercised over modern economic theory.

2. Scale economies can be said to exist when a commodity's cost of production falls, at least up to a certain point, with the volume of its output. Lower costs may be associated, in principle, with a high rate of production or with production over a long period. It seems likely, however, that the entrepreneur will generally be much more free to vary the scale of his equipment, in the ordinary sense, than its durability, and the following discussion will be limited to the economies which arise from the former source. I shall assume that the productive techniques available permit minimum costs to be achieved only at a substantial volume of output, beyond which neither economies or diseconomies of scale are of importance. The actual size of this minimum output will

naturally vary widely from one industry to another;[1] it will suffice to regard it, for present purposes, as being significant in relation to the size of the market for the commodity.

It is important to note that the relevant relation, in this context, is that which exists between costs of production and the volume of output, on the assumption that this volume of output is being produced in the best possible way. Economies will not result merely from the fact that a plant—even less a firm—is large, for the productive equipment and organization of any existing plant may have been built up gradually by successive small-scale investments. It is for this reason that the magnitude of the scale economies actually achieved will depend on the way in which, under the prevailing market conditions, firms are enabled to grow.[2]

It is also important to distinguish between those characteristics of the adjustment of supply to demand which result from the particular nature of the processes of adjustment in a competitive economy, and those which, by depending merely on the nature of the technical production possibilities available, would be common to any conceivable economic system. The fact that it may be cheaper per unit to produce large quantities rather than small, or to produce over a long period, rather than over a short one, necessarily implies that, if demand is limited and variable, supply may not always be produced at minimum cost. This involves of course no true imperfection or irrationality, no more than it does to refuse a bargain of things one cannot use or sell. Inevitably also, even in the best of all possible economic worlds, the structure of the productive equipment will normally be less than fully appropriate to the

[1] A very interesting account of the varying importance of scale economies is to be found in Professor J. S. Bain's *Barriers to New Competition; their Character and Consequences in Manufacturing Industry* (Harvard University Press), Ch. 3.

[2] 'In other words, it is the firm's rate of growth, or rather the size of the discrete steps by which it grows that determines what method of production is chosen as being the most profitable one,' 'Monopoly and Competition in Europe and America', by Professor T. Scitovsky (*Quarterly Journal of Economics*, November 1955). The analysis of this chapter borrows heavily from this article and from another by the same author, 'Economies of Scale, Competition and European Integration', in the *American Economic Review*, Vol. XLVI, No. 1, March 1956).

current demands for which it is catering, but will reflect also both the demands which were met in the past and those which have been anticipated for the future. Minimum cost outputs are not necessarily economic optima; a scale of plant, or degree of utilization, should not be called economically sub-optimal merely because it fails to secure all the possible scale economies irrespective of the level of demand. This analysis will be concerned with the effect of the adjustment process on the likelihood of attaining economic optima and not with the possible divergence between these and minimum cost outputs.

3. Let us now, therefore, consider once again the ways in which, in a decentralized system, competitive investments might come to be co-ordinated, our object being to discover how the different modes of adjustment might influence the scale of the equipment which firms will choose to employ. It was found convenient, in the earlier discussion, to distinguish between two principal forms of adjustment, neither of which, however, would often exist in the pure state. Successive adaptation was made possible by the fact that differences in the ability of firms to respond to a change in demand would give to one, or a few of them, a reasonably adequate expectation that the competitive supply of others would be temporarily held back. As the firms most able to respond would generally be different at different times, orderly supply changes could come about by their successive expansion. Simultaneous adaptation was made possible not by restraints on responsiveness at any particular time, but by barriers which separated the economic space of different firms and afforded to each of them an adequate expectation of maintaining its current share of total demand. The first mode of adjustment assumed that all firms were equally well placed to sell anywhere in the total market, whereas the other depended on this not being the case.

4. Let us first examine how successive adjustment would affect the scale of investments. An entrepreneur contemplating expansion would compare the expected trend of demand, which is here assumed to be rising, with that of the maximum possible (or at all likely) level of competitive supply. Provided that these two trends were so related as to leave some net demand available to him, he would be prepared to invest; and provided that this available demand were not less than the output of the minimum-cost plant, the additional capital installed would be sufficiently great to exploit all the economies of scale. If, however, as is clearly possible, the excess demand expected were not large enough to justify such a large step forward, the producer would be faced with a choice of policies.

His decision would be likely to be influenced, in the first place, by whether the productive techniques already in use offered full-scale economies. If they did, and if the price of the product reflected this fact, he would probably be unwilling to install equipment of less than the optimum scale even if this is all that his immediate expectation of demand would warrant. His choice, in these circumstances, would seem to lie between the immediate installation of optimal plant or the postponement of investment until demand had grown; the former course would result in temporary losses, until such time as demand had increased sufficiently, while the latter involves the risk that other firms will forestall him and remove his opportunity to expand. If we are to assume, however, that the now currently available minimum cost plant is larger, and can produce more cheaply than that already in use, the choice facing him is modified. If he installs the minimum cost equipment, he can afford to sell below the current level of price, thereby augmenting his expected sales to an extent depending on the elasticity of demand for the product and on any reduction of output which the lower price might force upon competitors. The available demand now may, or may not, be sufficient to sustain the minimum-cost plant. If it is not, a third course of action may be contemplated in addition to those just considered. The installation of sub-optimal plant, similar to that currently in use, will now allow normal profits, at least until such time as price may fall to the level associated with the lower average costs of the newer and larger plant.

Three policies have therefore been distinguished, none of which is clearly superior. Immediate installation of minimum-cost equipment will bring immediate, if only temporary losses; postponement will involve the risk either that others will

forestall his expansion or that their investments will coincide
with his so as to result in an excessive and unprofitable volume
of supply; and the choice of sub-optimal equipment may
result in losses at some future date. There remains yet one
further policy, but of a quite different kind. The firm contemplating the investment could amalgamate, or enter into an
agreement with other firms so as to bring the competitive
investments under planned co-ordination. The installation of
the new plant could be made to coincide with the deliberate
withdrawal of some of the older, and less efficient capacity;
alternatively, the new investment could be postponed until
demand had increased sufficiently, it being agreed that none
of the parties would install sub-optimal equipment in the
meantime.

General theory cannot indicate which of these alternatives
will be chosen. The relevant economic considerations are
easily recognized—the rate of growth and elasticity of demand,
the age structure of the existing capital stock, the size of firms
and of the total market, the exact difference between the unit
costs of the optimal and sub-optimal equipment, their short-run
cost functions and so on. Nor is it necessarily the case that the
economically optimal investment from society's point of view
will always involve the installation of minimum cost equipment.
If demand is inelastic and increases very slowly, if existing
capacity is very durable and will yield increased output only
at great cost, and if future satisfactions are heavily discounted,
it may prove preferable to install small-scale equipment rather
than install minimum-cost equipment either at a loss or after
a certain delay. This, however, is a problem in the theory of
resource allocation which lies outside our present scope; what
concerns us is that adjustment in a decentralized system need
not secure the installation of minimum cost equipment even
when this is socially desirable. Even where the existence of
restraints on the ability of different firms to respond to an
increase in demand does permit entrepreneurs to take investment decisions, the supply adjustment which they promote
may be less efficient than it might have been. Restraints, by
their very nature, can at most assure a firm that competitive
supply will not, for some time, increase; they cannot produce

the reduction in competitive supply which the profitable installation of large-scale equipment may require. Thus formal arrangements must supplement or replace the natural factors which facilitate adjustment. Amalgamation, or the taking over of one firm by another, is the policy which would seem most appropriate to this end; the likelihood that it will be chosen will depend not only on the gains to be made from the introduction of large-scale equipment, but also on many other economic and non-economic factors such as the desire for independence, on the one side, and the desire for power or size as such, on the other.

5. It remains to consider the influence on productive efficiency of the second pure type of adjustment process which was entitled 'simultaneous'. Each entrepreneur is enabled to obtain enough information for an investment decision, in this situation, by virtue of the market connexion which gives some protection against competitive sales. Any increase in total demand for a product will be shared out among producers according to the size of their 'particular markets'. Under these circumstances it is obvious that an efficient supply adjustment, taking advantage of available scale economies, will be much more unlikely to come about. Where adjustment is of the purely successive kind, a firm about to invest can count on all the accretion in total demand being available to it; but, if the forces of market connexion are strong, only a part of the increase, as determined by its share of the market, is available without the costs and risks which an attempt to enlarge this share would incur. The probability that a firm will install sub-optimal equipment is therefore greater if adaptation corresponds more closely to the simultaneous than to the successive form. The policy of investing in technically optimal equipment in the hope of a gradual increase in available demand will seem less attractive, in view of the difficulty of securing the necessary lion's share of any total increase. If the entrepreneur decides to postpone investment until the demand for his own product has grown sufficiently to justify a large-scale plant, then the presumed attachment of his customers would reduce the likelihood of other firms supplanting him during the interval; but this consideration may easily be offset by the fact that the time required for a sufficient accretion of demand to develop in his particular market may be very long.

It should be observed, however, that both the social desirability of installing the minimum-cost plant, and the likelihood of this happening, will depend on the particular forms which market connexion may assume. If a firm maintains the loyalty of its customers by offering them a highly differentiated product, then, accepting that consumers' preferences are the ultimate criterion, investment in sub-optimal equipment may be perfectly compatible with economic rationality. Similarly, if market connexion rests on geographical proximity, it may be socially appropriate to install sub-optimal equipment rather than incur heavy transport costs. Producers may enjoy the advantages of a particular market simply as the result of an established reputation, goodwill, trust, or personal loyalty. Although these bonds, if they are strong enough, might impede the introduction of minimum-cost equipment, this does not imply that their net effect, from the standpoint of general welfare, will necessarily be bad. In the absence of any more direct information about the quality of goods and the dependability of the seller, past experience and general reputation may be the best available basis for the buyer's choice. Given the informal nature of attachments of this kind, they are in any case unlikely to represent a very formidable barrier to the introduction of efficient equipment and resultant reductions in price.

It is chiefly where simultaneous adaptation is made possible by formal market connexion such as quota agreements and protective tariffs that its influence on the scale of investments is likely to be markedly adverse, although even here the social desirability of these arrangements has to be judged by their effects in more than one direction. Although the adjustment of supply which can take place within the context of these restrictive agreements may be less than perfectly efficient, their abolition can be recommended unreservedly only provided we can point to some alternative arrangements by which it would be practicable to replace them. It may appear tempting, although it would be erroneous, simply to attribute these imperfections in adjustment to imperfections in competition. It is quite possible for market connexions to make for a more efficient adaptation of supply than would take place in their absence, for they may enable producers to form at least some secure expectation of a market for their products, even although the market is not sufficient to induce them to install equipment of the optimal scale. The inhibiting uncertainty which would result from the abolition of such arrangements could cause a reduction, rather than an increase, in the scale of investments and the efficiency of adaptation. Whether it would do so in general is of course something which *a priori* reasoning cannot determine; attention would have to be given to the particular circumstances of each case. Improvement in the process of adjustment may be possible, on some occasions, only by the replacement of the restrictive connexions by far-reaching measures of planned co-ordination.

6. The effect, on the scale of production, of the different ways in which complementary investments may be co-ordinated, may be analysed along very much the same lines. It was observed, in the previous chapter, that adjustment requiring invest-ment in two or more complementary directions might, under suitable conditions, take place without measures of deliberate co-ordination. Provided that the equipment of the comple-mentary industries was capable of being worked more inten-sively, so that output could, to some extent, be increased at short notice, then the adjustment could result from successive expansion first in one direction and then in another; but there would be no guarantee that this spontaneous mode of adjust-ment would be compatible with the optimal exploitation of the available economies of scale. Let us consider an entrepreneur contemplating investment on the assumption that there will be no simultaneous addition to the fixed capacity of complementary industries. It would be reasonable for him to expect that his own investment, if undertaken, would itself stimulate comple-mentary investment, but only after a certain delay. Generally, therefore, the demand curve for his particular product will be lower and less elastic in the near future that it would be after the appropriate adjustments had been made in the industries which either purchased his output or which made goods with which his output was associated in consumption—provided, of course, that the supply produced by his competitors had not risen in the meantime to an extent sufficient to offset this. In the same way, the elasticity of his factor supply would be less than it would be once capital stock had been increased in those firms supplying him with raw materials or intermediate products. Although these influences would in general act together, it will be convenient to consider separately the effect that they might have on investment decisions.

I shall, therefore, begin by assuming that factors of production are available on terms corresponding to conditions of full adjustment in the firms which supply them, but that the market for the entrepreneur's product is expected to be smaller in the near future than it would be later, on the assumption that the appropriate complementary investment would ultimately be undertaken. For any particular scale of investment, therefore, the entrepreneur would associate different levels of expected profit with the period which would precede, and with the period which would follow the adjustment of capital stock in the related industries. His estimated profits for the later period would very probably be subjected to a heavy discount, because of their remoteness, and even more so, because of their uncertainty, for he will never be quite sure either that complementary investment will be undertaken in time or that competitive investment will not meanwhile itself be increased. Nevertheless, the attempt will be made to choose that level of investment which offers the best total prospect over both the near and further future. The higher this level, it is being assumed, the lower will be the unit of costs of production, up to the point where full-scale economies are reached.

If the scale of investment required for minimum cost production were small enough, it might yield positive profits in both the near and further periods, in which case it would almost certainly be undertaken. But this critical level might well be sufficiently large to offer profits only after, and not before, the installation of the appropriate complementary capital goods. Were this the case, the entrepreneur, always assuming he was unable to induce simultaneous investment in the required complementary directions, would have to choose one of three main courses. He might invest up to the critical level necessary for minimum costs, in the hope that his immediate losses would soon be reversed; or he might choose a lower scale of investment which offered positive profits (or at least smaller losses) in the nearer future, at the cost of a less favourable prospect in the longer run; or he might decide not to invest at all, on the grounds that no level of investment was likely to bring long-run gains large and secure enough to offset the temporary (but not necessarily short-lived) losses with which it was unavoidably associated. Without further information about the weights to be given to the relevant factors, all those courses seem equally possible; only the first of them is *prima facie* compatible with economic efficiency; the second secures an adjustment of supply to demand based on inferior techniques, while the third results in desirable adjustments failing to come about. The particular factors determining the outcome have been implicit in our discussion; though it would no doubt be possible, after a fashion, to incorporate them systematically as variables in a model of entrepreneurial choice, their variety and imperfect measurability necessarily reduce the value of such an exercise. Among the most obviously important considerations are the difference which complementary investment makes to the level and elasticity of demand; the time which must elapse before such investment can be induced and its effect felt; the shape of the long- and short-run cost functions of plants of different size; the relative uncertainty of the near and further futures, and the time preference between returns at different future periods.

The effects of complementarity between a firm and its suppliers can clearly be analysed in a similar way. Let us now assume that an entrepreneur does not expect the demand for his output to be significantly affected by investments which might take place, in the foreseeable future elsewhere, but that the cost or availability to him of the equipment required for additional expansion, or of the materials used in the production process, will depend on whether simultaneous expansion takes place in those firms which supply them. Here again, it is evident, the entrepreneur may be deterred from investing to the extent necessary to realize the available scale economies because of the losses which would be incurred during the period before complementary investment had been induced. The situation is the same, therefore, as that which has just been discussed; investments which are socially desirable might not appear profitable, if they had to be undertaken successively, although they would appear profitable if they were each part of a simultaneous and uniform advance. Where both the cost of the firm's inputs, and the demand for its outputs, would be reduced by complementary investment in other industries, the *prima facie* case for some kind of co-ordination is obviously reinforced.

7. The probability that productive efficiency would, in practice, be prejudiced by the unplanned mode of adjustment depends on a variety of circumstances; of these the relation between the size of the market in comparison with the minimum scale of efficient production may be the most important. Difficulties would seem most likely to occur in countries which have a small manufacturing sector and which, for one reason or another, cannot rely on foreign trade to afford all the desired elasticity in the demand for their products and in their factor supplies.[1] But the argument of this chapter is not to be summed up in the familiar principle that the size of the market sets limits to the possible exploitation of economies of scale; what it implies is that even those scale economies which are compatible with a given market size may in fact fail to be realized unless the investment decisions of related enterprises are taken jointly. The chances of them being realized, without measures of co-ordination, will depend on the rate of growth of the market as well as on its actual size. If there exists the widespread conviction that demand, as a whole, is on a rising trend, entrepreneurs will be more likely to take the risk that their own expansion will be matched, without much delay, by expansion in complementary directions. By engendering the appropriate state of confident expectation, experience of a high and sustained rate of growth may create conditions favourable to its continuance.

It would indeed be fair to say that the importance of the

[1] The effective market size will depend also on the extent of product differentiation: this consideration will be taken up in the following chapter.

general state of confidence has been understated, at least by implication, in this and in the preceding chapters. Because of the stress placed on the need for adequate information or evidence as a basis for investment decisions, entrepreneurs have been represented as being more cautious and calculating than they in fact—and probably fortunately—are. Keynes, in particular, was prepared to give very full recognition to the element of faith in long-run investment decisions. In his famous chapter on 'The State of Long Term Expectation', he has the following to say:

. . . a large proportion of our positive activities depend on spontaneous optimism rather than on a mathematical expectation, whether moral or hedonistic or economic. Most, probably, of our decisions to do something positive, the full consequences of which will be drawn out over many days to come, can only be taken as a result of animal spirits—of a spontaneous urge to action rather than to inaction, and not as the outcome of a weighted average of quantitative benefits multiplied by quantitative probabilities. Enterprise only pretends to itself to be mainly actuated by the statements in its own prospectus, however candid and sincere. Only a little more than an expedition to the South Pole, is it based on an exact calculation of benefits to come. Thus if the animal spirits are dimmed and the spontaneous optimism falters, leaving us to depend on nothing but a mathematical expectation, enterprise will fade and die;—though fears of loss may have a basis no more reasonable than hopes of profit had before.[1]

I am inclined to think that considerations of this kind do not wholly invalidate the conclusions of our analysis, although they should cause us to regard them with a good measure of scepticism. Almost all formal theory has a rationalistic bias which limits its applicability to the conditions of the real world. But it would surely be as foolish to deny the importance of reasonable

---

[1] *The General Theory of Employment, Interest & Money*, J. M. Keynes, Chapter 12, pp. 161–62. Cf. also the following: 'The outstanding fact is the extreme precariousness of the basis of knowledge on which our estimates of prospective yield have to be made. Our knowledge of the factors which will govern the yield of an investment some years hence is usually very slight and often negligible. If we speak frankly, we have to admit that our basis of knowledge for estimating the yield ten years hence of a railway, a copper mine, a textile factory, the goodwill of a patent medicine, an Atlantic liner, a building in the City of London amounts to little and sometimes to nothing' (ibid., pp. 149–50).

calculation as it would be to give it an exclusive place. Calculation, as Keynes himself remarks, must supplement and support animal spirits, not be replaced by them. My object, in the preceding analysis, was to stress that reasoned calculation must be based on relevant information, the availability of which depends on the nature of the particular market structure or economic arrangements within which entrepreneurs are presumed to operate.

VI

THE ASSORTMENT OF PRODUCTION

1. VERY frequently, both in the theory of resource allocation and in the construction of models of the competitive economy, we assume the existence of a fixed list of distinct goods and services. This simplification underlies the analysis in the previous chapters; it enabled us to view economic adjustment in terms of securing the right amount of any particular commodity by efficient means. But it is clearly important to deal explicitly with the qualitative composition, or 'assortment' of output; for as the possible differentiation or variety of production is unlimited, the economic problem might better be regarded as the filling-up of uncharted economic space, rather than the realization of optimal proportions between the quantities of distinct categories of output. This greater degree of realism imposes the sacrifice of much analytical convenience; yet, without considering systematically the kinds as well as the quantities of commodities, it is impossible to give an adequate account of the scope and limitations of a competitive system. This chapter, therefore, is concerned with the modifications which have to be imposed on the following analysis as a result of admitting the possibility of qualitative variation.

Formal demand theory assumes that consumers are able to determine an order of preference between different combinations from a fixed list of distinct commodities; it represents no more than a simple application of the logic of choice. If we wish to consider, as does an entrepreneur, which kinds and qualities of goods to produce, then this model of consumers' behaviour needs to be replaced. From a purely formal standpoint it might be legitimate to assume that the preference orderings embraced all possible goods rather than the small sample currently available. But it is surely more helpful to take account of the fact that commodities are desired not so much for themselves but because their purchaser expects them to enable him to enjoy certain experiences or produce certain effects. An analysis of these ultimate objectives of consumers' activity would be out of place here. But they can scarcely be described as the satisfaction of individual 'tastes', at least in any ordinary sense of this word; they are associated with psychological, as well as physical needs. Thus a commodity may typically be desired partly because it helps, let us say, to feed or clothe us agreeably, and partly also because of a symbolic value with which, perhaps unconsciously, we associate it. By possessing or consuming it, we may, for example, be made to feel the kind of person which we should like to be or with which we should like others to identify us. Although the psychology of such motivation lies outside our scope, it is worth while remarking that the decisions of consumers are not confined to the allocation of income between goods according to their preferences between them; for these preferences are not in any sense ultimate, having to be themselves determined by the consumer on the basis of the contribution made by each commodity towards the satisfaction of several desires. Any one article will in general realize more than one objective; a motor-car, for example, will offer not only the facility of transportation (which itself has several different dimensions—speed, comfort, safety, etc.), but also æsthetic satisfaction, prestige and so forth. Almost all commodities, that is to say, can be conceived as joint products, as possessing the power to meet, in varying degree, several needs. The richer the economy the greater the importance of the non-physical needs may be, but, even in the poorest countries, symbolic or prestige value is attached to the possession of at least some commodities. Preferences between various commodities are therefore not just 'given' to a consumer; he has to decide upon them by weighing up the contributions made by each of them to his several objectives. Each of them represents in itself a different combination of 'goods', or powers, which he cannot purchase separately.

Constancy or stability over time is much more likely to characterize the several desires which goods meet, rather than preferences between goods themselves. Some desires are indeed of such a nature as positively to require changing commodities for their satisfaction; the desire for novelty in itself is of such a character; so also in general will be the desire for social distinction, for the possession of any particular commodity is likely to offer prestige only so long as it is confined to relatively few people. Consumers buy goods because of the satisfaction which they are expected to provide; these expectations being uncertain, purchases will frequently be made experimentally as part of a constant endeavour to discover newer and better ways of meeting desires. Finally, businesses themselves will strive continuously to persuade people that their particular products do have the combination of real and symbolic properties which give the most satisfaction.

These considerations are in fact very well known and appreciated, even although they are ignored in most of our formal theorizing. Whether it is legitimate so to ignore them depends of course on the purpose in hand; if we wish only to highlight that aspect of consumers' behaviour which is most obviously related to allocative logic, then the pure theory of demand has some explanatory or heuristic value. But if we are to offer an adequate, even if simplified and formalized explanation of how an actual competitive economy works, then the picture to have in our minds will have to be the more realistic, if a less clear-cut one, which has just been summarized. Resources have to be seen as devoted to the production of goods designed to meet, in changing ways, a relatively stable, though ill-defined complex of desires. It will no longer be necessary to conceive of consumers, rather awkwardly, as endowed with a set of preferences between goods which is known imperfectly even to themselves; they can be regarded as endowed with a set of desires and as forming preferences between commodities on the basis of their imperfect knowledge of the power which the commodities have to cater to these desires.

2. Once we admit the possibility of indefinite qualitative variation in output, it is necessary to adopt a conception of entrepreneurial activity different from that appropriate to the hypothetical world of perfect competition. If we think in terms of a fixed list of goods, related to available factors by production functions of which everyone concerned has full knowledge, then entrepreneurial activity would seem to consist of two functions only. The first of these would be to form expectations about the demand for a product over a certain relevant period. (Models of the firm in perfect competition often assume away this function by taking demand as somehow 'given'.) The second function is merely to solve the problem of resource allocation posed in this model; to choose the factor combination and level of output which satisfy the marginal conditions and therefore maximize profits.

In our previous discussion we attempted to take a step nearer reality by assuming that production functions represented the best possible combination of factors, given the appropriate conditions, but that in fact entrepreneurs' information regarding them was, in varying degrees, imperfect. The situation in reality is, however, better described somewhat differently. It seems useful to conceive of there being, at any point of time, a state of scientific or technical knowledge which represents the same sort of conditioning influence as does the structure of consumers' desires. This state of technique will enable factors to be combined in a very large number of ways, only some of which will ever have been considered by entrepreneurs. Imagination, rather than information in any ordinary sense, is what entrepreneurs require in order to discover new ways of combining resources so as to meet consumers' desires; production functions exist unknown to entrepreneurs only in the sense that musical tunes await discovery; in either case originality, rather than the possession of 'information', as considered exclusively hitherto, is what is required for successful new combinations to be produced.

The scope of entrepreneurial, or competitive activity, is therefore much greater in reality than in the so-called purely competitive model. Very frequently, the competitiveness of a market is associated exclusively with, or even defined in terms of, the cross elasticity of demand for the products sold in it; yet a high or 'perfect' degree of competitiveness in this sense is wholly compatible with the absence of any of the activities which would be called competitive in the ordinary sense. One producer competes with another when he attempts to encroach upon his market; this he may do by charging a lower price for the same product or by offering a different product, which more fully satisfies the consumers' complex of desires. If producers make an identical commodity by means of the same process of production, the scope for competition between them is very limited; they can increase their market by reducing their selling price, but this is possible only to the extent that careful attention to the detailed operation of the common process enables them to reduce costs. But if manufacturers are free to contrive new 'production functions', to combine resources in different ways, whether to make the same or different commodities, the field for active competitive warfare is much enlarged. Even if the state of technical knowledge remained unchanged, the variety of ways in which factors might profitably be combined—the scope for innovation, in other words—would still be large; once technical advance is assumed to take place, entrepreneurs have the additional opportunity to discover the new combinations which it makes possible. In just the same way a change in consumers' desires, though not a condition for the profitable invention of new varieties, adds to the opportunities for such invention.

3. The preceding chapters offered a rather summary account of the processes by which, in a competitive, but not purely competitive economy, supply might adjust itself to a change in demand; they considered how the nature of these processes might affect the efficiency of the productive techniques in use. The discussion proceeded on the assumption of a 'fixed list' of commodities, so that adaptation was successful if these came to be produced in the right proportions and by the right methods; now we must consider the ways in which the account of adaptation requires modification to cover the qualitative, as well as the quantitative possibilities of variation.

The notion of adaptation implies, of course, some standard of appropriateness in the relationship of supply to consumers' desires and to available resources and techniques. Nowhere in the preceding chapters has the proper criterion or standard of efficiency been brought under examination. We committed ourselves, by implication, to the view that the volume of investment in any direction should be increased until potential profits, at the margin, were zero, though it was noted, in the discussion of complementary investments, that it was necessary to consider the potential profitability of a group of related projects rather than of individual projects taken in isolation. In adopting this approach there was implied an acceptance, as a criterion, of the Pareto optimum and of the belief that a divergence from it will set up potential profit, in the sense that the application (or withdrawal) of a marginal quantity of resources in any direction would yield revenue in excess of costs. I shall continue, in this section, to base the argument on the same general presuppositions, while conceding freely that, with the transition from a 'fixed' to an 'open list', their validity becomes increasingly doubtful. Even when our concern is with whether to produce a little more or less of a particular commodity, marginal profitability is a guide subject to a variety of qualifications; it becomes even less reliable when we have to decide what goods to produce from among all the available alternatives. Nevertheless, these are complications which, however important, will be put aside in this discussion. It will be necessary to recognize that the profitability of investment in any product variety will depend on whatever context of substitutes and complements might accompany it, as this has a direct bearing on the problem of market information which is our proper theme; but other important causes of divergence between private and social profitability will be ignored. The optimum will still be defined in terms of the impossibility of increasing the satisfaction of one person without reducing that of others.

I maintained earlier, when assuming a fixed list of goods, that a proper understanding and evaluation of the competitive economy was to be obtained by studying the actual process of adaptation and not by taking the illusory short cut represented by the identification of a supposed equilibrium state of the system, the properties of which could then be analysed. That which was regarded as an equilibrium was, it was argued, merely a special set of consistent, optimalizing activities, and not a position to which the perfectly competitive economy could be shown to gravitate. Precisely similar reasoning must lead us to question equilibrium analysis when applied to the 'open list', the analysis, that is to say, given by the theory of monopolistic competition.[1] No models of general equilibrium, such as would enable all prices and outputs to be deduced from initial conditions, have yet been constructed on the assumption of a state of monopolistic competition, and it may in fact be doubted whether this is a task capable of fulfilment.[2] Nevertheless particular equilibria appropriate to this assumption have been identified by a process of reasoning similar to that employed in the discussion of perfect competition. The procedure, in other words, is to determine the circumstances in which a producer will be unable to increase his profits, either by varying the nature or the quantity of his own product or by transferring to another industry. These circumstances, however, no longer imply the equality of price and marginal cost; since each firm is assumed to produce a slightly different commodity, the demand curve confronting it will be less than perfectly elastic, so that maximum profits will be obtained at a level of output at which price exceeds marginal cost. Nor need the level of profits in the economy be uniformly normal; they will be so only when entry is completely free, in the sense that firms can produce varieties which compete closely with existing output; where this is not so, pockets of abnormal profit will remain. The existence of normal profits no longer implies, as it did in perfect competition, that the firm was operating at that level of output which minimized its unit costs; on the contrary, the demand curve for the firm's output, being less than perfectly elastic, will touch its unit cost curve at a point above the minimum. Finally, we have to assume that no firm can increase its profits by changing the character of its product, again on the assumption that everything else in the economy remains unchanged.

4. What then is the justification for believing, that under the market conditions postulated, this equilibrium would actually be reached? No doubt the equilibrium, if attained at all, would persist for a very short period of time, for, on the assumption

[1] Vide E. H. Chamberlin, *The Theory of Monopolistic Competition* (5th Ed., 1947).
[2] 'No doubt the work of developing general equilibrium models in terms of monopolistic competition is yet to be done' (E. H. Chamberlin, *Towards a More General Theory of Value*, p. 11).

of an open list, it becomes particularly unplausible to regard consumers' preferences as constant, even if the underlying desires are constant. But it could be argued, nevertheless, that consideration of the equilibrium configuration would enable us to predict the directions in which the economy would start to change, even if its movement were continuously disturbed by alterations in the determining factors. In fact, however, it has never adequately been demonstrated that a hypothetical monopolistically competitive economy would gravitate towards this configuration, far less shown which particular path it would take.

According to the principle of its construction, the equilibrium, like that of perfect competition, is a set of consistent maximizing activities. In order that it should represent a set of activities which will be persisted in—i.e., a true equilibrium in the weak sense—it must be associated with appropriate conditions of belief. These can be elaborated in a way similar, but not identical, to that followed in our discussion of perfect competition; in this case it will not be enough for firms to expect the continuance of certain prices; they will need to be informed about the demand conditions which determine marginal revenue and expect them not to change. Whatever the exact nature of the beliefs postulated they will once again be performing in the same rôle, as the *deus ex machina* which gives to the configuration its equilibrium character. It is, to say the least, very doubtful whether the postulation of these beliefs would secure a direct movement to equilibrium as distinct from continuance in it. In any case, however, it is by some process of gradual adjustment that the equilibrium is generally supposed to be reached, even although the nature of the process, and the conditions for its efficiency, have not been very carefully examined. Some writers, including Professor Chamberlin himself,[1] conceive of the movement to equilibrium roughly as follows. Producers are assumed to know with certainty the current conditions of demand and supply and to expect them to remain unchanged; they then choose the particular commodity variety, and the particular scale of plant, that will maximize their profits under these assumptions. This policy

[1] *The Theory of Monopolistic Competition*, Ch. 5.

inevitably proves mistaken as more firms, who set up the production of close substitutes, alter the demand and supply conditions; the original firm, therefore, revises its price and output policies, but once more on the assumption of the *status quo*. By a sequence of such repeated revisions the equilibrium position, with the properties described earlier, is presumed to be reached. Acceptance of this demonstration requires a good deal of faith. As has been frequently pointed out,[1] the expectational assumptions on which it is based are highly unplausible and give entrepreneurs credit for much less foresight than they

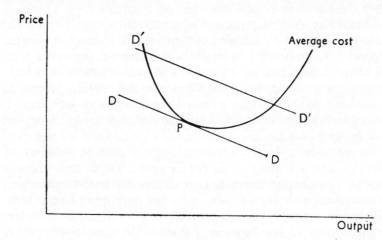

FIGURE 3

surely have. The process of repeated revision moreover will demand, as is sometimes forgotten, repeated alterations in the scale of the plant's equipment and not merely in the intensity of its use. A familiar diagram (Fig. 3) shows how the entry of competing firms will cause the demand curve for a producer to fall from say D^1D^1 until it is tangential with the

[1] The relevant literature is very extensive. The following articles are merely two examples of more explicit consideration of entrepreneurial expectations:

R. F. Harrod, 'Theory of Imperfect Competition Revised', in *Economic Essays* (1952).

J. R. Hicks, 'The Process of Imperfect Competition', *Oxford Economic Papers*, 1954.

curve of average cost at P; it implies that production plans are gradually revised downwards until the point of zero profits is reached and further entry ceases. This development is somewhat more plausible (although even then doubtfully so), if the cost function is short-run in character; but, if it is, the point of tangency is not the long-run equilibrium characterized by the equality of price and long-run average cost.

It is even more difficult to envisage how a determinate equilibrium could be reached in this way once the possibility of quality variation is introduced. Each producer is presumably supposed to regard the existing assortment of output as permanent and to determine the most profitable variety for his own product on this basis; the inevitable subsequent introduction of competitive varieties will, however, make his wish to vary his own product to suit the new context. It is at least questionable whether such a sequence of revisions would, if continued long enough, result in a particular equilibrium assortment determined by the unchanging state of consumers' desires and of technical possibilities.

These considerations seem to suggest that the theory of monopolistic competition is hardly more useful than that of perfect competition in enabling us to understand the working of an actual competitive economy. Its assumptions represent, in comparison with those of perfect competition, a step nearer reality; in particular it places a desirable emphasis on product variation and on selling costs; but, from other points of view, it represents a less radical theoretical departure than is sometimes supposed. In order to identify an equilibrium position, it is merely taken for granted that a general profit potential will not coexist for long with the freedom to exploit it, no attempt being made to ascertain the market conditions most likely to ensure that this potential creates particular profit opportunities for individual entrepreneurs. The theory, like that of perfect competition, effectively ignores the informational properties of economic systems; the question whether, under the arrangements postulated, entrepreneurs would be able to form reliable expectations, is simply not raised, and decisions are assumed to be taken merely on the basis of current demand and cost conditions. Both theories are dominated by the

concept of equilibrium, although neither really succeed in showing how in fact it could be attained; they fail to focus attention
on the process of change or adaptation in itself, although it is
this which is most urgently in need of explanation.

5. An explanation of this kind has already been offered,
under the assumption of a fixed list of goods, in the previous
chapters, and it will be convenient to begin by inquiring whether
it remains applicable, at least in rough outline, once this assumption is relaxed. We decided, in our earlier discussion, that a
producer contemplating investment would generally be obliged
to estimate, as well as the future demand for his class of
product as a whole, the likely volume of both competitive and
complementary output. Natural restraints, such as prevent a
rapid increase in either output or sales, may so regulate competitive production as to give him the necessary assurance that
investment in fixed capital would not be made unprofitable
through excess supply; alternatively they may fail to do this,
so that the competitive, purely decentralized process would
have to be supplemented or replaced by arrangements more or
less deliberately contrived to further successful co-ordination.
The integration of complementary investment plans, it was
recognized, could also come about automatically, but only under
favourable conditions; otherwise explicit co-operation would be
needed. These conclusions are by no means invalidated by the
possibility of indefinite product variation, but there are introduced additional complications which on balance further
restrict the conditions under which adaptation, without deliberate co-ordination, can successfully take place.

So long as we conceive resource allocation as being between
a fixed list of existing products, adjustment takes the form
of either addition to, or subtraction from, the outputs of
particular goods. Thus, leaving aside the question of the
efficiency of the production techniques employed, the actual
composition of output can be brought nearer the optimum
composition merely by increments or decrements of this kind.
Once the possibility of qualitative variation is admitted, however, and resources have to be allocated so as to fill up economic
space in some optimal way, adjustment may have to be more

complex; the nature, and not merely the quantity, of currently produced commodities may have to be altered. In addition, it may not be possible to approach an optimal pattern of production by successive investments. The difficulty is perhaps most easily realized if we think in terms of the attainment of an optimal spatial distribution of, for example, retail outlets. Let us imagine that the density of population, the economies of scale in retailing and the costs of transport are such that the ideal spacing of outlets is as in Fig. 4(a). If the outlets are to

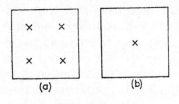

(a)   (b)

FIGURE 4

be set up without co-ordination, by successive entry, there is good reason to believe that the resultant pattern of distribution will diverge from this ideal; the first firm, let us say, may locate itself as in Fig. 4(b) in a position which, although the most profitable at the time, is inconsistent with the optimum arrangement. Later entrants may locate themselves largely with reference to the *status quo* as they see it and there seems no reason to believe that, without co-ordination, the optimum will ever be attained. This somewhat simplistic argument about the filling up of geographical space has an obvious extension in terms of the qualitative assortment of output. We can suppose, for example, that there are two products A and B, one of which is used in the manufacture of the other, and that cost or demand conditions are such that simultaneous modification of both of them, say to α and β, would be profitable. It may, however, be unprofitable for the producer of A to change to α unless he knew that B would simultaneously be changed to β; he might therefore continue to manufacture A or he might switch to say A_1, which was now the most profitable variety, on the assumption that B remained unchanged. The producer of B might later switch to B_1, as the variety most appropriate to the situation with A_1; and so on, there being no obvious reason to expect convergence on the optimum combination. Clearly a similar situation might arise where there were more than two firms in complementary relationship.

6. What practical importance is to be attached to these considerations? It is evident that, whatever the nature of the economy, the allocation of resources can never proceed on the basis of a *tabula rasa*; the existing pattern of production, and not merely current objectives and technical possibilities, will affect the composition of additional output. In the economic sphere, as indeed in any other, societies have a history or inheritance which inevitably conditions current developments. Precisely for this reason, it is dangerous to regard the structure of production as tending towards some determinate equilibrium form, deducible from preference and production functions and independent of its previous states. This of course is the principle underlying the 'age of industry argument' sometimes adduced to account for differences in productivity between different industries or areas. Correctly interpreted, the argument does not imply that the older industry still employs the equipment set up initially; it is rather that the individual additional investments or replacements, taken at different points of time, had to be shaped to fit the inherited structure of complementary assets—the available factory buildings or sites, the gauge of the railway track, the size of harbours and so on. Considerations of this kind suggest there are economies not only in the size of the market, but in its rate of growth, for it is this which in part determines the extent to which the past will trammel the future.[1]

Our present interest, however, is not so much in the way in which the *status quo* will inevitably influence, in any economy, the character of investment, but in whether a better assortment of production can be obtained by some deliberate co-ordination of investment decisions. The desirability of producing goods

---

[1] For a discussion of these influences, see Marvin Frankel, 'Obsolescence and Technological Change in a Maturing Economy', *American Economic Review*, Vol. XLV, No. 3, June 1955.

of the right kinds, related to each other in the right way, gives rise, it can scarcely be doubted, at least to a new prima facie case for co-ordination. It is probably in the sphere of the relationship between intermediate and final production that the practical importance of obtaining the correct assortment of output is greatest. It may be possible to achieve substantial economies by large-scale manufacture of standardized intermediate products; but unless appropriate modifications are made in the nature of the products or the processes of firms which might use them, the intermediate production will not find a market. Let us imagine, for example, that a manufacturer of metal cans wishes to realize the economies offered by the large-scale production of a standard size. Before the canning industry could use this size, however, it might require new equipment in its factories, or different packing cases from other suppliers. Only deliberate co-ordination, embracing several independent concerns, might suffice to secure the changes necessary for the exploitation of the available economies.

7. What possibilities are there that an optimal assortment of related products could be obtained automatically without agreement or co-ordination? The co-ordination of complementary investments was considered earlier in terms of the need for additional investment in fixed capital, in related, and already existing, lines of production. This might ultimately be secured, it was argued, by investments made successively in the different complementary directions, provided that the existing equipment offered sufficient short-run elasticity of output; in this case the firm which expanded production, to the extent required to obtain scale economies, would find that the supply of necessary inputs and the market for its products were both sufficient to afford it a tolerable return throughout the period which would have to elapse before the complementary adjustments were made. But where these adjustments take the form of change in the nature of the product or production processes, as opposed to an increase in existing capacity, there is no very close analogue to the short-run elasticity which makes spontaneous, unplanned co-ordination possible. It is of course possible that if one firm changes its product to the variety appropriate to the optimum combination without others simultaneously doing likewise, it will nevertheless still be able to use the same inputs and still find a market for its product with the same customers; in this case co-ordination could be achieved through a series of successive adjustments. But it seems likely that the relevant technical complementarities may frequently be much too rigid for this to be the case; a motor-car, for example, with wheels of a certain diameter, has very inelastic requirements for tyres.

So long as we were concerned with quantitative variation only, even if it had to be by substantial finite amounts, simultaneous adjustment could come about, given favourable conditions, through implicit or tacit collusion. Several producers, that is to say, all being aware of conditions which would make their combined expansion profitable, might well advance in step without formally agreeing to do so. But where the optimal adjustment requires a particular set of related quality variations, of which the precise nature could scarcely be immediately apparent to all concerned, consultation and agreement are likely to be essential.

8. The above observations do not of course purport even to summarize the complex problems associated with standardization, far less the general problem of an optimum assortment. They are, moreover, in the context of these problems, very familiar. At the theoretical level with which we are concerned, however, and in connexion with the general theme of the relative merits of centralized and decentralized allocation, they are usually denied appropriate emphasis. Only by ignoring such essential issues of change and adjustment can the modern protagonists of perfect competition and comparative statics give any plausibility to their claims that this kind of conceptual apparatus, despite apparent inappropriateness, is well-suited to explain and predict actual economic developments. The concentration by economists on supposed equilibrium situations is surely responsible for much of the weakness and limitations of our conventional tools of analysis. Its dangers are well exemplified by the way in which some writers have attempted

to assess the efficiency of allocation in actual competitive economies purely on the basis of a study of the properties of the
presumed equilibrium state of monopolistic competition, in
which prices exceed both marginal, and minimum average,
costs. This, in itself, is a difficult undertaking, for the criteria
by which we define ideal allocation—the optimum conditions
of production and exchange—were originally worked out under
the assumption of a fixed list of goods and become very difficult
to apply once this assumption is relaxed. The equality of price
and marginal cost, for example, ceases to be a desideratum as
soon as we decide that goods should be provided in appropriate
variety as well as in appropriate proportions.[1] If products are
to be differentiated so as to meet the almost unlimited variety
of consumers' preferences, then some economies of scale will
inevitably have to be sacrificed.[2] Without wishing to deny that
useful information about the possible divergences between
private and public profitability has been yielded by analysis
of the so-called equilibrium conditions, I am nevertheless
inclined to believe that it is upon the actual processes of adaptation by which supply adjusts to changing circumstances that
the efficiency of the final assortment and composition of output, as well as of the manner in which it is produced, will
chiefly depend.

The prima facie case for co-ordination, which the foregoing
analysis would appear to support, should not be misinterpreted;
the issue in question is not that of free enterprise versus a
controlled economy, but of the area over which there should be
co-ordination of some kind. Voluntary co-operation between
independent enterprises may be the form which this co-ordination can most conveniently take and, at least in the field of

[1] In order to decide whether a commodity should be produced at all, as
opposed to deciding how much of it to produce, the 'total' and not merely
the 'marginal' conditions for optimum allocation are relevant. (These are
the terms employed by Professor Hicks, in his article 'The Foundations of
Welfare Economics', *Economic Journal*, December 1939.) An estimate would
have to be made of the total net increase or decrease in producers' and
consumers' surpluses as a result of the change; the immense difficulties in
the way of applying this test are clearly evident.

[2] '. . . the final welfare equilibrium . . . would inevitably involve product
heterogeneity; and it would be characterized neither by the equation of price
and marginal cost nor by production at minimum cost for the firms involved'
(E. H. Chamberlin, *Towards a More General Theory of Value*, p. 99.)

standardization, American experience argues for its effectiveness. But if the common policy demands different degrees of risk and sacrifice from the different firms, some more intimate form of association is likely to be required. The large multiproduct firm, or the vertical integration of several stages of production, are themselves means by which, over a certain area, an appropriate assortment of intermediate and final output can be planned. Nor, finally, should it be forgotten that co-ordination is not the only requirement for economic efficiency and that economic efficiency is not the only, nor even an ultimate, good. One might reasonably choose to accept an imperfect degree of co-ordination if it were thought that the measures necessary to improve it further would seriously impair the flexibility of the whole investment programme, or would, by unduly restricting the freedom of individual entrepreneurs, dampen their energy and initiative. The discussion of these further considerations, however, is reserved for later chapters.

VII

COMPETITION, SELECTION AND MARKET DISCIPLINE

1. THROUGHOUT all the preceding discussion, attention was focused exclusively on one essential requirement—the informational requirement—for the effective operation of a competitive system, our object being to ascertain the nature of the conditions which would or would not enable entrepreneurs to obtain information sufficient for them to identify profitable investment opportunities. By carrying out this investigation, we were made better able to judge when the integration of investment plans might take place spontaneously and when some measures of deliberate co-ordination would have to be introduced. The decision to give priority to the informational requirements of the system could be justified both by their obviously fundamental importance and by the equally obvious fact of their neglect in the greater part of the accepted theoretical analysis.

But we must now transfer our scrutiny to two other requirements which any efficient competitive system must meet. The first of these is that control over the resources of the economy should tend to pass to those who possess entrepreneurial talent from those who do not; this can be called the need for Efficient Selection. The second is that entrepreneurs should not be able to restrict the investment in any particular direction so as to maintain in it a rate of profit permanently in excess of the normal level; this we may call the need for Market Discipline. These objectives can conveniently be discussed together, as both are promoted, in the private enterprise system, by the same means—by the force of free competition. Both seem at least at first glance to require the maximum freedom of competition, so that any producer can invade the markets of others, either because he is more efficient than they are, or because they are enjoying abnormally high returns. This condition, however, would appear to be manifestly incompatible with the informational requirements of the system as they were previously elaborated, for, in that context, we found ourselves obliged to recognize that no single firm would be induced to take advantage of a general profit opportunity if all others were equally free and able to do so. The provision of adequate market information, and therefore the successful integration of competitive investment plans, required, it appeared, the existence of certain restraints either natural or contrived; yet restraints would seem to be the very antithesis of the freedom of competition by which both selection and market discipline have to be furthered. There would seem to be a need that the markets of individual producers should both be secure, in order to give them the confidence to invest, and at the same time vulnerable, lest their policies are inefficient or restrictionist. Must we admit this incompatibility to be genuine and ineluctable? Is it possible to find a compromise between the conflicting requirements, an optimum degree of inertia or restraint, which will best favour the process of resource allocation taken as a whole? Let us begin by considering, rather more fully, what precisely the need for efficient selection and for market discipline can be taken to imply.

2. In earlier chapters, the selective function of competition was wholly neglected, in that the power to command resources was assumed to be distributed among entrepreneurs in some particular way, the nature of which was merely taken for granted. For the purpose of short-run analysis this attitude is justifiable, for, as the distribution of command over resources changes only slowly, it may be adequate to regard the efficiency of the allocation achieved by any economic arrangements as determined solely by the information and incentives it makes available to entrepreneurs. Nevertheless, this is a simplification, for, in the long run, the pattern of control over resources must be recognized as partially determined by, and partially determining, the course of economic activity. The efficiency of allocation will depend not only on what individual entrepreneurs do, but also on which entrepreneurs have resources put at their disposal.

The volume of resources under the command of particular entrepreneurs may vary automatically or as a result of deliberate decision. To the extent that it is varied directly by the profits and losses incurred in economic activity I shall say that Automatic Selection is in operation. Selection will be termed Planned when the resources available to an entrepreneur are altered by the deliberate decision of an authority with a superior position in an organizational hierarchy, or by the owners of wealth who entrust the entrepreneurs with funds. In a competitive economy, both forms of selection operate simultaneously, as firms generally grow both from undistributed profits and from external finance.

I have argued that the competitive economy must further the efficient selection of entrepreneurs; but what are the agencies, in modern capitalist economies, to which the entrepreneurial function, featuring so prominently in this analysis, can properly be attributed? For present purposes, the function itself can be conceived quite simply as that of responsibility for policy decisions as to resource allocation; the owner-manager of a small private business would represent its most obvious embodiment. Direct responsibility for the allocation of productive resources now rests, most typically, with the directors of public companies, who, though nominally elected by shareholders, will only rarely be under their control in the making of investment decisions. Moreover they are subject to automatic selection, in that they are generally able to decide by themselves on the employment of the undistributed part of the profits accruing to their company. Yet clearly some influence on allocation, if only an indirect one, remains with private wealth owners themselves and with those intermediaries, such as investment and insurance companies, who connect them with firms actually engaged in productive activity; they also perform an entrepreneurial function, and according to their ability in doing so, their command over resources will automatically grow or decline. Although the term entrepreneur will normally be used, in the following discussion, to denote the management of ordinary businesses, it should be borne in mind that it is not they alone who are subject to the selective forces.

Automatic selection is essentially a consequence of the institution of private property, which gives to individuals the right to employ their capital as they please and to enjoy

the gains or losses which result from its employment. Under
the conditions of modern capitalism, however, neither right is
unqualified; government regulation and taxation will interfere
with both of them. Within a centrally directed economy, as
within an individual private firm, there will be no private
property and therefore, in general, no automatic selection; but
even here it is possible that something analogous to it may be
deliberately built in, by, for example, allowing managers to
decide upon the use to be made of at least some part of the
surpluses made by their concerns.[1]

3. One further preliminary observation, bearing on the
efficiency of automatic selection, should be made. In a world of
uncertainty, the profits and losses made by entrepreneurs will
be the result of luck as well as of good or bad management.
While it is desirable that the funds available to entrepreneurs
should vary in accordance with the quality of their foresight,
imagination and administrative capacity, there is no social
rationale in gains and losses which are the inevitable result of
unforeseeable developments. Performance will be a guide to
efficiency only if assessed over a period long enough for the
influence of skill to outweigh the influence of chance. Entrepreneurial ability will not necessarily be reflected in profits
unless a sufficiently long run is available for its exercise, which
demands that firms should not be too vulnerable to single errors
of judgement. This has a clearly important bearing on what was
said earlier about the compatibility of efficient selection with
limitations on the freedom of competition; efficient selection
itself requires, it would seem, some degree of stability for the
individual firm. The informational and selective requirements
of the system are related also in another, and more direct way;
the more adequate the information made available to entrepreneurs, the smaller will be the rôle of chance and the greater
the likelihood that profits and losses will reflect the level of an
entrepreneur's efficiency.

[1] Vide János Kornai, *Overcentralisation in Economic Administration* (Trans.
John Knapp), pp. 101–03. It would appear that the management of state
enterprises may retain a certain percentage of profits in excess of their
planned amount and decide themselves how this 'development fund' may be
employed.

An excessive vulnerability of firms and wealth owners to unforeseeable events would in any case be objectionable, quite apart from its effect on selective efficiency. An element of gambling is present in almost all business activity, but if factors' limiting its scope do not already exist they will be, and of course are, invented. People will be unwilling to expose themselves beyond a certain extent to the danger that they may suffer a sudden reduction in wealth; there will be a maximum degree of risk-bearing which the members of any economy will voluntarily assume, given the existing framework of economic organization. We shall later have to consider how this framework may come to be modified in order to deal with risk and what the effects of this on selection and on market discipline are likely to be.

4. Meanwhile, however, let us turn to consider the nature of the requirement for market discipline. This was intended to secure, it will be remembered, that the returns from investment in all directions should tend towards a uniform level; the desirability of this result follows, of course, from the principles of formal welfare theory, of which it forms perhaps the essential core. This is not the place to examine the validity of these principles or to elaborate the many qualifications by which they should be hedged; something should be said, however, about how they are related to the rest of our analysis. Formal welfare theory is concerned essentially with the logic of resource allocation; it sets itself to find what distributions of resources satisfy a stipulated criterion while being consistent with certain postulated objective conditions, such as preferences, production functions, and the like. It can be used to identify in particular, an important kind of configuration, known as a Pareto optimum, in which everyone is as well off as he can be (in a specially defined sense) subject to the condition that no one is made worse off. The special properties of such a configuration are usually called the 'optimum conditions of production and exchange' and the allocative efficiency of any actual economic system is judged by the extent to which they are realized by it.

What then are the institutional arrangements most likely to impose the appropriate market discipline and thereby to ensure

that the optimum conditions will be realized? An answer to
this question, at least at a high level of abstraction, is supposed
to have been provided by the theory of perfect competition
which was considered in the first part of this book. Allocative
efficiency is represented by this theory as depending on the
existence of a particular market structure characterized by the
presence in each industry of many independent firms making
identical commodities, by the absence of any collusion and by
the unencumbered mobility of all resources. Misallocation,
conversely, appears as the result of monopoly, restriction, or
immobility. In the light of the analysis of perfect competition
given in Chapters I and II, these conclusions must be rejected;
the conditions supposed to ensure allocative efficiency are in
fact such as would prevent purposive economic activity of any
kind, for they are incompatible with the availability to entrepreneurs of the necessary market information. The construction of the theory of perfect competition did prove historically
to be of great value in so far as it enabled economists, although
almost incidentally, to discover what the conditions of optimum
allocation, in fact, were; but in appearing to prescribe the
institutional requirements for the achievement of this optimum
allocation by a decentralized system, it surely did much harm.

In fact, of course, misallocation cannot always be attributed to
the deliberate restriction of supply by a monopolist or trade
association. Whenever the rôle of expectations in economic
activity is explicitly recognized, influences of a wholly different
kind can be shown to be at least as important. The efficiency
of adjustment can be shown to depend on the availability of
market information, the conditions for which were discussed
in earlier chapters. It depends in addition on the influence
exercised by uncertainty on the policies of individual entrepreneurs, for the supply of technical and market information
will never be such as to remove from entrepreneurs' estimates
any element of uncertainty and, therefore, of risk. The inevitable presence of risk, attaching in different degrees to different
investment opportunities, will have a substantial influence on
the policies of the entrepreneur and, therefore, on the allocation
of resources achieved. Consideration of this influence will be
deferred until later chapters, but I refer to it here in order to

stress the plurality of the determinants of allocative efficiency. The need for market discipline, in order to prevent deliberate restriction, must be appreciated in conjunction with the other requirements for efficiency, with the need, that is, for adequate information, for selection, and for an appropriate response to uncertainty.

5. Having discussed the general implications of these two further requirements, automatic selection and market discipline, I shall now attempt to judge the extent to which they are compatible with the conditions which we found necessary for the provision of adequate market information, and therefore for the automatic co-ordination of competitive investments and the adjustment of supply to demand. I shall review first those natural restraints which appeared as roughly analogous to inertia and friction, and then turn to the formal arrangements which producers may adopt in order to co-ordinate their activities.

The existence between firms, at any point of time, of differences in the ability either to foresee a profit opportunity or to increase production in response to it, might sometimes be sufficient, it was decided, to secure the satisfactory adaptation of supply by means of successive investment decisions. Automatic co-ordination of this kind, when possible, would seem to be most in harmony with the other conditions for the efficient working of the system, for it depends on the existence of restraints on competitive activity which are essentially short-lived. A firm is enabled to expand output without the threat of excess competitive supply, but it will have no protection against ultimate encroachment of more efficient rivals and no opportunity to maintain profits at a permanently abnormal level. Moreover the frequency and extent to which it is itself able to respond by an increase in supply will depend on the amount of the profits which its efficiency has earned it in the past.

The effectiveness of competition, in both its selective and disciplinary functions, may be impaired, however, by the presence of significant scale economies in production. The levels of profits in an industry may be abnormally high, or its operations may be conducted with less than normal efficiency, yet it may not be profitable for a new firm to enter it if the minimum efficient scale were such as would produce additional output sufficient to cause a large fall in price. Neither might it pay an existing firm to introduce larger capacity, on the occasion, let us say, of replacing its old equipment; for, already possessing a significant share of the market, it would realize that expansion would, in the long run, merely reduce the profit rate to a normal level. Yet, the likely frequency or practical importance of such a situation may not be very great. An outsider with an important efficiency advantage could afford to reduce price by an amount which, under very common conditions of demand elasticity, would give a substantial extension to the market; and it does not seem likely that the firms already in the industry could succeed, without formal collusion, in preserving deliberately a deficiency in supply which was both great enough to cause significant misallocation and small enough not to induce entry. All depends, needless to say, on the actual circumstances of each case. It should be observed, moreover, that the difficulty in question is not that of incompatibility between the conditions necessary for automatic co-ordination, on the one hand, and selection and market discipline, on the other; it is rather that large-scale economies may happen to be inimical, in some degree, to all three requirements.

6. Let us now turn to the category of restraints which limited the ability of firms to increase their sales rather than their output. It was observed earlier that established firms might have, to use Marshall's term, a 'particular market' in which they could sell more easily than could competitors. This, it was claimed, might increase the supply of the information necessary to efficient adjustment; but might it not, at the same time, hinder entrepreneurs from obtaining an increase in sales which either their superior efficiency or the prevalence of abnormal profits would seem to justify? Marshall himself, it will be remembered, held that a producer with a particular market 'does not expect to get better prices . . . but he expects to sell more easily'. A firm may enjoy the attachment of his customers through goodwill or reputation; but these are benefits to be preserved rather than exploited. They give to existing firms a measure of advantage which affords them an assured market, but only on condition that they continue to offer a product which is no more expensive than comparable alternatives. There is a good deal of evidence that business men place great store on having a body of reliable customers; the common policy of maintaining prices in the face of excess demand frequently has, at least in part, this aim in view. An attempt is made to keep customers on the waiting-lists as contented as circumstances allow, while at the same time increasing capacity to the degree required to satisfy them and thereby prevent other firms from entering the market. It has been suggested that firms may also be prepared deliberately to preserve some excess productive capacity, in order that they may not fail to meet the demands of their more loyal customers.[1] The short-run stability of prices has, in addition, definite advantages from the informational point of view, for the length of order books is, as an index of excess demand, clearly superior to a rise in price. Whether such stability has a directly harmful effect on allocative efficiency is, as we shall argue later, very doubtful.

All the factors making for market attachment, or particular markets, may not, however, be equally innocuous. The guaranteed market afforded by location and the protection of transport costs, for example, may permit inefficiency or the deliberate restriction of supply. Here again trouble arises from the fact that the minimum scale of efficient operation may be large compared to the market. The existence of a natural monopoly, it has to be admitted, disposes of the problem of obtaining market information about the plans of competitors; at the same time, however, it is the obvious negation of both automatic selection and market discipline.

The protection, or particular market, provided by a special product variety, associated perhaps with a brand or trade name, is unlikely to prove an enduring shelter for inefficiency or a source of permanently abnormal profits. This is so, first and foremost, because of the changing nature of consumers' demands and the ever-widening range of technological possibility. Short-run protection there may be, and this may be a

[1] See P. W. S. Andrews, *Manufacturing Business,* p. 88.

condition of orderly adjustment, but abnormal profits are likely to result, in the long-run, from superior ability to judge or to mould consumers' desires.

The effects then of restraints of the natural variety just considered will vary from one situation to another and have to be judged accordingly; but one is inclined to conclude, at least tentatively, that they will rarely impede competition very seriously in either its selective or disciplinary function. Advantages in particular markets will be given to some firms rather than to others and this may afford them sufficiently secure demand expectations to induce them to assume the risks of investment; but it is doubtful if protection of this kind would enable firms to persist for very long if inefficient or restrictionist. Natural restraints by themselves, however, cannot be guaranteed to promote efficient adjustment; they need not, in all cases, make adequate market information available and, where scale economies are substantial, the automatic coordination of competitive investments may not always secure productive efficiency.

7. Let us now turn to the second category of restraints, to those which are deliberately contrived. Although their effects are qualitatively similar to those of the natural category, they are likely to be much more strong, and may therefore represent a more serious threat to the other requirements of efficient allocation. They exist, needless to say, in a great variety of forms, only a few of which will be mentioned here. Our intention is not to provide an adequate assessment of the balance of merits and demerits for each type of restriction, but rather to underline their relationship to our primary theme— the creation of informational conditions appropriate to successful adjustment.

I will consider first the agreements which are made between firms and their customers. Of these the most common is the simple contract to buy and sell certain volumes of goods, at agreed prices and for a stipulated period of time; though generally regarded as innocuous, it is, in principle, restrictionist in character. By guaranteeing a definite market to one producer it necessarily closes it to others; the incentive to efficiency remains in the effect on profits of reducing costs, but the force of automatic selection, which would deprive the inefficient producer of his market, is temporarily suspended. It is not, however, permanently withdrawn, because the customer will, on termination of the agreement, be free to switch his custom; contracts emerge, therefore, as a way in which entrepreneurs may be afforded at least some measure of predictability for future sales without impairment to the other requirements for efficiency.

But customers may, on occasion, be induced or compelled to enter into agreements of a probably more harmful character. They may agree to give a certain producer their exclusive custom in return for a certain rebate. If we assume that only one good is covered by the contract, no harm would seem to be done, for if a more efficient producer were able to offer a sufficiently cheaper alternative, the customer could sacrifice the rebate and go elsewhere. But if the contract covers a variety of goods, the conditions for automatic selection may be contravened, for the customer may be persuaded to buy from the producer a commodity which he would prefer to buy elsewhere if he were free to do so. This may merely amount to saying that a multi-product firm, which is able to practise some form of internal subsidization, is not subject to automatic selection in terms of each of its activities taken separately; for the effect of the discount will be to charge the customer rather less than he would be prepared to pay for some things and rather more than he would be prepared to pay for others. It may, however, be that the producer has a monopoly in some but not all of his products and endeavours to extend his monopoly power by making the purchase of some of them conditional, by some means or other, on the purchase of all. Such an arrangement would seem to give him a degree of protection for his total market by which both selection and market discipline would be seriously inhibited; it has to be based, of course, on a presumed monopoly in one particular line.[1]

---

[1] A more thorough discussion of this point can be found in an article by Mr. B. S. Yamey, 'Aggregated Rebate Schemes and Independent Competition', *Oxford Economic Papers*, 1960.

Exclusive contracts of this kind may be similar in effect to full vertical integration, the advantages of which for the co-ordination of complementary activities were elaborated at an earlier stage. Here again automatic selection will now operate only on the group of related activities as a whole, as inefficiency in one of them can be supported by efficiency in others. The effect of such selection will manifestly become less particular or detailed the wider the area under single ownership, although an extension of ownership over several activities may, on occasions, be a condition of their successful integration.

8. Let us now turn to the agreements which competing firms may make with each other; we shall consider first the fixing of common prices. The stability of prices under conditions of changing demand does not, of course, in itself require agreement, but may be the policy of each firm individually. But it is likely to be reinforced, in times of falling demand, by a sense of common interest which could be regarded as implicit collusion. Each entrepreneur may recognize that it would pay him to cut his own price provided his competitors did not follow him, but that a general price reduction, given the demand elasticity for the type of product being made, would reduce the profits of all concerned. There may thus develop a quasi-moral scruple or inhibition against 'spoiling the market' in this way.[1] The influence of this conventional practice on selective efficiency is more likely to be favourable than not. It is true that it prevents the more efficient producers from using price reductions as a means of encroaching on the markets of others, but its more important effect may be to mitigate the losses which would otherwise prove seriously harmful to efficient and inefficient alike. A firm's actual performance, and therefore the profits available for its expansion, will be a more accurate index to its efficiency the less the vulnerability to short-run, unforeseeable disturbances. Under conditions of low elasticity of demand and high fixed costs, downward flexibility of prices

---

[1] Vide Marshall (*Principles*, Bk. V, Chap. V, Sect. 6), who says that an entrepreneur 'is more or less in fear of incurring the resentment of other producers, should he sell needlessly at a price that spoils the common market for all'.

might result in severe losses and widespread bankruptcy, both without economic justification.

Neither need the practice be harmful in its disciplinary or allocative effects. Here one must distinguish between two aspects of allocative efficiency, that of the appropriate amount of capacity invested in a particular direction and that of the intensity at which, at any point of time, a given capacity is employed. Efficiency in the former, or long-run sense, is likely to be furthered by the convention in question; for, were not firms able, by maintaining prices, to mitigate the effect of sudden, temporary falls in demand, the risk of investment in the industry would be the greater and volume of resources allocated to it consequently less. One might argue that firms might make themselves viable in the face of short-run disturbances by some other means; they might, for example, carry greater reserves. But this would also restrict investment in the industry, as a profit large enough to offset the charge of these reserves would be required.

Stable prices may appear more injurious to short-run allocative efficiency, as prices will then exceed short-run marginal costs. But if demand is, in fact, inelastic the principal effect of a fall in prices may be merely a pointless (or indeed harmful) redistribution of income from firms to their customers. In the short run, demand is, in fact, likely to be highly inelastic for it may be difficult for customers to alter their consumption patterns, or factor inputs, as the case may be; a price fall might indeed stimulate speculative purchases, but the introduction of a speculative element into consumer demand would be no unmixed benefit. Stable prices may facilitate planning by the firms or individuals who consume the product.

This assessment rests on the assumption, however, that the fall in demand is to be short-lived. Price stability in the face of a permanent reduction in demand cannot be similarly justified; nor indeed is it likely to be maintained, if mere convention or implicit collusion is to be the only support. We should, therefore, turn to consider price-fixing which results from formal agreement and which may give rise not merely to stable prices but to profits which remain at a level permanently equal to or greater than normal. The injurious effects of such arrangements are well known. They take away from the efficient producer an important weapon of competition with which he can enlarge his share of the market. They may permit an excessive number of competitors to remain in an industry, the under-utilization of capacity being sustained by a high profit margin; or they may enable producers to restrict investment so as to earn a monopoly revenue. The forces producing selection and market discipline will be damped, but they may still work behind the scenes. The more efficient firms have interests as individuals which run contrary to their interests as members of the group, and, unless they can expand as they wish, they may break the price agreement. The threat of entry by other firms may force existing firms to set a price which is no higher than the costs of efficient production, so that unless supported by restrictions on entry the effects of price agreements may not be very harmful.

Nevertheless, as far as selection and discipline is concerned, price agreements, at least prima facie, are undesirable. Is there anything to be set against this judgement by virtue of effects which they may have in other directions? Might they, in particular, facilitate the adjustment of supply by affording entrepreneurs greater assurance of a market for their products? We have just admitted one way in which such agreements might, under certain conditions of costs and of demand elasticity, reduce the risks of investment, namely by stabilizing receipts in the face of fluctuating demand. They may also reduce uncertainty by stabilizing individual market shares. Where common prices are fixed, a firm's volume of sales will depend upon the extent of its established connexions, on goodwill and reputation and on the quality of the product; it is less likely, therefore, to be capable of sudden increase. Moreover, the losses resulting from any excess supply will bear principally on the firm responsible for introducing it; whereas, if price were flexible, they would be distributed more widely over all producers. In so far as this reduces the fear which producers may have of losses resulting from competitive supply, it may be beneficial; at the same time, it may, as we have already observed, prevent the introduction of efficient large-scale equipment.

9. There would seem, on general grounds, to be a further argument in justification of formal price agreements, but I find it difficult to judge what weight to attach to it. Let us accept that production planning will be facilitated if entrepreneurs know the price at which their output is likely to sell, on the grounds that this will enable them more easily to estimate both ultimate consumer demand and also (at least to some extent) likely competitive supply. Will they not be able to do this, however, merely by assuming that price will approximately correspond to average costs of production, including a normal profit, in an efficient firm? There seem to be good reasons, in competitive conditions, why price should gravitate towards this level; and entrepreneurs' own preferences for stability, which we have just considered, would tend to maintain this price in the face of short-run demand fluctuations. One could argue, therefore, that, ruling out a serious deficiency in demand, a price less than this normal average cost need be feared only if one producer were to discover a superior product or method of production—this being precisely the condition in which a loss of sales by other producers might be socially justified. If this is so, must not price agreements give to the markets of individual producers a degree of stability greater than that needed for production planning and greater also than that consistent with selective efficiency?

This general argument carries a reasonable amount of conviction so long as the economy is conceived as being composed of single-product firms, for then assuming common factor prices and the general state of technique, any commodity will have a fairly determinate level of average costs. Entrepreneurs will then be able, from the beginning, to set their price appropriately, in the justifiable belief that others will do likewise. Whenever we admit, however, that multi-product firms are the rule rather than the exception, and that the allocation of common overhead costs is arbitrary, then this method of estimating, and proceeding directly towards, the long-run equilibrium price is available no longer. According to our textbook theory, the prices of joint products would ultimately settle down to an equilibrium level after a succession of adjustments, by the individual entrepreneurs, of their price and output policies. But one may wonder whether such a process might not involve a degree of instability in price and sales volume in excess of that which entrepreneurs would willingly tolerate. If this were so, one would expect to find firms seeking agreement either on the prices to be set or at least on uniform accounting procedures to which to conform.[1] When single-product firms are considered, mutual understanding, or implicit collusion, may suffice to give firms a general idea of what the 'right price' (to employ a term in business use) might be; where a more or less arbitrary decision about the allocation of overheads is required, only explicit collusion could produce this result.

There are obvious alternatives to direct or indirect agreement about a common price. One such would be to accept the actual, historically given price for the joint product as the 'right' or 'conventional' price; but such a policy, though it would give producers a price to depend on, would be difficult to maintain under changing cost and demand conditions. In addition, it is quite likely to produce allocation which would be inferior to that resulting from deliberate price-fixing agreements. The other alternative would be for individual firms to alter the prices of their products freely and at will, according to their own judgements as to profitability; by such a procedure an ideal equilibrium price might indeed ultimately be arrived at, but it is surely possible, at least in certain industries, that the unpredictable fluctuations in prices and sales accompanying this process would seriously hamper the efficient forward planning of production. In industries with high fixed costs, and much arbitrariness in the allocation of costs common to several products or services, this consideration may be of

[1] The adoption of agreed accounting procedures may be a way in which firms might come to set approximately uniform prices without recourse to overt price fixing to which public disapproval may be attached. See, for example, *Cost Accounting* by W. B. Lawrence, revised by John W. Ruswinckle, 4th Ed., 1954. According to these authors 'A constantly growing number of trade associations within the manufacturing industries have adopted uniform cost systems and have, with more or less success, secured their use by members of their industries. Industries in which uniform cost systems are in use cover almost the entire range of manufacturing activity and include both the large and powerful trades and those which are either so small or so specialised as to be practically unknown to the general public.' (These remarks refer to the United States.)

substantial importance, although, in our systematic theory of
the attainment of equilibrium, it is given little place.

In the field of transport, for example, the need for planned
co-ordination is widely accepted. The original case for control
rested mainly on the possession, by the railways, of a natural
monopoly, on the fact, that is, that it would generally be
impracticable to have more than one company operating
between two localities. Nowadays, however, alternative forms
of transport—rail, road, and air—are generally available, and
the problem is to ensure that they are used in the optimal way.
It would be very difficult to maintain that the efficient integration of the different forms of transport and of the activities
of the different operators within them would be reliably and
rapidly produced merely by the operation of unrestricted
competition. An important, but not the only reason why more
deliberate co-ordination will be required is the significance of
indirect costs. As the transport services provided in different
areas and at different times are frequently joint products, their
pricing admits, at least in some degree, of arbitrary decision.
In the absence of some form of agreement between the agencies
concerned, therefore, an irrational and unstable price structure
might result and the possibility of making informed investment
decisions would be seriously prejudiced.

Co-ordination is therefore usually desirable in both the
national and international spheres, but there remains the need
to reconcile it, where possible, with market discipline and
efficient selection. No doubt some of the problems of the
transport industry are peculiar to itself; others, however, have
their counterparts within the field of ordinary manufacturing.
In many branches of production, it is necessary to allocate
overhead costs between the several products with which they
are associated, and without some agreement or convention
about how this is to be done, competition could result in
instability in prices and outputs.

This kind of difficulty naturally remains hidden so long as
analysis is focused on the determinants of so-called equilibrium
situations, in which firms would be pursuing mutually consistent, profit-maximizing activities, rather than on the conditions appropriate to successful adjustment. Once we are

prepared to give these conditions explicit attention, it becomes apparent that, at least in certain cases, price agreements, although possibly prejudicial to market discipline and to selection, may be the indispensible condition of informed investment decisions and the orderly adjustment of output to demand.

10. Price agreements between competitors may reduce, but will by no means eliminate, the uncertainty of producers about the future market for their products. This uncertainty may be further reduced, however, in so far as the likely actions of competitors are concerned, by arrangements, either formal or informal, which are designed to divide up the total market among individual suppliers. The effect of this on the efficiency of automatic selection is easy to see; the low-cost producer may no longer use even the weapons of non-price competition in order to draw customers from his rivals, although, of course, he may employ the threat of breaking the agreements as a means of obtaining favourable treatment in the allocation of market areas or quotas, as the case may be. The efficacy of this policy will depend on whatever powers of coercion the association of producers is able to command. Market sharing may also lead to an undesirable restriction of supply, at least if entry to the industry can somehow be blocked.

There exists, therefore, a strong prima facie case against this particular obstruction to free competitive activity. Other practices, such as the attempt to destroy competitors by deliberately operating at a loss, or to exclude new entrants by monopolizing the supply of an essential factor of production, are subject to even more severe indictment. It would be exceedingly convenient if we could say of at least some restrictionist measures that, whatever the circumstances, they were, on balance, economically objectionable; but, however desirable for the purposes of practical judgement and of a legislative criterion, this is very difficult to do. The case against practices of this kind results from a balance of considerations, the importance of each of which will undoubtedly vary from one industry to another. Measures such as selling at a loss to destroy competitors and establish a monopoly will perhaps almost always be unjustifiable, on the grounds that although a monopolist can undoubtedly estimate his likely future sales more accurately than could competing producers, yet this benefit is bought at too great a cost in terms of the loss of automatic checks against restriction and inefficiency. When we consider market-sharing and the restriction of entry, however, this conclusion would already require qualification. Let us take the case of an industry in which fixed costs are very high and in which a long period must elapse between the decision to create additional equipment and the availability of output from it; and let us assume, in addition, that demand is both fluctuating yet, in the short-run, inelastic. These conditions, it must be conceded, are very unfavourable to the automatic co-ordination or adjustment of competitive production, the requirements for which were discussed in Chapter III. Such conditions are not universal, but they certainly exist. They characterize, let us say, the production of natural rubber. Indeed, in the production of primary commodities in general, the requirements for automatic co-ordination are rarely met; our experience in this field both of maladjustment and of attempts at deliberate, centralized control clearly bear this out. It is true that automatic adjustment appears to proceed more smoothly in manufacturing industry, but this is because of, rather than in spite of, such deviations from the perfectly competitive ideal as market connexion, etc. And even here there are particular industries, such as steel, in which measures of planned co-ordination can be shown to be likely to be required—and where, of course, they have in fact been introduced.

11. Over a wide area of our twentieth-century capitalist economy, therefore, the adjustment of supply to demand is accomplished with the assistance of deliberate co-ordination, whether with or without participation by governments.[1] This

---

[1] Cf. A. A. Berle, *The Twentieth Century Capitalist Revolution*: 'In some industries like transportation and public utilities, solution by competition was discarded from the very outset, and state regulation adopted in its place. Today, the system of more or less planned industry has spread far beyond the enterprise classically assumed to be "natural monopoly". An incomplete list of the areas of American economy presently controlled would include: banks, and banking—via the Federal Reserve legislation; railroads and

is a fact which has, of course, been far from wholly neglected by economists, yet could one claim that they have taken as full account of it, in their theoretical work, as it deserves? And even when the existence of measures of planned co-ordination is freely admitted, are these then not frequently represented as aberrations or as expedients, temporary and regrettable?

This incapacity to appreciate fully and vividly at a theoretical level the importance of such aspects of our industrial life, and the related incapacity to explain their rationale satisfactorily, stems, I should argue, from deficiencies in the analytical apparatus of our subject. Over and over again, the history of economics demonstrates how awareness of important aspects of reality may be inhibited (just as it may be promoted) by the particular conceptual framework we employ.[1] Modern equilibrium analysis, I have maintained, almost entirely neglects the relationship of the structure of an economic system to the availability within it of the market information without which entrepreneurs cannot take the actions required of them; for this reason, it cannot properly deal with the problems of economic adjustment. In particular the idea, or ideal, of a system of self-regulating perfect competition, which still occupies so

trucks—via the Interstate Commerce Act and companion legislation; electric light and power—via the Federal Power Commission Act; and certain sections of the Securities and Exchange Commission legislation; radio and television—via the Federal Communications Act; oil and petroleum—via the Interstate Oil Compact of 1925 and the Connally Hot Oil Act; shipping and merchant marine—through the Maritime Commission legislation; meat products—through the Packers and Stockyards legislation. In lesser degree of development, the aluminum industry is at the moment operating under a jerry-rigged plan combined out of an antitrust decree against Alcoa and federal administrative action constructing the Reynolds Metal Company and Kaiser Aluminum Company; the sugar refining industry under the Sugar Act of 1948; the aviation transport industry under the Civil Aeronautics Act, and aviation production chiefly by administrative action through the purchasing agencies of the Department of Defense. Lesser, but effective private arrangements, often achieved by mere balance of power in a concentrate, and without agreement-violating antitrust laws, are often more numerous.'

[1] Cf. J. A. Schumpeter, *History of Economic Analysis*, p. 1115. Schumpeter refers to the reluctance of economists to recognize that bank loans create deposits and remarks: 'This is a most interesting illustration of the inhibitions with which analytical advance has to contend and in particular of the fact that people may be perfectly familiar with a phenomenon for ages and even discuss it frequently without realising its true significance and without admitting it into their general scheme of thought.'

central a position in this analysis, exercises a powerful and baneful, even if unconscious, influence on our minds.

We should recognize that it may not always be possible to have economic arrangements which make available the market information necessary for the integration of competitive and complementary production decisions, without sacrificing, to some degree, the benefits of automatic selection and market discipline. Entrepreneurial efficiency within an economy does not, of course, depend solely on the process of automatic selection, which in any case does not operate inside large companies or government organizations. Neither is competition the only check on restrictive policies by an industry; the threat of government intervention or the exercise of 'countervailing power'[1] on the other side of the market may also serve to prevent exploitation. Nevertheless it may sometimes be desirable to accept looseness of co-ordination, and corresponding uncertainty, in order to preserve the competitive controls. But limits to doing so will be set by the attitude to uncertainty of business men themselves, of whom Mr. Berle says, with much truth, that 'fundamentally, they all want, not a perpetual struggle, but a steady job—the job of producing goods at a roughly predictable cost under roughly predictable conditions so that goods can be sold in the market at a roughly predictable price'.[2]

Enough has already been said for it to be clear that no single market structure can be regarded as the universal ideal; the requirements for efficient allocation are several, and on occasions, conflicting; and the institutional arrangements most likely to meet them will vary with the nature of the productive techniques and of the demand conditions associated with each particular commodity. In appraising such different arrangements, attention has so far been concentrated on the need for adequate information, for efficient selection and for market discipline. In the third part of this book, yet a further condition for efficient allocation will come under discussion. Whatever the prevailing arrangements, the information at the disposal

[1] The term is, of course, Professor Galbraith's. See his *American Capitalism* (1952).
[2] A. A. Berle, *The Twentieth Century Capitalist Revolution*, pp. 51–52.

of entrepreneurs will inevitably be imperfect and the investment programmes which they undertake will be modified by this fact. It will be necessary, therefore, to study the nature of these modifications, to judge how they might vary with the kind of economic system in force, and to appraise their influence on the whole pattern of resource allocation.[1]

---

[1] With respect to this whole discussion, one cautionary observation ought perhaps to be made. The selective function attributed to the economic system in this chapter should not be confused with that claimed for it by Mr. Armen A. Alchian, in his article 'Uncertainty, Evolution and Economic Theory' (*Journal of Political Economy*, June 1950, Vol. LVIII, No. 3, p. 217), I have been at pains to show the necessity of appropriate expectations and the information on which to base them; Mr. Alchian is intent to demonstrate their superfluity. Thus he argues that 'individual motivation and foresight while sufficient, are not necessary; even if all firms were to act in a wholly random fashion the surviving ones would be those which happened to act appropriately.' Mr. Alchian does not maintain that economies actually do operate wholly on the basis of random decisions but that they could do so. Thus the economist is enabled to relate cause and effect by predicting 'the effects of environmental changes on the surviving class of living organisms' (op. cit., p. 220).

Mr. Alchian's thesis rests on a very uncritical and unqualified extension of Darwin's theory of natural selection into the sphere of economic activity, where important conditions for its applicability are surely lacking. A central aspect of the process of natural selection is the existence of sexual reproduction, which produces new varieties. Another is the highly prolific character of this production, which enables the population to be maintained even although the less suited perish in very large numbers. Yet another is the very slow change in environmental conditions which affords the process of selection the long periods of time necessary for its successful operation.

Mr. Alchian's model envisages the selection of particular investment policies (such as producing such and such a product variety or input combination) from out of what is a potentially infinite set of random policy decisions. I have suggested that selection operates between entrepreneurs and, ideally, according to the abilities displayed in their long-run performance, while admitting the influence of unforeseeable or chance factors on their fortunes. Perhaps the most fundamental difference between our approaches is this: I have insisted throughout on the purposive character of economic action and the importance, therefore, of adequate information on which to form rational beliefs. Mr. Alchian's arguments lead us in precisely the contrary directions; they seek to minimize the importance of foresight and informed action, and, by implication, to justify the comparative neglect of these elements in much of formal theory.

PART III

THE INFLUENCE OF UNCERTAINTY

VIII

THE NEED FOR ADAPTABILITY

1. OUR chief concern, in previous chapters, was to inquire whether, under various different market arrangements, the information available to entrepreneurs would, or would not, provide an adequate basis for the investment decisions required for successful economic adjustment. It became clear that this information would inevitably be incomplete; technical uncertainty could never wholly be eradicated and, for this and other reasons, market uncertainty would persist also, whatever the measures designed to reduce it. I shall now turn from the ways in which business men seek to increase the information at their disposal to a consideration of how they will respond to the uncertainty which remains. We shall ask ourselves, that is to say, how investment strategies will be influenced by the fact that they are based on knowledge which is inevitably imperfect. Rather, however, than offer any systematic and exhaustive review of all the measures with which entrepreneurs meet uncertainty, the analysis will be focused on one particular object of business policy—that of increasing the adaptability of an investment programme.

The entrepreneur will be regarded as having formulated a variety of alternative hypotheses about each of the particular present and future circumstances which are relevant to his investment decision, and as having attached to these hypotheses degrees of probability conceived by him, at least approximately, in quantitative terms. These probabilities may be taken to represent a particular relationship between the hypotheses and the information upon which they are based; they indicate, in other words, the degrees of belief which it is rational to associate with the hypotheses on the evidence available. By assuming that the probabilities are quantitative, and that the hypotheses refer to the magnitude of some measurable variable, such as the price of a product or the income from an investment, it becomes possible to represent the entrepreneur's expectations in categories borrowed from frequency distributions; his prospect can then be represented as depending on the mathematical expectation of relevant variables and on the degree of dispersion of their possible values. Throughout the following discussion this mathematical expectation will be referred to as the 'expected value' of the variable and will be taken to represent the sum of the values given by the alternative hypotheses weighted by their respective probability coefficients, where these are so measured as to add up to unity. By the 'uncertainty' of the variable, I shall denote the degree of dispersion of its possible values as measured in terms of the standard deviation. No doubt other characteristics of the probability distribution are relevant to business decisions, but it will not be necessary to refer to them specially.

The reader will be aware that there are very serious objections to this conventional way of representing business expectations. Probabilities, as they usually occur in ordinary affairs, are certainly not measurable, in any ordinary sense of the word, and they cannot, therefore, be used to calculate expected values or uncertainties in the way that I have defined them. Nevertheless it may be desirable for us to assume that entrepreneurs can, in some rough way, make calculations analogous to those which we know to be impossible. It is interesting to note that Keynes, in his *Treatise on Probability*, is at great pains to stress that the notion of probability is, in most contexts, immeasurable, while he admits elsewhere that we may have to act as if this were not the case. As regards the uncertainties which confront the business man, he argues:

. . . there is no scientific basis on which to form any capable probability whatever. We simply do not know. Nevertheless, the necessity for action and for decision compels us as practical men to do our best to overlook this awkward fact and to behave exactly as we should if we had behind us a good Benthamite calculation of a series of prospective advantages and disadvantages, each multiplied by its appropriate probability, waiting to be summed.[1]

There are, of course, alternative ways of representing the

---

[1] J. M. Keynes, 'The General Theory of Employment', *Quarterly Journal of Economics*, February, 1937.

expectations of entrepreneurs, such as that suggested by Professor Shackle, but I am inclined to doubt whether they are less open to objection than the very familiar one which I have chosen to adopt.[1] Those who prefer them would, I imagine, be able to restate the greater part of the argument of this chapter in different terms. It is certainly uncomfortable to have to employ, for the purposes of analysis, notions, such as that of quantitative probability, which we know to be open to justifiable objection; but economics cannot stand still until the very highly perplexing logical problems which surround this whole subject have been solved.

2. In discussing the strategies which it would be appropriate for an entrepreneur, with imperfect knowledge, to adopt, the first task is to establish what his objectives, under these conditions, are likely to be. I shall assume, for the time being, that the objective is to maximize expected income irrespective of its uncertainty. An entrepreneur will be assumed, that is to say, to adopt that investment programme which offers the highest mathematical expectation of income, irrespective of the degree of dispersion which the possible values of income may show. It will be convenient to refer to this briefly as the 'neutrality assumption', as it implies entrepreneurial indifference between certain and uncertain returns. Whether this assumption is justified, is a question which we shall take up in the succeeding chapter. It will be instructive to consider first whether measures, the adoption of which is sometimes attributed to a positive aversion to uncertainty, would be taken even in the absence of any such attitude.[2]

If the neutrality assumption is to be interpreted properly, however, the expected income from an investment has to be

---

[1] G. L. S. Shackle, *Expectation in Economics*, 1949. A review of the different accounts of how entrepreneurs form expectations and react to them is given in two articles by Professor K. J. Arrow, 'Alternative Approaches to the Theory of Choice in Risk-Taking Situations', *Econometrica*, Vol. 19 (1951), pp. 404–437, and 'Utilities, Attitudes, Choices; a Review Note', *Econometrica*, Vol. 26 (1958), pp. 1–23.

[2] That the greater part of business men's reaction towards uncertainty may be independent of any psychological aversion to it, has been stressed by Professor A. G. Hart, in his book, *Anticipations, Uncertainty and Dynamic Planning* (1951). This chapter has been influenced by his discussion.

defined with some care. It has to be regarded in terms not of the investment's immediate outcome, but of its effects on the entrepreneur's long-run business prospects. The possible gains or losses which could be the direct result from the placing of a bet, for example, may be capable of precise stipulation, but in deciding whether to make the gamble it would be prudent to estimate in addition the indirect financial consequences which this result might bring in train. The gain, for example, might provide the gambler with the funds necessary to exploit some other promising opportunity, while the loss, by necessitating a forced sale of assets, or by prejudicing the continuance of some profitable business activity, might bring other serious losses in its wake. In a similar way, it would be dangerously short-sighted to neglect the effects which a particular investment might have on the whole set of activities which the entrepreneur is undertaking currently or which he might undertake in the future. Investments are not to be regarded in isolation, like the single throw of a dice, but as part of a succession of related decisions, each one of which will in general modify those which follow it. It may be convenient, on occasions, to distinguish between primary and secondary elements in an expected yield, the former being the immediate and direct outcome of the investment decision, while the latter are the effects of this decision on long-term prospects. The primary element will depend chiefly on the nature of the particular investment with which it is associated, while the secondary element will depend on the particular situation of the investor, taken to include his wealth, the forms in which he holds his assets and his other business activities, whether actual or planned. But it is upon the total expected income, comprising both these elements, that the appeal of an investment will depend; and if we are to postulate an attitude towards uncertainty—whether neutral or otherwise—which is to be invariant to the changing nature of the entrepreneur's business situation, it is with this total expected income that it must be associated. It is easy to point out the difficulty of appraising a decision in terms of direct and indirect consequences which will, in principle, stretch out indefinitely into the farthest future; all that is implied here is the need for the investor to include in his computation of the expected yield all those indirect effects which he is in some measure able to foresee.

3. The reader may be inclined to sense a contradiction between the assumptions of this chapter and the argument of those which have preceded it. In view of all that has been said of the ways in which producers will endeavour to obtain information, and thereby to reduce the uncertainty of their estimates regarding the many factors upon which the profitability of their investment decisions depends, is it legitimate to attribute to them an attitude of indifference between certain and uncertain income expectations? In fact, if we bear in mind the distinction between expectations and the information on which they are constructed, this paradox is easily resolved.

In discussing the choices open to an entrepreneur, it is frequently assumed that the probabilities associated with each of the relevant variables are given to him in a cut and dried form, no reference being made to the information upon which the probabilities depend. For some purposes this procedure may be justifiable, but it is important to recognize that it focuses attention on only part of the problem of choice with which the man has to deal. In selecting a policy under conditions of imperfect knowledge, it is necessary not only to construct the probability estimates, but also to judge how far the relevant information could be augmented, by inquiry, by experiment or by the mere postponement of the decisions to be taken. In order to simplify the choices available, let us assume, provisionally, that the investor can either commit his resources fully on the basis of his expectations as they currently stand, or may first endeavour to obtain more information by which these expectations may be modified. (We shall have to take account presently of intermediate courses of action which commit the entrepreneur to an investment programme, but to a programme which is capable of some modification according to any changes in the relevant information and expectations.) If the policy of prior investigation is resorted to, some small part of the entrepreneur's resources will be required to meet its cost and there may be some further loss resulting from the postponement of the investment, on the assumption that the investigation showed it to be profitable. On the other hand, however, the entrepreneur will be enabled to revise his opinions about the opportunities open to him, the expected yield of one or more of which may now be higher than previously appeared. One may imagine, for example, that a man is contemplating the purchase of one of two articles, to both of which, on the basis of superficial examination, he attaches the same rough estimate of worth. Further scrutiny will not only make his estimates more secure but may enable him to choose between the two articles. Provided the cost and trouble of the inquiry is not excessive, this course of action may offer a higher net expected income than that which dispensed with further investigation. At the risk of trying the reader's patience, I shall give a further example in illustration of this principle.

Let us suppose that an entrepreneur is prepared to invest if the net expected yield from a project exceeds zero. On the basis of the information currently available, it may be supposed that the yield is expected to lie somewhere between -8 and $+8$, but that no more precise prediction can be made. Let us further assume, however, that for an expenditure of x, information can be obtained which is certain to narrow the range of possible outcomes to a size of 4, as compared with the present one of 16. The entrepreneur will learn, that is to say, that the outcome will lie between -8 and -4, or in any similar interval up to that between $+4$ and $+8$, although he cannot say in advance which of these intervals will be shown by the inquiry to be the relevant one.

If the expected outcome is shown to lie in one of the intervals between -8 to -4 and -2 to $+2$, investment will not be undertaken and the sum x spent on the inquiry will have been forfeited. If, on the other hand, the interval proves to be one of those between -2 to $+2$ and $+4$ to $+8$, then the entrepreneur will invest; as the expected value of the yield will lie between 0 and 6 (corresponding to the interval -2 to $+2$ and the interval $+4$ to $+8$ respectively), the average value of the expectation, on the assumption that it will be shown to be positive, will be 3. If the inquiry is being contemplated therefore, two hypotheses will be entertained; one of them, with a probability of $\frac{1}{2}$, is that the outcome will lie in one of the lower ranges so that the project is put aside and a total loss of x is incurred, the other, with an equal probability, is that the outcome will lie in one of the upper ranges so that investment is undertaken in the expectation of a mean outcome of 3. The total expected value of this prospect is therefore $\frac{1}{2}(-x) +$ $\frac{1}{2}(3 - x)$, i.e., $1.5 - x$, which, provided that x does not exceed 1.5, is positive and therefore greater than the expected yield from the policy of committing resources without further investigation. It is easy to show that if the further information were to produce a greater narrowing of the possible range of outcomes, then the maximum sum which can justifiably be spent in obtaining it would be greater.

Needless to say, the choices which are ever likely to confront us in reality will bear little resemblances to this naïve example, which is constructed on the basis of several serious simplifications. Expectations regarding a prospective outcome will rarely, if ever, take the form of a range within which the outcome is equally likely to fall; in addition, the results to be produced by the inquiry will themselves be the subject of a probability estimate and they will scarcely ever narrow down the range of possible outcomes in the precise way which was supposed. Nevertheless, it is not difficult to construct more realistic, if more complicated, examples which would illustrate the same point—that expenditure designed to increase the information upon which an investment decision is to be based need imply no reluctance to take risks, but is compatible with neutrality towards uncertainty of its expected yield.

One would generally expect that, by obtaining additional information, profit expectations could be made less uncertain; but this need not be so, and the possibility cannot be ruled out that the entrepreneur's estimates will remain unaffected both as regards the expected value and the uncertainty of the yield. Are we to judge, in this case, that nothing of value has resulted from the trouble and expense of the investigation? We are not entitled to conclude that the information collected must have been irrelevent, for it might have served merely to strengthen both the favourable and unfavourable hypotheses in equal degree. One can certainly say that the informational base of the estimates has been enlarged, but whether this makes the entrepreneur more justified in acting upon them is a problem of some perplexity to which I can see no easy answer. How should one evaluate, for purposes of action, two hypotheses of equal probability but founded on different quantities of information? The issue is a quite general one about the logic of choice under conditions of uncertainty, but it is difficult to say whether it has any bearing on the practical matters which are our present concern. One might perhaps argue that the greater the amount of information on which an entrepreneur's estimates are based, the less likely is it that these estimates will have to be substantially revised as a result of further information which the implementation of his plan brings to light; if this were in fact so, then there would be less need for the kind of measures, to be discussed later, which are specially designed to deal with subsequent revision of expectations. The costs of inquiry might therefore have been worth while, not because they altered the expectations in question, but because they rendered them less likely to require modification in the future. The reader, however, will detect difficulties in this line of thought.[1]

4. Entrepreneurs may endeavour to increase the amount of information relevant to their plans in a variety of ways, of which the most obvious is represented by investigation designed to ascertain more precisely the preferences of consumers or the technical possibilities of production. 'Market research' can be conducted in different ways, each of which involves more or less expenditure; production possibilities can be explored and confirmed by industrial research, development, testing, and the like. But additional information may also be sought by policies of a more indirect nature. We have already discussed in some detail how market information, in the sense which includes

---

[1] The issue which we have been discussing is considered by Keynes in his *Treatise on Probability*, Chapter VI, 'The Weight of Arguments'. Here he points out that the probability of an argument is distinct from the weight of evidence, or relevant information, in favour of it; the probability depends on the balance between the favourable and unfavourable evidence and not on the absolute amounts of these. He shows also that the 'evidential weight' of an estimate is also distinct from its 'probable error', so that there is no necessity that the latter should be diminished as the former is increased (ibid., Ch. VI, Section 6).

information about competitive investment projects, can be increased by agreements of various kinds; the cost of doing so is, in this case, difficult to estimate simply in financial terms, as it will consist chiefly in a certain loss of independence and of the chances of exceptional gain which this may sometimes appear to offer. It may also be possible to obtain firmer estimates on which to base an investment decision simply by waiting, in the hope that clarification may take place merely with the passing of time; in this case the chief cost may be the loss of opportunities to less cautious rivals.

Beyond a certain point, however, neither investigation, nor procrastination, nor the other possible measures are likely to reduce much farther the uncertainty inherent in business estimates. The entrepreneur will be obliged to take the decision to invest even although his expectations concerning the future circumstances determining its most profitable form are still represented by a more or less restricted variety of alternative hypotheses. Ideally, the investment programme should be so designed as to offer positive profits under all the possible situations which are considered at all likely to develop. In practice, however, such perfect adaptability will be out of reach. So long as the investor holds his resources in the form of money, he remains free to engage, whenever he chooses, in a variety of activities, the range of which is limited only by current technical and legal restraints and by the magnitude of the sum at his disposal. But whenever he decides to commit his resources in a form other than money, the scope of his future activities henceforth becomes, to some extent, and for some period of time, thereby curtailed. The boundless sea of possibility which had lain before him is replaced by certain particular lanes along which he will, for a time, be obliged to proceed. Should he have chosen to invest in manufacturing business, the range of activities which remain open in the future will have been drastically narrowed.

This sacrifice of adaptability which any act of real investment inevitably imposes should be regarded as simply the obverse side of the gains from specialization. Under any technological conditions, except the most primitive, production requires the services of skills, experience, and equipment which are highly specific in character. There may, of course, be occasion when the maximum adaptability, such as is conferred by investment exclusively in money, provides the expectation of greatest gain or smallest loss. Where the investor is confident that future opportunities will be greatly superior to those of the present, or merely where the existing uncertainty seems so great as to preclude any tolerably firm expectation, then money, or its close substitutes, may present the strongest appeal. (Any very widespread attempt to adopt a policy of this kind may have, as we know, serious repercussions on the general level of incomes and employment, but all such considerations lie outside our present scope.) Generally, however, it is only by allowing himself to be trammelled by a particular production programme that the entrepreneur can hope to make any substantial return.

It should not be concluded, however, that profitable investment requires the complete sacrifice of adaptability; on the contrary, the inevitable uncertainty about the detailed circumstances in which the investment programme is to be implemented will oblige its promoters to compromise, where practicable, between the gains from specialization on the one hand, and those from versatility on the other. Although the scope for striking such a balance will vary very widely with circumstances, it will rarely be non-existent. An investment programme will generally envisage the purchase and conversion of a variety of inputs, of particular kinds and at particular prices, in order to produce and sell a particular variety of products; its adaptability can therefore be regarded as having two dimensions, represented by the extent and the rapidity of the possible variation in these inputs and outputs, whether in respect of timing, quantity, or kind.

5. The adaptability of an investment programme will depend, in the first instance, on the technical nature of the production process adopted. The more highly capitalized the process, and therefore the greater the importance of fixed costs, the greater will be the costs incurred per unit output if the total volume of production has to be adapted to a lower level of demand. The longer the physical life of particular equipment, the greater will be the loss incurred in switching to kinds of output or

input to which it is unsuited, and the probability that it will be so unsuited depends on how specialized was the purpose for which it was designed. Management may therefore have to choose, for example, between the use of 'special purpose' and 'general purpose' machine tools, or between the techniques known as 'flow' or 'batch' production; in each case, it will have to weigh against each other the desirability of carrying out one activity as economically as possible and that of being able to modify the nature of the activity should the need arise. From some points of view, management itself, together with the skills, experience, and traditions which it embodies, may restrict a firm's freedom of manœuvre as much as, if not more than, the fixed equipment which it owns. In recruiting to its ranks, therefore, it may have to weigh up the versatility of candidates against their special expertise.

Adaptability is also provided by the holding of stocks and of storage space. The process of production consists of a large number of different activities, whether of buying, selling, or transforming, which are undertaken simultaneously or in succession. The degree of synchronization between these various stages will, for a variety of reasons, rarely be complete, with the result that stocks of original inputs, or work in progress, and of final products will be required to link them together. It may be frequently possible to estimate minimum values for these stock holdings on the basis of whatever failure of synchronization the desirability of bulk purchase, the seasonality of demand, or any comparable influence is thought to render inevitable, but by carrying a volume of stocks in excess of these amounts, the flexibility, and therefore—up to a certain point—the expected yield of the programme will be increased. The degree of synchronization between the different phases of production cannot be foreseen precisely; the delivery of inputs may be delayed, there may be a temporary stoppage of one stage of the production process, it may be desirable to meet unexpectedly large demands from loyal customers with the minimum delay, or, when demand unexpectedly falls off, to produce for stock. A similar case can be made for the holding of spare tools in order to ensure the uninterrupted continuity of production in the case of a breakdown.

6. Any investment programme will involve, extended in a pattern over time, flows of total revenue and of total expenditure. In one sense these will of necessity be out of balance, for the original capital expenditure initiating the programme will be recouped only gradually over the life of the equipment; during the carrying out of the programme, however, current income will generally be expected to cover current outgoings, and, these being both related to the volume of output, there will be some tendency for them to move together. The degree of this synchronization will be neither complete nor wholly pre-dictable, although, as the making and the timing of expenditures will sometimes be a matter of choice, it will not be wholly outside the entrepreneur's control. The greater the adapta-bility with which he wishes to endow his programme, the greater will be the likelihood that, in any short period, revenue will fall short of the expenditure which appears desirable; for many of the modifications which, as expectations are revised, the entrepreneur may wish to impose on the pro-gramme, will require some net outlay.

Should, for example, the level of demand fall temporarily below that which was originally considered most likely, it may be in the interest of the firm to produce for stock, rather than to reduce output or to attempt to stimulate demand by a reduction in price; it may even be, if demand were temporarily very low, that the receipts of the enterprise would be insufficient to enable it to meet those fixed and contractual expenditures which it was absolutely obliged to make. The ability to make expenditures in excess of income would be a condition for adaptation in the former case and of survival in the latter. Nor need this ability be of service only when disagreeable contingencies arise; the profits of the firm might, for example, be capable of substantial increase if only some small change in the nature of the product or the process of production could be made, while this, in turn, might require expenditure in excess of receipts.

Adaptability will consequently be enhanced by the power to make such net expenditures and by the possession, therefore, of some source of readily-available purchasing power. The efficiency of such a source, like that of adaptability itself, has two dimensions, the one relating to the amount of purchasing power which the entrepreneur can command and the other to the speed with which he can do so. Adaptability of this special kind, we have safely conjectured, is at the heart of the somewhat fugitive notion of *liquidity*, which although exceedingly familiar to both business men and economists, is difficult to associate with any single, precise definition. Having originated in ordinary business life and been subsequently borrowed for the purposes of theoretical analysis, it manifests the shifts and variety of meaning characteristic of many terms which have not been specially minted for scientific work. The following discussion will, I hope, cast some light on the significance of the concept, although it will stop short of the concept's most important applications. Our concern with the measures which an entrepreneur may adopt in order to meet uncertainty obliges us to analyse the function of liquidity and the means by which it is provided, but the focus of the analysis will be restricted to the individual business; an account of the liquidity of the economy as a whole, of how it may vary and of its relation to aggregate demand, would lie outside our scope.

7. We must now turn from the reasons why liquidity is required to the ways in which it may be provided. An entrepreneur's ability to obtain general purchasing power at short notice will be determined by the quantity and nature of the assets in his possession and by the state of his credit; these two factors, which are not wholly independent, will have to be examined in turn.

Money itself, in the sense of bank deposits, represents purchasing power which can be realized without cost or delay and which, at any rate in terms of the unit of account, is of predictable magnitude. But although the best, it is not the only source of general purchasing power; other assets, which can readily be converted into money, may also serve as such. These are, however, subject to several disadvantages which must now be considered. It is our very general practice to refer to 'the' price of an asset, thereby implying that there is a unique rate at which it would, at any particular time, exchange against money. In fact, however, it would be more correct to regard all assets as having at least two prices, one at which they can be bought and another at which they can be sold. In making any association between particular assets and particular prices, we presume the existence of an organized market, for otherwise it would be possible to refer only to the exchange rates at which individual transactions took place. But, however well organized the market, it will not be costless in operation; buyers and sellers are normally separated in time and space and may be ignorant of each other's existence, and if they are to be brought effectively into contact, expenses of transport, of storage and of providing information will all have to be incurred. The seller will not generally undertake these activities himself, there being economies of specialization in this direction as in most others; they will be undertaken by dealers, who are remunerated by the differences between the two prices at which they buy and sell. Should the seller choose to find a buyer himself, however, he should deduct from the nominal price which he receives a money sum equivalent to the value of the time and trouble which he has been obliged to expend in doing so.

By the expression *buying price*, I shall simply mean the amount of money for which the entrepreneur can acquire an asset. I shall use the term *value in sale* to denote the sum which he will normally expect it to fetch in a quick sale, assuming that he himself does not bear the expense and trouble of finding a final purchaser. The justification for burdening the reader with a new term will, I hope, be obvious; the more familiar expression 'selling price' would be in danger of being identified with the price charged by a dealer rather than that paid by him. The efficiency of an asset, considered as a means of holding readily-available purchasing power, depends, therefore, on the relationship between its buying price and its value in sale, thus defined; and I shall entitle the ratio of these two sums the *coefficient of marketability* of the asset in question.

The value of this coefficient, it has to be admitted, cannot be regarded as a comprehensive measure of the marketability of an asset, as this has in effect two dimensions. If the owner of the asset did not have to sell it immediately, he might expect to get a better price, but both the gain to be made by taking time about the sale, and the loss incurred by the delay in obtaining the proceeds, will vary according to the circumstances of each case and cannot, therefore, be easily summed up in any single coefficient. All we can do, therefore, is to regard the measure suggested as providing some indication of an asset's market-ability, rather than a full representation of it.

The value of the coefficient will depend on three principal considerations. Of first importance will be the frequency with which the good is normally bought and sold, and this will vary with the extent to which it is in common demand; the more specific the purpose for which the asset is desired, the fewer, at any particular time, will be the number of potential purchasers. Secondly, there are the costs of storage and transport and the risk of price fluctuations, all of which will be borne by the dealers who operate the market. Finally, there is what, for want of a better term, we may call the 'recognizability' of the asset. The precise worth, for example, of a second-hand car, a complex item of machinery, or the shares of a little-known firm may be difficult to determine, and the buyer may be obliged to put himself to the expense of an investigation, the cost of which ought to be added to the buying price in calculating the coefficient of marketability. He may, alternatively, be prepared to trust that the asset has the properties claimed for it on the strength of the repute of the dealer, but, in this case, the dealer will be able to claim a return for his possession of this reputation and for the costs of investigation which he himself has to incur in order to sustain it.[1]

Money itself is then the only asset which has a coefficient of marketability which is not less than unity. Financial assets, generally, if they are bought and sold on an organized stock market, will have a high marketability, as determined by the size of the brokers margin and any duties on transfer. Private loans, on the other hand, for which there is no organized market, will generally have a very low value in sale, chiefly

---

[1] The first systematic treatment of these questions of marketability, as far as I am aware, is that given by Menger. In explicitly considering assets from the point of view of their similarity to money, he anticipates some of the much later analysis provided by Keynes. Cf. C. Menger, *Grundsätze der Volkswirtschaftslehre*, Ch. 9, 'Die Lehre vom Gelde', and J. M. Keynes, *The General Theory of Employment, Interest and Money*, Ch. 17.

attributable to their lack of recognizability, there being few persons in a position to form an estimate of the credit worthiness of the borrower. Physical assets will have various, but generally rather low, coefficients of marketability, depending on their specificity, storage costs, recognizability, etc., in any particular case.

8. Anyone who is considering the purchase of an asset and is concerned, in part, with its efficiency as a source of readily-available purchasing power, will have in mind, not only the difference, at any point of time, between its buying price and value in sale, but, in addition, with the uncertainty which may surround the future magnitudes of both of these. By the *reliability* of an asset, I shall mean the predictability of its value in sale at any particular time in the future, this being inversely related to the uncertainty of the expectations which are formed regarding it. One reason for this uncertainty may, of course, be the unpredictability of the marketability coefficient itself, but its principal determinant will be instability in the demand and supply for the asset in question, which will affect both the buying price and the value in sale to a similar degree. The amount of general purchasing power to which, in the future, any particular asset will be equivalent, will depend, first, on the value of the asset in terms of money, and, secondly, on the value of money itself in terms of goods. It will be convenient to assume for the time being that the value of money, as appropriately measured, is invariant; the additional complexities which result from the waiving of this restriction will be touched on later.

Money itself, in the form of notes or current bank accounts, is perfectly reliable in our sense; so are deposit accounts in a bank or building society, although both of these, if they are cashable only after notice has been given, will be less than perfectly marketable. Reliability, like marketability, however, is not to be summed up in any single measure. A dated Government security gives the certain expectation of obtaining a precise sum at a specified time in the future, although it may be an unreliable source of purchasing power during the intervening period. It is, therefore, less suited as a general contingency reserve than it is as a store of purchasing power which will be required at some definite future date. Irredeemable securities are unreliable in a more general sense, as their value in sale in any future period will vary with the movement of interest rates. Physical assets of whatever kind will always be unreliable, their price being dependent on particular demand and supply conditions.

It seems safe to say that, as a source of readily available purchasing power, and apart from other relative advantages, money would always be preferred to securities or other assets. This preference—liquidity preference in Keynes's sense—is sometimes seen to depend on an attitude of aversion to uncertainty or risk; can we regard it as consistent, therefore, with the neutrality assumption which underlies the argument of this chapter? That this is in fact so, follows, I believe, from the fact that the marginal yield or efficiency of readily available purchasing power, viewed as a contribution to the adaptability of the programme, will fall as the quantity of such purchasing power increases. The reasons for this diminishing marginal efficiency are fairly readily apparent. The entrepreneur will wish to anticipate, as we have seen, some failure of synchronization between the receipts and outgoings of future periods, but he will generally be able to set some upper limits to the gaps which are at all likely. The modifications which he might later wish to impose upon his production programme, and for which he will wish to retain ready purchasing power, are more likely to be small than large, if only because his fixed equipment will generally limit the scope of practicable variation. Granted, therefore, that the marginal efficiency of liquid resources will diminish with the amount held, any uncertainty about their future selling value will reduce the expected yield of the programme with which they are associated. Let us assume, for example, that the value in sale of an asset is considered by its owner to be as likely to rise as to fall. Should it rise, readily available purchasing power will have increased, and with it the adaptability and, therefore, the expected yield of the programme. Should it fall, adaptability will be correspondingly reduced, but in this case the resulting change in the expected yield will be larger than in the previous case, as well, of course, as being in the opposite direction. It follows, therefore, that the contribution to the expected yield of the programme which is made by assets, as sources of ready purchasing power, will increase with their reliability, other things being equal.

Both marketability and reliability, therefore, are important determinants of the liquidity of an asset, this being taken to mean its suitability as a reserve of spending power. But it is reliability in terms of real purchasing power, rather than in terms of the unit of account, which is of fundamental significance. The importance of this distinction will depend on the degree of uncertainty which surrounds the future value of money and upon the length of the period for which the asset is to be held. If an entrepreneur values an asset chiefly in order to provide liquidity, he will generally expect to have to convert it into money in the reasonably near future; under these circumstances, marketability will probably be the dominant consideration, and in any case, unless prices are to change very rapidly, those assets which are most reliable in money terms will be the most reliable in real terms also—the price of individual assets being normally more subject to fluctuation than the general price level of assets as a whole. Money reliability, therefore, will usually be a good substitute for real reliability, although there may be exceptions to this general rule. Millers, for example, who expect to have to buy so much, at some future date, of a particular grade of wheat, might buy 'futures' in some standard variety. In doing so they would have acquired an asset which was very reliable in terms of the expenditure which it was ultimately designed to finance, for, on the assumption that the prices of different grades of wheat varied together, the asset could be sold for a sum of money approximately equal to that which would be required. This, however, it must be admitted, is a rather special case.

9. In buying an asset, an entrepreneur, assuming that he is interested in adapability, will in principle give some weight to its liquidity value as determined by the factors which we have been reviewing. Needless to say, however, this will not be the only, or generally the most important of the asset's attributes; the entrepreneur will be chiefly concerned with the contribution which it makes more directly to the expected income from his programme. Where highly liquid assets, such as securities, are concerned, this contribution may take the form of interest or dividends, but more usually of course the asset will play a direct part in the process of transformation and sale. Where this is so, it may be difficult to identify the contribution of any particular asset, such as a machine, which yields services only as part of the whole apparatus of production, but it will always be possible to make some estimate of the extent to which the total expected income from the programme would be reduced if the asset had to be disposed of in order to obtain ready purchasing power. It is in fact this sacrifice of future prospects which will influence the entrepreneur in deciding whether to make the particular expenditure which adaptation appears to require; he will weigh up, that is to say, the loss from parting with the asset against the gain to be expected from the modification in his programme which the proceeds of the asset could be used to make. The *liquidity position* of a firm, as contrasted with the liquidity value of the assets which it may possess, is best conceived of in these terms, as referring, in other words, to the relationship which exists between the firm's likely need to make net expenditure and the costs or sacrifices incurred in obtaining the money required.

It will be convenient to refer to the *value in use* of an asset, this being defined as the discounted value of the loss of expected income which would result if the asset were given up in order to obtain ready money. The difference between the value in sale and the value in use may be called the *separation loss*; the ratio between these two magnitudes may then be regarded as the *coefficient of dispensability* which relates the asset to its particular context. The larger this coefficient, the less will be the cost of parting with the asset; should it exceed unity, the asset would not be held.

Fixed equipment will, in almost all cases, be highly indispensable to the carrying out of the firm's programme; its value in sale, which in any case will fall far short of its cost, will not, therefore, be regarded as contributing to liquidity. Stocks, on the other hand, will generally represent a liquid reserve, even if not one to which the entrepreneur will frequently wish to resort. But it is important to distinguish between the various kinds of stock holding. Stocks of raw materials, as was observed earlier, will be held in order to match the various processes of purchase and transformation; generally, however, the amount required will not be determined quite rigidly, but will admit of some variation according to the adaptability to be provided. It should be possible, therefore, to run down such stocks at a cost (in terms of the increased likelihood of future interruptions to production, etc.) which will not initially be crippling, even although it will rise sharply after a certain point. Much the same can be said of stocks of final output. The yield which they provide in terms of adaptability can be temporarily foregone if money is required for some urgent purpose. This money could be made available either by reducing the rate of production relative to that of sales, by borrowing on the security of the stocks, or by their quick sale. If such a sale is forced upon the entrepreneur, he will suffer a loss both because of a reduction in the flexibility afforded by the stocks and because their value in sale will fall short of the price which could have been obtained from them had they been marketed in the normal way.

Work in progress is distinguished from the stocks just considered in having a much lower coefficient of marketability; partly finished goods may be of value only as scrap unless there are purchasers who have the facilities to enable them to complete the process of transformation. Their dispensability will also be very low. If they have to be liquidated, both the cost of transforming them up to the stage which they have reached, as well as those fixed costs associated with the further stages of production which they would normally pass through, will have been incurred without the corresponding yield expected from their normal sale. The sale of stocks of this kind, therefore, would be undertaken only very exceptionally.

From the point of view of reliability, as I have defined it, stocks suffer from a notable defect. Their value in sale will frequently be low precisely at such times as ready purchasing power is urgently required. One circumstance—though not the only one—which may make the entrepreneur wish to obtain ready purchasing power will be a fall, which is believed to be temporary, in the demand for his product. At such a time, however, the value in sale of his stocks of final output, and perhaps also of inputs, will be exceptionally low. Indeed the policy which is most appropriate, if storage costs are not too high, may be to build up stocks rather than run them down; for this reason it is important to have alternative sources of ready money.[1]

Let us now consider those assets which are held specifically as a reserve of ready purchasing power—financial securities and money itself. Securities offer some form of running yield, the sacrifice of which is one of the costs of realizing them in order to spend the proceeds. Money, however, unlike other assets, is held solely because of its liquidity value, because, that is, of the need to make expenditures in excess of current receipts. It would be misleading to say that its yield was zero, for it contributes indirectly to the total expected income of the investment programme by affording adaptability. For this reason, a stock of money, though perfectly marketable and perfectly reliable, is not perfectly dispensable and it cannot be drawn upon without impairing—other things being equal— future prospects. In deciding whether to use this reserve in order to make an expenditure, therefore, the entrepreneur will weigh up the gain to be expected from the expenditure against the weakening of the adaptability with which, until his liquidity position is restored, he can meet the future. He will have to recognize, in other words, that the use of his reserve at one point of time is associated with an opportunity cost represented by the possible gains to be made (or losses to be avoided) from using it later. The magnitude of this cost will clearly depend on the size of the reserve relative to likely requirements; if it is

[1] Keynes, in his *Treatise on Money* (Chs. 28 and 29), offers strong arguments to show that firms will very rarely be able to accumulate stocks in this way, because of the high costs and risks which would be incurred. He makes a distinction between Working and Liquid Capital. The former is defined as 'the aggregate of goods . . . in course of production, manufacture and retailing, including such minimum stocks, whether of raw materials or of finished products, as are required to avoid risks of interruption of process or to tide over seasonal irregularities'. Liquid Capital is then all stocks in excess of this. He assumes therefore, in our terms, that the function relating the volume of stocks to their coefficient of dispensability exhibits discontinuity at a certain point; this discontinuity, however, need not be very sharp and Keynes admits that his distinction is a broad one.

very small, the entrepreneur will draw on it only when the expenditure for which it is to be used will make a large difference to his expected income. The marginal efficiency of money falls, and, therefore, its dispensability rises, the greater the amount of it which is held; indeed, the increase in expected income which would result from a marginal addition to money stocks offers a measure of the liquidity position of a firm.

How then are we to sum up this discussion of the contribution which a firm's assets make to its liquidity position? Each asset can, in principle, be viewed as providing an amount of readily available purchasing power equal to its expected value in sale, this being related to its marketability and reliability. If the asset is sold, in order to realize its value in sale, the expected income of the investment programme with which it is associated will generally be reduced. The extent of this reduction measures the indispensability of the asset and will differ according to the part played by it in the production process. Thus the liquidity position of the firm, at least in so far as it depends upon its asset structure, can be viewed in terms of the cost of obtaining various sums of ready purchasing power, in terms, that is, of a relation between quantities of money for immediate expenditure on the one hand and the loss of expected income caused by making them available on the other.

10. We recognized earlier that the liquidity position of a firm would depend, not only on its assets, but also on its borrowing power. Unexhausted borrowing power, or potential credit as I shall call it, might itself be regarded as a particular kind of asset, but it is more convenient to treat it separately. The notions of marketability and reliability which were associated with the liquidity value of assets, are relevant also to the liquidity value of potential credit. The time taken to negotiate a loan, and the costs of doing so, may vary very widely, as will the confidence with which it is expected that a particular line of credit will be made available at any time in the future. Some forms of borrowing, such as the issue of share capital, are clearly unsuitable as a means of obtaining money at short notice in order to meet a contingency. In other cases, however, credit potential may be almost as convenient as money itself; an overdraft facility gives the power to obtain money immediately without any special transaction taking place and is inferior to money only in respect of reliability—there being no certain assurance that the overdraft right may not be cancelled at some date in the future. Trade credit, which may be of very great importance in permitting expenditure to exceed revenue, is likely to be particularly unreliable, its availability depending on the general state of business confidence. Indeed the entrepreneur's ability to borrow money will frequently vary inversely with his need to do so, for should conditions be poor, either for his particular firm or for the industry or the economy as a whole, the willingness to lend will be seriously reduced.

Potential credit and the possession of assets are not wholly independent sources of liquidity. Where an owner of wealth has little knowledge of the standing and prospects of a borrower, he may be prepared to lend on the security of his assets, their value in sale being realizable therefore without the need to part with them; thus even highly indispensable assets may, in this indirect way, have liquidity value.

The recognition of potential credit as a source of ready purchasing power does not oblige us to revise the way in which it was found convenient to describe a firm's liquidity position —in terms of the relationship, that is to say, between the amount of ready money which the firm could obtain and the cost of doing so. If funds are borrowed, this cost will be represented by the expenses of the negotiation and the rate of interest, as well as by the reduction in future adaptability caused by the using up of the potential credit. Whether the entrepreneur obtains cash by the realization either of assets or of potential credit, the cost of doing so will rise with the amount obtained, becoming prohibitive after a certain point. It is worth pointing out that it is the entrepreneur's beliefs about his liquidity position, rather than his liquidity position in some objective sense, which will affect his business decisions; for this reason, it may be difficult to separate the influence of liquidity from that of the state of business confidence. If expectations are buoyant, firms may be confident, for example, that further credit will be extended to them if required, so that the risk of running short of ready money will be a less effective check on the scope of their activities.

It cannot be denied that a firm's liquidity position, as I have defined it, would in practice be very difficult, if not impossible, to measure—at least with any degree of precision; for both the sums of money which could rapidly be obtained, and the likely costs of doing so, appear as subjective and uncertain estimates in the mind of particular entrepreneurs. This difficulty, however, is inherent in the nature of the phenomena and nothing is to be gained from pretending that it does not exist. Of first importance is to analyse what in fact are the circumstances which make up the liquidity position of a firm, as it is normally conceived and as it affects the policies of its management; having done so, we can then discuss how the quantitative aspects of the liquidity position can, at least approximately, be gauged.

11. It is of interest, for example, to inquire as to how far the liquidity position of a firm, as I have defined it, can be deduced from its printed accounts. Information will be obtainable about holdings of money and securities, but these, although they form the firm's first reserve of liquid assets, do not represent the maximum amount of ready money which the firm, if it so desired, could acquire; nor is the magnitude of these reserves of much significance except in relation to the size of the calls which would be likely to be made upon them. A better indication of liquidity position could be deduced, it might be imagined, from a comparison of the items usually entitled Current Liabilities and Current Assets in a firm's balance sheet. The difference between these two totals could at best give no more than a very rough indication of liquidity position as I have defined it, for this was conceived as a schedule which related the quantities of cash which could be realized to the cost of doing so, rather than as simply a sum of money. Nevertheless, it will be worth while considering how the magnitudes of these two items, and of their components, affect liquidity in our sense.

Current Assets are normally taken to comprise stocks, whether of raw materials or finished goods, work in progress, cash and securities and money owed to the firm. It will be best to consider each of these in turn.

There are two good reasons why the total value of stocks, as normally recorded, should not be taken as representing an equivalent amount of cash readily available. The first and least important of these is concerned with the principle of valuation. It is the value in sale of stocks, as I previously defined it, which is the relevant measure of their contribution to liquidity, whereas it is normally at cost or at market value, whichever is the lower, that they will be entered in the accounts. Between these different methods of evaluation there will be no simple and consistent relationship; if stocks have to be sold off very rapidly, they may fetch less than their market price and less even than their cost, whereas, if reduced more gradually, the full market price may be obtained. Even, however, if stocks were to be estimated at their value in sale, it would obviously be wrong to regard them as perfectly dispensable and to neglect the separation loss which would follow from their liquidation. Stocks are usually held because they contribute to the expected yield of the programme, and if they are run down, this yield will suffer a reduction which, after a certain point, will become very sharp indeed. The selling value of the total stock-holding represents a sum of money which the entrepreneur would be able to realize only if he were prepared to close down the business, and it greatly exceeds the sum which it would be practicable to obtain under other circumstances. The genuine contribution of stocks to liquidity would be more easily assessed if a distinction could be made in the accounts between those stocks which were reasonably dispensable and those which were absolutely essential to business operations; dispensability, it is true, is a matter of degree, but it may be legitimate, for accounting purposes, to assume that there is some point beyond which further stock reductions would be an intolerable obstacle to the carrying out of the firm's operations. Whether it would be practicable to amend the printed accounts in this way, I am unable to say.

Work in progress will generally represent a source of liquidity very considerably less significant than its magnitude as set down in the list of current assets. Its value in sale may be very small; highly fabricated, but unfinished products may command a price hardly greater than their value as scrap, and, in addition, they will be highly indispensable, as they could be sold only by forfeiting the profit to be expected from their further transformation and ultimate sale. It would normally be advisable, therefore, if the object were merely to assess a firm's liquidity position, to neglect this item entirely.

Securities, at market value, and cash, indubitably represent a liquid reserve equal to the sum at which they are entered in the accounts; nevertheless, they do not represent the amount of money which would be available for expenditure at any particular time. Cash holdings, like stocks, can be reduced only at the sacrifice, other things being equal, of adaptability and, therefore, of expected yield; were they to fall below a certain point, the implementation of the firm's programmes would prove impracticable. Here again it might be useful, as a first approximation, to separate that part of the firm's cash holding without which it could not carry out normal operations from the remainder, which could be held either to provide adaptability or merely as the unexpected result of recent business transactions. But the distinction between cash held for normal operations and cash held to provide adaptability is essentially arbitrary, for, in a world of uncertainty, a variety of possible alternative developments, and the need to adapt to them, is itself the norm. There is more logic, we may note in passing, in the distinction between reserves which are held as a matter of policy and reserves which are the unintended result of changes in the stock position or of other causes. It would be wrong to identify the actual volume of a firm's cash, or near cash reserves, with the desired volume, for it is of the very nature of a reserve that it should fluctuate about its planned level. The degree of this fluctuation will depend in part on the practicability of frequent adjustment of the firm's asset structure; where the costs of investment are high, and the chief business of management is not that of choosing an optimum portfolio, cash may be permitted to increase, for a time, well above its planned level. Different firms will differ, in Professor Hicks's words, in terms of sensitivity, and there is good reason to believe that a manufacturing business will be less sensitive, in respect of the balance of its asset holdings, than would be a finance house or a bank.[1]

Finally, as an item of Current Assets, there are the debts which are owed to the firm by others. They clearly cannot be regarded, without further scrutiny, as a liquidity reserve equal to their book value; the contribution to liquidity which they do make will depend on the date and the reliability of the payments which are due.

No information is provided by the Balance Sheet about the magnitude of a firm's potential credit, and the reasons for this are obvious; nevertheless, the relevance of this factor to the firm's liquidity position is no less important than that of those which we have just been considering.

Let us now turn to the other side of the Balance Sheet. Under the heading of Current Liabilities, there are listed some of the purposes for which cash is known to be required in the near future, but these are usually confined to future obligations of a contractual or semi-contractual nature. Details may be given, for example, of future taxation liabilities or of payments related to schemes already sanctioned but not yet carried out. Given that printed accounts have to include only hard and fast figures, this restriction is probably inevitable, but it means that no satisfactory estimate of cash requirements, as determined by the future pattern of revenue and expenditure, can be obtained from this source.

It would appear, therefore, from all this discussion, that the liquidity position of a firm, as I have defined it, cannot be deduced from its printed accounts, even although these may throw some light upon it. It may be that some suitable revision of the way in which accounts are presented might enable more of the relevant information to be obtained, but it is not my present concern to assess the practicability of reform along these lines. That it is not wholly deducible from the printed accounts is no serious criticism of the definition of liquidity which I have suggested; entrepreneurs could never safely confine their attention to such information as their accountants could present to them in precise and quantitative terms.

---

[1] J. R. Hicks, 'A Suggestion for Simplifying the Theory of Money', *Economica*, 1935.

12. In concluding this chapter, it may be of interest to comment very briefly on the relation between this account of liquidity and that offered by Keynes, for it is probably his analysis which has had most influence on subsequent thinking. Keynes gave very full attention to the fact that 'our knowledge of the future is fluctuating, vague and uncertain', and showed how 'our desire to hold money as a store of wealth is a barometer of the degree of our distrust of our own calculations and conventions concerning the future'.[1] In addition, he indicated that all assets, by affording some 'power of disposal', have, in principle, some liquidity value. It could be argued, however, that the classification which he adopted for his analysis of the motives for holding money is not entirely satisfactory. Being principally concerned in this connexion with the determination of the rate of interest, he lists the motives for holding money rather than securities; we have been discussing the demand for liquidity in general, in terms of the desire to be able to adapt investment plans to an uncertain future. Thus the famous 'speculative motive', which induces wealth owners to hold money in the expectation of a fall in security prices, has not featured in our analysis—though this is not to say that entrepreneurs, if they are sufficiently sensitive in this respect, may not choose to hold their liquidity reserve in money rather than in securities for this reason.

It does seem, however, that Keynes's distinction between a 'transactions' and a 'precautionary' motive for holding money would fit rather uneasily into our analysis. The transactions motive, it will be remembered, referred to the need to hold money during the interval between receipts and disbursements; the precautionary motive to the need 'to provide for contingencies requiring sudden expenditure and for unforeseen opportunities of advantageous purchases, and also to hold an asset of which the value is fixed in terms of money to meet a subsequent liability fixed in terms of money . . .'.[2] The function of any money reserve, however, is to bridge the gap between the revenue and expenditure of any particular period; presumably,

---

[1] 'The General Theory of Employment', *Quarterly Journal of Economics*, February, 1937.

[2] *The General Theory of Employment, Interest and Money*, p. 196.

therefore, the motives for holding it are to be regarded as transactions or precautionary according to whether the expenditures to be made are expected or unforeseen. But this approach implies a rather half-hearted acceptance of the fact that business expectations characteristically refer to a number of alternative possible developments; it is inappropriate in this case to distinguish between money needed to carry out a set of planned transactions and money held in case plans have to be changed, for the plans themselves will generally envisage a variety of possible occurrences of different degrees of probability and implying different cash requirements. Thus it is impossible to make any sharp division between the desire to hold money 'for transactions' and the desire to hold it 'to provide adaptability'. Any investment programme will require, from time to time, expenditures in excess of current revenue, the magnitude and frequency of these expenditures being dependent both on the scope of operations and on the amount of adaptability which the entrepreneur considers future conditions likely to require. In deciding upon his optimum liquidity position, the entrepreneur will have to weigh up, in a rough and ready way, the cost of a marginal addition to liquidity against the increase in adaptability, and therefore in expected yield, which it affords. The best way of building up the desired liquidity position will depend on a variety of circumstances; cash and overdraft facilities will form the first line of reserve, while, for more remote and problematic contingencies it may be better to rely on the possession of marketable assets and potential credit of a less reliable kind.

Here again, however, it is important to remember that a firm's *actual* liquidity position may differ quite markedly from that which its management would consider optimal; all that we have said about the importance of the costs of realizing assets and of negotiating loans serves to indicate the impracticability of continuous adjustment designed to maintain the optimum liquidity structure. The actual liquidity position of enterprises at any particular time, therefore, may have to be accounted for not in terms of the intentions or motives of entrepreneurs but as the unplanned result of recent transactions —of unexpected variations in costs or in receipts, of stock changes and so on. Cash balances are in fact associated with transactions, therefore, in this *ex post* sense, but it would be wrong to account for them in the *ex ante* terms of a 'transactions motive'.

We have been concerned with liquidity in connexion with the measures which an entrepreneur could adopt in order to be able to deal with changing and uncertain business conditions. These measures were all shown as furthering the objective initially postulated, which was that of maximizing the expected value of future profits; their usefulness, that is to say, was independent of any preference for security, or aversion to risk, in the ordinary sense. But is the objective of business men in fact that which we postulated? Is there an alternative assumption which would form the basis of a more realistic analysis of entrepreneurial decisions? It is with these highly perplexing problems that the following chapter will be concerned.

IX

ATTITUDES TOWARDS RISK

1. THROUGHOUT the previous chapter, it was assumed without further argument, that entrepreneurs were neutral towards uncertainty, in the sense that they preferred the investment programme with the highest yield, irrespective of the range or dispersion of its possible outcomes. I endeavoured to show that this indifference towards the uncertainty of expected profits was consistent with attitudes and policies frequently attributed to risk aversion of some kind. It was consistent, for example, with attempts to increase information and with measures designed to improve the flexibility of an investment programme, such as the choice of versatile equipment and the retention of a liquidity reserve. Nor did neutrality towards the uncertainty of total expected income in any way preclude discrimination against investments in accordance with the degree of uncertainty of the estimates on which they were based; the less precise these estimates, the wider would be the range of possible circumstances for which programmes would have to be adaptable, and the provision of adaptability, where practicable, would entail a sacrifice of the gains from specialization and a consequent reduction in expected yield.

But the fact that business practice, in conditions of imperfect knowledge, can be explained without the postulation of any special preference for certain or for uncertain returns, does not imply that such a preference is non-existent. We remain obliged, therefore, to consider whether there is a sufficient case for assuming that some general psychological aversion from, or attraction towards, risk is a factor in entrepreneurial motivation.

2. Many writers have attempted to deduce the existence of some positive attitude towards uncertain expectations (as opposed to the neutrality which we have assumed hitherto) from the hypothesis of utility maximization. It is assumed that the investor is able to associate with each of the possible financial outcomes of a decision numerical measures of both probability and utility, where utility represents the significance attached by him to a change in income equal to the value of the outcome regarded as certain. The decision which he will take, it is further assumed, will be that offering the highest mathematical expectation of utility, this being defined as the sum of the products of the estimated utilities and probabilities corresponding to each of the alternative outcomes. The decisions of any one person are presumed to be consistent with each other and with the particular function which relates his income to the utility provided by it.

Now the principle which would seem to underlie the hypothesis of utility maximization is that money is desired not for its own sake but for the satisfaction to be obtained from its expenditure. It has immediate relevance, therefore, to the way in which an individual consumer would choose between different uncertain income expectations; but it is not relevant, or at least not directly so, to the decisions of an entrepreneur, the outcome of which cannot readily be identified with changes in his personal income and changes in consumption induced thereby. It will be convenient, therefore, first to consider the value of the hypothesis as a rationalization of the choices of an individual consumer and then go on to inquire whether it can be put to any further use in connexion with the wider, and to us more important, problem of determining the objectives of entrepreneurial policy.

In the traditional formulation of the doctrine under discussion, it was assumed, as a matter of psychological fact, that the utility or satisfaction to be obtained from an income would increase with its size, but at a decreasing rate. This being so, the objective of utility maximization would entail discrimination against income expectations in accordance with their uncertainty, as the gain in utility from a particular increase in income would be less than the loss resulting from a decrease in income of the same amount. Rationality therefore implied risk aversion. Insurance, for example, was consistent with utility maximization, whereas gambling was not. More recently, however, Professors Friedman and Savage have endeavoured to bring both these apparently contradictory forms of human behaviour within the scope of the hypothesis, by postulating a utility function with the particular shape shown in Fig. 5.[1] The marginal utility of income, it is suggested, will fall at low levels of income, will rise again for yet higher levels and will again fall when the highest levels of incomes are reached. Given such a shape to the utility function, it could be rational to discriminate either against or in favour of the uncertainty of an income expectation according to the range of incomes within which the alternative outcomes were expected to fall. Were all

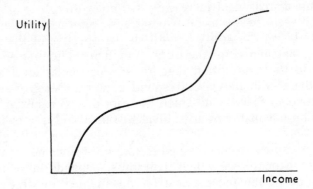

FIGURE 5

the outcomes to lie within the range of diminishing marginal utility, the greater their dispersion the less would be the utility value of the prospect; if, however, they lay within the range of increasing marginal utility, dispersion would appear advantageous. In this way, it is claimed that both insurance and gambling may be consistent with the desire to obtain the maximum utility. One is naturally tempted to ask why the utility function should have this somewhat special shape, but the authors who have suggested it characteristically insist that any doubts on this score are beside the point. All that matters, they maintain, is that individuals behave as if they maximized utility on the basis of the function supposed; the hypothesis therefore has 'predictive value' and cannot be

[1] M. Friedman and C. J. Savage, 'The Utility Analysis of Choices Involving Risk', *Journal of Political Economy*, Vol. LVI (1948), pp. 279–304.

declared invalid until a prediction based on it is proved false. They do, however, in addition, suggest a possible interpretation of the undulatory nature of the curve, according to which the two convex segments correspond to 'qualitatively different socioeconomic levels' and the concave segment to 'the transition between these two levels. According to this interpretation, 'increases in income that raise the relative position of the consumer unit in its own class but do not shift the unit out of its class yield diminishing marginal utility, while increases that shift it into a new class, that give it a new social and economic status, yield increasing marginal utility'.

There seem to me to be two serious objections to this way of formulating the utility hypothesis, irrespective of the shape which is postulated for the utility function. The first of these relates to the assumption that for any particular level of income there will always correspond a unique level of utility, the second to the way in which the gain or loss resulting from a decision is equated to an equivalent rise or fall in income.

3. The utility to be obtained from a given income, or rather from the expenditure which it permits, depends both on the magnitude of the income and on the manner in which it is allocated among different commodities. If we are to assume, following the ordinary theory of consumer demand, that there is one unique optimal pattern of expenditure appropriate to any level of income, then we can construct a schedule relating income to the maximum utility which can be obtained from it. It seems clear that the function employed by Professors Friedman and Savage, as well as by many other writers, is to be interpreted as such a 'maximum utility function' as indicating, that is to say, the amount of utility which would be obtained from a given income by allocating it in the best possible way. What seems to me to be very much in doubt is the justifiability of using such a relationship within the context of an explanation of choice under conditions of uncertainty. The formal theory of consumer's choice, it will be remembered, abstracts from any consideration of knowledge or of time. The optimum pattern of expenditure which is deduced from it has to be understood as appropriate to a consumer who is confident that neither his requirements, nor his income, nor the prices and availability of goods would alter in the future, and whose choices were untrammelled by any purchases which he made in the past. In reality, however, consumers are not in this position, and, if our explicit aim is to consider their behaviour in conditions of uncertainty, we are not at liberty to assume away the complications which these conditions entail. We are not entitled, in particular, to take it for granted that the consumer will be able to realize the optimum consumption pattern appropriate to a new level of income even although this level could not be perfectly foreseen.

An adequate reformulation of the utility hypothesis would have to be based on a less half-hearted admission of the fact of imperfect knowledge. It should be recognized that the consumer will form estimates of varying uncertainty about the magnitude of his prospective receipts, about the prices at which goods can be bought, and about the utility to be yielded by various commodity combinations. On the basis of these he will formulate, in the same way as did an entrepreneur, a particular expenditure programme. Such a consumption expenditure programme, like the investment programmes considered in the previous chapter, will inevitably be characterized by some degree of rigidity, of specificity, that is, to the particular situations which are thought most probable. This is the natural consequence of the fact that much of a consumer's utility is derived from the possession of durable assets such as houses, cars, clothes, and domestic equipment, which yield a flow of services over some extended period. It results also from the fact that assets may be complementary with each other or with other commodities; a house in the country may yield little utility without a car, and the car will in turn require petrol.

This inevitable rigidity of a consumption programme will affect the gain or loss of utility which will result from any occurrence which has not been perfectly foreseen. Should a consumer be obliged, for example, to adapt his expenditure rapidly to an unexpected fall in income, the full strain of the adjustment will have to be borne by the more variable items in his budget. His consumption of the flow of services from his more durable possessions could be cut back only if these were sold, but the realization losses incurred by doing so would act as a strong deterrent to this course of action. His loss of utility will, therefore, exceed that which he would in any case have suffered had the fall in income been foreseen, the magnitude of this additional loss depending on the extent to which the new pattern of his consumption diverges from that appropriate to the new expenditure level, and on the size of any realization losses which the enforced sale of assets has involved. Unexpected developments, therefore, have what may be termed a *dislocation effect* on the consumption programme, which will prevent it from being perfectly adapted to current circumstances. The effect could be brought about, as we assumed, by a short-fall of income, but it could equally well be the consequence of an unexpected increase in income, a change in prices, or by the fact that consumption requirements had changed. It is misleading, we may note in passing, to regard the consumption pattern of any particular person as determined directly by what are normally called 'tastes'; they depend also on not wholly predictable elements in his general circumstances, such as his location, occupation, health and family obligations, which are very inadequately described by this word.

The dislocation effect which an unexpected development has on a consumption programme, has its obvious counterpart in the domain of entrepreneurial activity. A short-fall in the demand for a certain product will not only reduce the profits which could be made from investing in this direction, but will also cause the production programmes of those firms which are already in the business to be less than perfectly adapted to the new situation. Consumers therefore have motives similar to those of entrepreneurs for deliberately introducing adaptability into their expenditure programmes and can adopt similar ways of doing so. The greater the uncertainty of their future income, the less willing will they normally be to purchase expensive indivisible articles which are durable or which require the consumption of various complementary goods in order to yield utility; like entrepreneurs, they will discriminate against programmes of a highly capitalistic nature. In the same way, also, they will be unwilling to incur substantial fixed interest commitments. They will likewise recognize the advantages to be gained from liquidity, as provided by assets or by potential credit.

4. These considerations lead us naturally to the second of the criticisms of the way in which the utility hypothesis is employed by Professors Friedman and Savage and by others. The first criticism, which we have just considered, was based on the neglect of the dislocation effect which would result from the rapid adjustment of consumption expenditure to a new and unexpected permitted level. The second related to the way in which the authors equated the outcome of a risky decision to a change in expenditure. In their treatment, gains and losses from risky decisions (such as the purchase of a lottery ticket), are regarded as equivalent to changes in income of the same money value, and the corresponding utility yield is then deduced directly from the function which relates utility to income. Such a procedure, however, involves a host of simplifications which, I would suggest, are unwarranted. It is not clear, in the first place, what is to be meant by income. It could be defined, for example, as net receipts within the current period, in which case the outcome of the risky decisions, as represented by the gain or loss of a particular sum of money, would be part of these receipts. But here we must note that the effect which the outcome will have on the magnitude of income will depend on whatever length we attribute to the current period in our definition. The shorter this period, the net receipts during which constitute income, the greater will be the fluctuations in income which result from unpredictable gains or losses occurring within it. To avoid this difficulty it might be considered more useful to define income as the amount which would be spent in the current period without impairment of future prospects.[1] In this case, it would not be appropriate to treat the gains and losses of one particular period as part of the income to be attributed to it; if the receipts of the current period were believed, for example, to be higher than those which would be obtained in the future, then some part of them would be allocated to capital account. Defined in

[1] The intricacies of this particular definition are set out by Professor Hicks, in his book *Value and Capital*, Ch. XIV.

this way, a man's income would represent some sort of average of the receipts which he expected to accrue to him over an indefinite future period of time.

Now, as has been said, Professors Friedman and Savage are content to represent the financial outcome of choices involving uncertainty as simple additions or subtractions, of the same money value, to income; in doing so, they would appear to commit themselves to the definition of income in terms of the net receipts of the current period. Utility is therefore presumably to be taken as a function of income in this sense. But utility is presumably related most directly not to income but to expenditure, so that we are obliged to assume that expenditure is always equal to the net receipts of the period in which it is made. The implications of this assumption in terms of the effect on expenditure of a particular gain or loss will depend, of course, on the length of the period on which the definition of income is based; if the period were a week, then a gain of £20 might be considered to double the recipient's income, while if it were a year, then it would increase his income by a small percentage only. The utility value of an uncertain financial return will depend, therefore, on the length of the period chosen for the definition of income and can be made higher or lower at will, simply by varying this length.

It is only by taking a more realistic view of the way in which a consumer will plan his expenditure that ambiguities of this kind can be removed. We must allow him to recognize that his future stream of receipts is uncertain and is likely to be variable, and to realize, that if dislocation effects are to be avoided, the level of his consumption expenditure must not be subject to frequent and unplanned variation. If this expenditure is to be kept constant, or nearly so, under the pressure of falling receipts, then he will have to be able to draw upon wealth or upon potential credit. The retention of such wealth, and in a liquid form, is one of the costs of obtaining the adaptability which we recognized to be desirable in conditions of uncertainty; the alternative to incurring such costs would be to suffer the full force of the dislocation effect, on his pattern of consumption, of unexpected developments.

5. What then are the implications of this kind of analysis on the question at issue—the attitude of the consumer towards the uncertainty of his income expectations? It suggests, quite clearly, that discrimination against income expectations on the ground of their uncertainty can be justified without the need to postulate that the maximum utility to be obtained from income rises less rapidly than does income itself. If the maximum utility function were in fact linear, then the pursuit of the greatest utility would still require this discrimination. An uncertain yield of a particular expected value will then give less utility than that given by a certain yield of this value, precisely because, being uncertain, it prevents the consumer from planning his expenditure in the best possible way. Either he is obliged to pay the cost of measures designed to give adaptability such, for example, as the holding of liquid reserves, or he will have to pay the penalty of having the pattern of his consumption imperfectly adjusted to the permitted level of expenditure. Such problems of adjustment are neglected by Professors Friedman and Savage; although they seek explicitly to introduce uncertainty, they seem unwilling to admit the full scope of its effects. The utility function which they employ is an analytical instrument which has no reference to knowledge or to time, although they apply it in a context of uncertainty and lagged adjustment.

6. It is readily apparent, therefore, on the basis of these considerations, that insurance can be shown to be quite compatible with the hypothesis of utility maximization without the necessity of assuming that the utility from a given income will rise less than proportionately to it. A linear relationship between expenditure and maximum utility is sufficient to justify this and similar practices. The insurance company, it can be safely assumed, consider the expected value of any payments which they may have to make (in the sense of their magnitude multiplied by their probability) to be less than the value of the premium which they charge, or otherwise their business would not be profitable. Provided, therefore, that the individual insurer does not attach a higher estimate of probability than does the company to the eventuality against which he desires protection, he will judge the premium which he pays to exceed the expected value of any payments which might be made to him. From his point of view therefore the contract appears to have a negative yield in financial terms. Nevertheless, it may offer a positive expectation of utility. His annual premium constitutes a known and fixed deduction from the sum which he can expect to devote to expenditure; although it will reduce the amount of utility which he can enjoy, it in no way impairs his ability to plan his expenditure in such a way as to obtain the greatest benefit from it. On the other hand, the possibilities of loss against which he has insured, had they eventuated, would have seriously dislocated his consumption programme—unless of course he had taken special measures to ensure its adaptability. Very frequently, the cost of such measures would exceed the cost of insurance; the retention of liquid reserves, for example, in order to stabilize expenditure in the face of fluctuating receipts, is undertaken more appropriately by a company which can spread its risks than by an individual person with less opportunity to do so.

It is worth noting, however, that insurance may be perfectly justifiable even where the objective is merely to maximize expected receipts, rather than the utility to be derived from them; it is perfectly consistent, in other words, with the assumption of neutrality towards uncertainty which we made in the previous chapter. At first glance, this assertion may seem difficult to reconcile with the statement, made in the previous paragraph, that the expected value of the receipts to be obtained by the insurer will fall short of the amount of the premium he has to pay. But a moment's reflection suffices to show that the total expected yield from the contract is not to be calculated simply by subtracting the premium from the mathematical expectation of payments to be received. What we have to compare is the reductions in expected yield which would be caused, on the one hand, by having to pay a certain annual premium, and, on the other, by the occurrence of the unfavourable event without the cover offered by the insurance. Let us suppose, for example, that an entrepreneur is able to insure against the nonpayment of a particular debt, as he might do with the Export Credit Guarantees Department. With such cover, he would be able to regard the sum due as a certain and dependable component of future receipts; without it, however, he would have to allow for the possibility that receipts might fall to the extent of the sum on which his debtors had defaulted and that he might be obliged to cut his expenditure, to sell assets, or to borrow, in order to bridge the gap. Now there need be no close relationship between the size of the payment he expects to receive and the consequences, in terms of a reduction in his future income, of his expectation being disappointed; for we have to bear in mind the importance of secondary losses which may result from the dislocation of the entrepreneur's investment programme and from any realizations which this may oblige him to make. In the case of insurance against fire and theft, the same argument applies. The receipt of a certain sum of money, on the occasion of the destruction of certain buildings and equipment from fire, may enable the entrepreneur to replace these assets and re-establish his productive activities. Were this money not obtainable from the insurance company, however, it might be difficult, costly, or even impossible to obtain it from any other source; neither the firm's liquid assets nor its potential credit might suffice to raise the funds necessary to carry out the production plan, and the consequent reduction in expected income might be out of all proportion to the amount of money involved. It follows, therefore, that an entrepreneur, in entering into an insurance contract, may increase his expected income even although the value of the premium exceeds his mathematical expectation of any payments which he might receive.

This discussion of insurance serves to illustrate once more the true nature of the disadvantages of uncertainty and of the reasons for discrimination against it. Expenditure programmes, whether for investment or for consumption, are, to some extent, naturally inflexible and cannot be varied at will in such a way as to ensure continuous appropriateness to the relevant circumstances; yet these circumstances are, in varying degrees, unpredictable. Uncertainty about future receipts and payments will oblige the entrepreneur, bent on maximizing expected income, to take steps to introduce some adaptability into his plans. In an analogous way, uncertainty about income prospects will oblige the consumer to adopt a less satisfactory expenditure plan than he might have chosen had these prospects been dependable.

7. But we must now return to the consideration of the utility hypothesis. I have endeavoured to show that, given a linear relationship between income and the maximum utility to be derived from it, the consumer would be justified in discrimination against uncertainty in his income prospects. But I have offered no reasons for believing that this relationship is in fact linear. If, in fact, utility increased less rapidly than did income, then the case for discrimination would be all the stronger; but, if, within certain ranges, utility rose more than in proportion to income, then the consumer's attitude to an uncertain income expectation would depend on the resultant of two opposing forces. He would be biased against it because of the demands for flexibility (or the risk of dislocation effects) created by the fact of the uncertainty, but this might be offset by the fact that the utility value of the favourable outcomes, even allowing for dislocation losses, was very high. We are therefore still obliged to attempt to decide whether there is any particular shape which the utility function is most likely to have.

This, it must straight away be admitted, is very difficult to do. I have argued above that discrimination against an uncertain income prospect was justified because of the difficulty in planning an optimal distribution of expenditure on the basis of unpredictable receipts. These difficulties would be experienced by any consumer, and therefore the arguments founded on them is of quite general validity. But there seems to be no reason why all consumers should estimate the utility which they expect to derive from different levels of expenditure in the same way. Very little can be said *a priori* to suggest that the utility function is of one shape or another, and even that is conjectural and inconclusive. One can argue, for example, that the consumer will have requirements of varying degrees of urgency and that he will naturally use his disposable income to satisfy them in the order of their importance; from this it would seem prima facie that successive increments of income, by being devoted to items lower in the hierarchy of significance, would yield decreasing amounts of utility. This conclusion, however, would have to be modified to take account of the fact of indivisibility and complementarity in consumers' expenditure. A certain increment in disposable income might just fall short of that sufficient to enable a consumer to run a car; an increment twice that size, by sufficing for this purpose, might therefore afford him more than twice the amount of utility. Whether this consideration is of great importance in practice, however, is open to doubt; one has to remember that the consumer is at liberty to accumulate income over a period long enough to permit him to make the large indivisible expenditure. More weight might be given to the fact that various forms of expenditure are complementary, so that the utility derived from the aggregate exceeds the sum of the utilities which would be provided by each of them individually. Increasing marginal utility might then result from increased expenditure, in the same way as increased investment would produce increasing returns in an industry which exhibited external economies. The scope of this argument could even be widened to take account of the fact that the utility derived from consumption may be obtained, in part, from the social status of which particular levels of consumption are taken to be symbolic. What weight would be given to these considerations by the average consumer, in choosing between different and uncertain income prospects, I do not feel confident to judge. If obliged to form an opinion, I should hazard that utility would be judged, by most consumers, to rise less rapidly than expenditure over the greater part of the range, but I see no way that this assertion can be put on any very firm footing.

8. Given the weakness of *a priori* reasoning in this matter, it is natural to consider the possibilities of empirical determination of the relationship in question. Would not an extensive study of actual choices made under uncertainty, together perhaps with results obtained by the issue of questionnaires, enable us to deduce the most typical shape of the utility function? Research along these lines has already been undertaken, but there would seem to me to be very serious grounds for doubt as to whether it is likely to prove of value. Let us very briefly review the difficulties which beset such an approach, even on the assumption that the utility hypothesis is valid; we can then turn to the question of whether the hypothesis is really able to bear the weight of explanation which is being put upon it.

From what has already been said, it appears that a consumer would have to base his evaluation of an uncertain financial outcome on three considerations. He would, in principle, have to estimate, first, the effect of different outcomes on his level of expenditure. It was apparent that the gain or loss from the venture cannot be treated simply as an equivalent addition or reduction in income available for expenditure purposes; the relation between the outcome and changes in expenditure will depend on the consumer's capital and potential credit, as well as on his future expectations. He would have to estimate, secondly, the extent of the dislocation effect of an unplanned change in his expenditure on his consumption pattern, and, thirdly, the maximum utility yielded by different levels of expenditure before any deduction is made for this dislocation effect. Given the relevance of all these three considerations, therefore, it is clear that we cannot, from evidence of actual choices, obtain directly any information about the shape of the maximum utility function, and that, even if we had this information, it would not suffice to enable us to predict actual choices. That is to say, in other words, that the choices of the consumer depend not only on whatever basic psychological attitudes determine his evaluation of the utility to be obtained from different levels of expenditure, but also, and very sub-stantially, on various aspects of his general financial situation, such as the value and structure of his asset holdings, his fixed obligations and the flexibility of his consumption pattern. The difficulties of disentangling these various influences, in any empirical investigation, would be very formidable.

At a more fundamental level of criticism, I am also inclined to doubt whether the utility hypothesis is really able to bear the weight of explanation which this sort of investigation would seem to put upon it. It is reasonable to believe that we can throw some light on the consumer's evaluation of uncertainty by considering the satisfaction which he could obtain from whatever changes in expenditure the alternative money receipts might give rise to; but it is surely unreasonable to ignore other factors which we have no reason to regard as of slight or secondary importance. Professors Friedman and Savage themselves remark that consumers' choices, in conditions of uncertainty, may be affected by considerations other than the utility value of possible outcomes, and admit that this fact greatly enhances the difficulty of getting evidence from their reactions about the shape of the utility function. They mention, for example, that 'in much so-called gambling the individual chooses not only to bear risk but also to participate in the mechanics of a game of chance; he buys, that is, a gamble in our technical sense, and entertainment'. But they go on to say that one can conceive of the separation of these two commodities; the person concerned 'could buy entertainment alone by paying admission to participate in a game using valueless chips; he could buy the gamble alone by having an agent play the game of chance for him according to detailed instructions'. It is doubtful, however, whether this distinction goes to the heart of the matter. Is the special satisfaction (or dissatisfaction) given by risk-bearing adequately described as entertainment derived from the actual playing of the game, and is it easily separable from the suspense and excitements associated with the possibility of real gains and losses? One's doubts on this score acquire rather more significance if we reflect that the activities of the world of business, although they involve risk-bearing, may differ very significantly from games of chance. An entrepreneur undertaking a risky venture may be said to be taking a gamble on the quality of his own foresight and skill, and the attraction which it holds for him may depend precisely on the challenge which it offers and on the sense of achievement and the reputation which success may bring. The same man might find games of chance to have no appeal, while believing that only through success in difficult and risky ventures could the psychological satisfaction from achievement be realized.

This suggests that a man's attitude to uncertainty will depend on the particular context of the choices to be made, on circumstances—such as the extent of the challenge to his own powers—which are not wholly specified in terms of the value of probabilities and outcomes. Two ventures, in other words, may be indistinguishable in terms of the expectation of the outcomes and yet the one may appeal more than the other. This consideration seems to underline the great difficulty—if not the impossibility—of isolating any general psychological propensity to take risks, quite apart from deducing the shape of the maximum utility function; it casts doubt, in fact, on the feasibility of presenting any formalized account of choice in conditions of uncertainty which will be of other than limited use. The impression is sometimes given that, either by further refinement of our hypotheses, or by a more extended empirical inquiry, we might ultimately be in the position adequately to rationalize, or to predict, choices of this kind. One of the obstacles to advance in this direction is represented by the difficulties which we have just been discussing, the difficulties inherent in any attempt to specify a consumer's relative evaluation of certain and uncertain expectations of financial return. But even if these were to be overcome, we should still be very far from being able to construct a formalized model of choice.

9. It is characteristic of elementary models of consumers' or of entrepreneurs' decisions that they assume perfect knowledge, and that, by doing so, they permit us to represent choice as determined directly by specified external conditions and subjective preferences. Given these determinants, we can deduce the optimum choice, and then, by assuming that the agent has the same knowledge as the model builders, it is possible to convert this theorem about rational allocation into a model of individual behaviour. Once the assumption of perfect knowledge is relaxed, however, this simple procedure can no longer be followed, for we have to admit that the connexion between objective reality and individual responses is no longer so direct. It may be necessary, first, to distinguish between external circumstances and a man's information regarding them; the factors affecting the availability of this information were a principal focus of our attention in earlier chapters. We have then to recognize, secondly, that different people may form different expectations or beliefs on the basis of identical information. It is inevitable that we should interpret the significance of current indicators according to the nature of our relevant past experience, and this will never be precisely the same for different persons; it is for this reason that the estimates on which business decisions are based are properly termed personal or subjective. Only when these two stages of the analysis have been passed, can we turn to consider what actions would be planned on the basis of the particular subjective beliefs held.

Most formal analysis of choice in conditions of uncertainty ignores at least some of these complications. The estimates on which the individual has to reach a decision are normally represented as available in a processed, and more or less precise form; such, for example, is the case with the lottery type analogy, where the possible outcomes from alternative courses of action are clearly specified in terms of value and of likelihood. Sometimes it is assumed that everyone would form his estimates in the same way, according to some simple rules such as that of the projection of current prices into the future; in this way we abstract from the subjective element which makes it so difficult to relate the information available to the beliefs for which it forms the basis. In some circumstances, where we are dealing with large aggregates, where it is easy to say what information is generally available, and where this information obviously points one way, the simplifications inherent in this approach may be relatively innocuous, but it seems fair to say that highly formalized models based on short cuts of this kind will not be of general applicability.

We have to conclude, therefore, that although the utility hypothesis offers a mental framework enabling us to analyse consumer responses to uncertainty in a general qualitative way, it fails to account for all the factors which will influence choice, and it provides no adequate basis for quantitative prediction. Some people, regarding this view as unduly pessimistic, would hold that further effort of analysis and inquiry would bring these goals within reach. My own scepticism about the probability of substantial progress in this direction is matched by the belief that the marginal yield of intellectual effort is likely to be much greater in other directions. I am inclined to hold that the greater part of any attempt to predict the probable reactions of entrepreneurs or others consists in establishing, with reasonable accuracy, the nature of the information and opportunities available to them. In earlier chapters, I did in fact endeavour to study, in a more systematic and realistic manner than appears to be usual, how differences in market structure could affect the information available to entrepreneurs and therefore the choices with which they were confronted. No doubt there will be cases where even a full and accurate specification of the entrepreneur's information and circumstances will not permit us to say anything useful about the nature of his reaction. More generally, however, it may be possible to say, at least in general terms, what he would do; precise and detailed prediction, which would rarely if ever be possible, is not always required.

Some general principles about the nature of this reaction have already been established. It was shown, in the previous chapter, that to the extent that the information about investment opportunities was uncertain, their expected yield would be lower, the entrepreneur being required to adopt an adaptable programme; such opportunities would be discriminated against, therefore, even on the assumption of neutrality towards the uncertainty of expected income. These considerations had their counterpart, it later appeared, in the situation of a consumer who was obliged by an uncertain income expectation to choose an adaptable programme of expenditure. This provided us with one substantial reason for believing that, other things being equal, an outcome of known magnitude would be preferred to an uncertain outcome of equivalent expected value. This reason was not conclusive, but the factors which were seen to work the other way did not appear to have the same generality or strength. Positive preference for uncertain returns of particular kinds might be exercised by some people in some situations, but the balance of argument seems to suggest that discrimination against this uncertainty is the general rule.

X

RISK AND WELFARE, I:
PRIVATE AND SOCIAL PROFITABILITY

IN the two previous chapters, we studied the ways in which uncertainty would influence the policies of entrepreneurs and of consumers. The greater the uncertainty of the estimates on which an investment programme was based, the less, it was concluded, would be the total income to be expected from it; and the greater the uncertainty of this expected income, the less would be its utility to the person to whom it accrued. All this lay within the sphere of positive economics. I shall now endeavour to extend the inquiry into the area of welfare or normative economics, by seeking to evaluate individual responses to uncertainty from the point of view of the allocative efficiency of the economy as a whole. Can we say whether the measures adopted by entrepreneurs and others in order to maximize their own expected income or utility are likely also to promote the general economic welfare? Is there reason to believe, for example, that the individual responses previously discussed, which are in part the consequence of the particular institutional arrangements of the private enterprise system, are likely to result in a misallocation of resources, in that they cause an excessive (or insufficient) discrimination against the more risky lines of investment? This question, and those related to it, raise a number of highly perplexing problems towards the solution of which formal welfare theory takes us only a very little way; yet, on the face of it, they are meaningful and important problems, and without some kind of answer to them, any assessment of the efficiency of the competitive economy will be incomplete. It seems better to examine these questions, therefore, rather than to ignore them altogether, even although any conclusions which we can reach will be only tentative and imprecise.

One of the chief difficulties of the problem in hand is that of its proper delimitation. Uncertainty is only one of many factors which may affect the degree of correspondence between private and social profitability. The study of this correspondence forms, in fact, the central core of a great part of economic science. We noted earlier that, according to generally accepted welfare analysis, individual profit maximization would lead to an optimum allocation of resources in a hypothetical system of perfect competition, subject to certain qualifications such as the possibility of economies or diseconomies external to the firm. My reasons for rejecting this conclusion have been set out in earlier chapters, where it was maintained that the co-ordination of both competitive and complementary investment decisions required the presence of circumstances and arrangements additional to, or inconsistent with, the condition of market perfection. Competition, I argued, was necessary both for allocative and selective efficiency, but it had to be balanced by other elements on which the availability of adequate information for investment decisions would depend. The possibility of correspondence between private profitability and social utility was not denied, but the conditions for its realization appeared to be different, and more complex, than formal welfare theory would lead us to believe.

I wish now, without having to re-open all these issues, to confine the discussion to the ways in which the correspondence between private and public profitability is affected by the nature of individual responses to uncertainty. The question can conveniently be discussed in three stages. It is necessary, first, to inquire how the criteria of optimum allocation, as given to us by static welfare analysis, have to be modified to take acount of uncertainty. Secondly, we should endeavour to assess the degree of correspondence between a socially optimal investment programme and the corresponding programme which an entrepreneur would adopt if he wished to maximize his expected total income. Thirdly, we shall have to take account of the general preference for certain as against uncertain returns and appraise its effects, from the general welfare point of view, on the pattern of investment within the economy. This last question will be taken up in the following chapter.

The attempt has not yet been made, as far as I am aware, to set out, fully and systematically, criteria for optimum allocation which are appropriate to conditions of imperfect knowledge; the task would be a most formidable one and lies quite outside my scope and competence. I shall therefore limit myself to suggesting, in broad outline, the kind of modifications to which the familiar marginal criteria would be subject in one important particular case. Let us assume that we have estimates, expressed in terms of quantitative probability, of the demand for a certain commodity and of the cost of producing it. Let us also take it for granted, without further argument, that the total utility which the commodity affords to society is measured by the maximum amount of money which people would be prepared to pay for it, as measured by the area under its demand curve, and that its costs of production will represent the value to society of the alternative output which the factors could have made available if applied at the margin in other directions. The validity of this somewhat naïve procedure is of course questionable; partial analysis of this kind is hazardous even within the context of static welfare analysis, quite apart from any additional complications introduced by uncertainty. But this does not seem the place to discuss all the conditions and reservations with which these simple assumptions would have to be hedged in order to make them less liable to objection, and I do not in any case believe that the general nature of our conclusions would be altered if the argument were presented in more sophisticated form.

Were the demand and cost functions for the product known with certainty, then, according to the accepted principles of optimum allocation, it would be desirable to plan that level of output for which the selling price equalled the long-run marginal cost of production. At first sight it might seem that the replacement of certain values by best estimates, or mean expected values, would be all that was required in order to prescribe the optimum amount of investment in conditions of imperfect knowledge. But a moment's reflection shows the inadequacy of this simple modification.

In Fig. 6(a) are represented the true demand and marginal cost curves for the product in question. The point (P, O), at the intersection of these two curves, corresponds therefore to the volume of output which it is desirable to produce. O_1

and O_2 correspond to levels of output which are respectively less and greater than this optimum by the same amount, so that the triangles C_1P_1P and C_2P_2P measure the loss to society in each case. (This follows from the fact that, under our assumptions, the area under the demand curve equals the utility afforded by the commodity, while the area under the marginal cost curve equals the value of the goods which could have been produced as an alternative.) The extent of these losses clearly depends on the elasticity of the two schedules. I have assumed in the diagram that the demand for the product is highly inelastic at prices above the optimum, and much

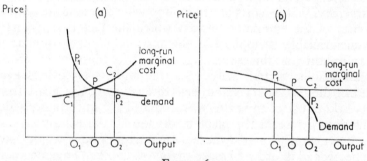

FIGURE 6

more elastic at prices below it, so that a deficient, rather than an excessive supply would produce the greater loss. Had it not been assumed, in the construction of the marginal cost curve, that supply became less elastic at higher levels of output, the relative seriousness of the loss from deficient supply would have been even greater. If we were to assume, as in Fig. 6(b) that demand became less rather than more elastic with increased output, while marginal cost was constant over the relevant range, then excessive, rather than deficient supply would involve the greater waste.

It is apparent from these relationships that the optimum investment programme would not be that which simply equated the best estimates of price and marginal cost; it would have to take account of the possibility that demand and cost conditions might prove to be different from those considered most likely and of the losses which would result from error in either direction. If there were reason to believe for example, that consumers' demand for the product would be highly inelastic for volumes of supply below a certain critical amount, then it would be desirable to make the programme such that the rate of sales could be expanded cheaply and quickly above the level which, on the basis of the best estimate or mean expectation of demand, appeared optimal. A supply reserve of this kind might require the construction of more capacity than the best estimate of demand seemed to justify; alternatively, the need might be met by a versatile production process or simply by the holding of stocks.

A situation of this kind, in which under-investment would have much more serious consequences than over-investment of an equivalent amount, could easily be found in practice. It is more likely to exist in the market for producers' goods than in that for consumers' goods, as a consequence of rather rigid complementary relationships between factors of production in the short run. (These relationships were discussed in Chapter IV when we considered the co-ordination of complementary investments.) A temporary shortage of coal or steel, for example, such as was dramatically evident in the economies of Western Europe after the Second World War, may result in the unemployment of a variety of co-operating factors and cause serious economic loss.

The aim of the investment programme should therefore be, not the equation of the expected value of price and marginal cost, but the minimization of the expected value of waste, defined as the social loss resulting from misallocation, and determined by the probabilities associated with alternative outcomes and by the shape of the demand and cost schedules. On the one hand, the authority would have to estimate the losses, as determined by the specificity or inelasticity of consumer requirements, which would result from over- or under-shooting the optimum output target. On the other, it would have to weigh up the gains from an adaptable programme against the increase in costs which, as we saw in Chapter VIII, adaptability entails. A more realistic estimate of expected waste would take account not only of its rate, as determined by the demand and cost schedules given in the diagram, but also of its likely duration. If, for example, it were possible to make piecemeal additions to capital stock fairly quickly and without much loss of scale economies, then waste resulting from deficient supply would be short-lived and might be avoided entirely by holding sufficient stocks. In a similar way, the duration of waste would be determined, on the demand side, by the ease with which production processes of consumer firms could be adjusted to the factor supply available. The analysis could be further improved if it were made to take account of the possibility of qualitative as well as quantitative variation in output, but extension along these lines is precluded by the summary nature of this treatment.

Let us now proceed to the second stage of our inquiry and consider whether the desire to maximize expected profits would lead entrepreneurs to adopt socially optimal investment programmes. Chapters III and IV endeavoured to provide an outline account of the ways in which supply could successfully adjust to demand in different types of market; they were chiefly concerned with whether entrepreneurs would be able to obtain adequate information on which to base expectations sufficiently secure for their investment decisions. We now recognize explicitly that adequacy is a matter of degree, and that the knowledge possessed by entrepreneurs will necessarily be imperfect; our present problem is to decide whether the modifications imposed on investment programmes as a result of this uncertainty will be socially appropriate.

Let us first consider the type of market in which there are restraints on production but not on selling and where price is flexible and outside the control of any one seller. In this case, it is clear that the price expectations of entrepreneurs will be influenced not only by what they consider to be the likely balance of future demand and supply, but also by the elasticity which they attribute to the two schedules. If demand were believed to be highly inelastic, then the typical entrepreneur's expectation of future price would show a wide dispersion; this being so, profit maximization would require a flexible investment programme which would enable him to cut his losses in the case of a very low price and expand his operations in the case of a high one. The more elastic the demand curve, over its whole length, the less would be the need for such a policy. Were it believed, however, that an excessive supply could be absorbed with only a small fall in price, whereas an equivalent shortage would produce a sharp rise, then the probability distribution of expected future price would be skewed. In order to maximize his expected income, the entrepreneur would then concentrate on measures, such as reserve capacity or large stock holdings, which would enable him to meet the highly profitable, even if unlikely, event of a general shortage.

In markets in which there were restraints on selling as well as on production, where each firm had its particular following of traditional customers and where price was kept relatively stable, the nature of the incentives would be different. An excess or deficiency of supply would not create the possibility of large gains or losses resulting from large price changes. Should supply be generally excessive, losses would be incurred as a result of under-capacity working rather than of a low price, so that, although there will be an incentive to provide for a flexible rate of output, the individual producer's loss will not vary with the extent of the elasticity of demand for the product. The welfare consequences of making output, rather than price, bear the chief burden of adjustment were discussed previously in Chapter VII. In the case of general deficiency of supply, the producer with stocks or capacity in reserve will not be able, by charging what the market would bear, to make exceptionally high profits, but he may succeed in attracting customers away from his competitors and thereby, perhaps permanently, increasing his share of the market. It seems likely that this sort of consideration would carry a good deal of weight with producers in deciding whether to adopt investment programmes which would permit supply to be increased, at short notice, above the normal level. If the forces of competition are very weak, entrepreneurs being unwilling or unable to encroach on each other's markets, then they will have little to gain from making provision against the possible occurrence of a shortage. These, however, are precisely the circumstances in which private and public profitability will diverge, quite apart from the complications introduced by uncertainty.

It would seem, therefore, on the basis of this very cursory discussion, that, given reasonably strong competition, private producers will modify their investment programmes to take account of uncertainty in ways which are also socially appropriate. But there are reasons why we should hesitate before concluding that the presence of uncertainty does not interfere with that correspondence between private and public interest on which any justification of the competitive economy has inevitably to be grounded. An implicit assumption of the above analysis was that the degree of uncertainty confronting the state planning authority, in framing the optimum investment programme, would be the same as that envisaged by individual entrepreneurs in a competitive economy. But, in general, this would not be the case. The chief uncertainties, in the collectivist economy, will relate to technical possibilities and consumers' requirements; market uncertainty about what other agencies in the economy propose to do would be eliminated, in principle, by the national plan. In the decentralized economy, on the other hand, market uncertainty of this kind is unlikely to be wholly eliminated, whatever the arrangements designed to reduce it. On *a priori* grounds, therefore, one would expect to have, in competitive economies, investment programmes which were more adaptable than could be justified by technical uncertainty alone, and more adaptable, therefore, than those of fully planned economies. If this is, in fact, the case, costs of production—other things being equal—would be higher in competitive economies, as adaptability can be provided only at some sacrifice of the gains from specialization.

This simple analysis requires further qualification in certain very significant respects. In discussing the criterion for the socially optimal investment programme, we employed a marginal cost function for the product which was deemed to measure the value of the alternative goods which could have been obtained from the factors of production if applied in other directions. Implicit in this reasoning was the assumption that the prices of factors would be equal to the value of their marginal products in other lines, which would be the cause if optimum organization (in Pareto's sense) prevailed throughout the rest of the economy. Now if the cost functions of particular

individual firms are also to be interpreted as giving a reasonably good indication of the opportunity cost of their products,
then clearly similar assumptions must be made; all firms must
be presumed to purchase factors at the same prices, and these
prices must correspond—at least approximately—to the value
of the marginal products of the factors in other uses. The
validity of these assumptions, with reference to any actual
competitive economy, is obviously a matter of degree and I
do not propose to discuss here the numerous and complex
circumstances on which it depends. There is, however, one
particular aspect of the relationship between the money costs
of the entrepreneur and the social opportunity costs of his
output, which, because of its concern with the imperfections of
knowledge, we cannot properly ignore.

It will frequently be legitimate to assume, for purposes of
simplification, that firms all pay the same prices for factors of
production, these being taken to include labour, raw materials,
and equipment. But their total production expenses will be
determined not by these prices alone, but also by the cost to
them of raising capital. These costs, as we know from abundant
evidence, are certainly not the same for all; there is no perfect
market for capital and both its price and availability differ
considerably between firms. This circumstance, although it
will have a potent influence on the scope and nature of the
investment programmes of individual firms, has at yet played
no part in our analysis. The relevance of interest charges to the
socially optimum investment programme is reasonably obvious;
they would have to be included in the costs of production, the
rate being chosen to reflect the community's preferences
between present and future goods. But the social rationale or
justification of the effect on private investment programmes of
differences in the costs and availability of finance has yet to be
considered. Do these differences prejudice the attainment of
an optimum allocation of resources or are they in some way
conducive to it?

The answer to this question will become more readily
apparent if we pause to consider the different ways in which the
knowledge of investment opportunities can be said to be imperfect. It has been taken for granted, in connexion both

with the socially optimum investment programme and with the investment decisions of individual entrepreneurs, that the relevant expectations were in the form of a range of alternative hypotheses with differing degrees of probability. We should recognize in addition, however, that these expectations are in the form of personal, subjective and commonly divergent estimates made by different people. In determining the socially optimum investment programme, these factors could be ignored, for we were concerned merely with the appropriateness of the programme relative to the expectations. In seeking to appraise the investment decisions taken by individual entrepreneurs in a competitive economy, however, our analysis cannot stop short at this point; we are obliged to pay more attention to the variety of possible subjective estimates upon which the decisions are based. We have to ask ourselves, that is to say, not only whether the investment programmes undertaken are socially appropriate relative to the expectations or opinions on which they are based, but also whether there is any reason to believe that these opinions are likely to be correct.

Now in a competitive economy, the command over resources exercised by any particular entrepreneur, and therefore the weight to be given to his estimates depends on the extent of his capital and of his credit; this represents what may be called the *mandate* given to him by the system. (In this context, the directors of a joint stock company are to be regarded as an entrepreneur, their capital being the sum which has been subscribed in the past by shareholders and built up by undistributed profits.) There will be a maximum permitted scope, as determined by this mandate, to the operation of any single firm. Its own capital will be limited and capable of augmentation by borrowing only up to a certain point. The number of wealth-owners with independent information about the likely profitability of its projected operations will be comparatively small; others will rely on general reputation and past performance, but will not generally be prepared to commit all their capital to one firm. The rationality of the mandate, as thus determined, will depend on the degree to which the possession of wealth and reputation are correlated with the ability to invest successfully. That this correlation is not perfect, no one would deny; the significant question is whether it would be higher under an alternative set of arrangements. In the collectivist economy, the weight to be given to particular opinions is decided in a less impersonal way; all ultimate authority in the allocation of resources is possessed by the central planning agency and the extent of the activities of individual enterprises is determined by the amount of it which is expressly delegated to them. We shall have occasion to consider, at a later stage in this chapter, some of the consequences of these different institutional arrangements; my immediate concern is to stress the fact that the need to choose between different opinions, and therefore the need to specify the mandates to be given to particular decentralized agencies, will impose itself on any economic system, however organized.

In view of this consideration, it is misleading to regard the differences between firms, with respect to borrowing power, as evidence of 'imperfections in the capital market'; they are merely evidence of the particular weighting system which the competitive economy employs in distributing the authority to allocate resources. Unequal access to sources of finance is indeed inconsistent with the defining conditions of the perfect competition model, according to which every entrepreneur can borrow indefinitely at the same rate of interest; in this special sense, therefore, it may be termed an 'imperfection'. That this is so, however, merely underlines the total neglect, by the perfect competition model, of the whole question of the mandate. The distribution, among entrepreneurs, of the power to command resources is clearly not determined, in this hypothetical system, by varying availability of capital; anyone is presumed able to obtain as large a quantity of funds as he pleases and to expand the scope of his operations up to the point where rising costs, occasioned presumably by limits to his managerial capacities, make further growth unprofitable. The absence of any need to attach weights, in the form of mandates, to the opinions of individual entrepreneurs, follows, it would generally be argued, from the assumption of perfect knowledge with which perfect competition is sometimes associated. The legitimacy of such an assumption, however, within the context of a decentralized system, is exceedingly doubtful. One could conceive of an economy in which all investment decisions were taken by one central agency which was presumed to have full knowledge of all the circumstances on which these decisions had to be based. But the theory of perfect competition is designed to explain how an economy can work despite the dispersion of knowledge and of the power of decision among many autonomous units; it seems highly inappropriate to graft on to these circumstances the assumption of perfect knowledge, however interpreted. This assumption, as we have had previous occasion to recognize, is appropriate and useful so long as we are chiefly concerned with the problem of determining an optimum allocation of resources, it being convenient to presume that the relevant ends and means are known or 'given'; it is not appropriate—nor indeed does it have any clear meaning—in connexion with the analysis of the working of a decentralized economy. At the roots of the failure to appreciate this point may be the confusion of perspective which has already been mentioned, the confusion, that is between the point of view of a model builder, who is acquainted with all the determinants of the system, and of the agents which he conceives as operating within it.

This discussion of the significance of the availability of finance in determining the mandate to be given to particular entrepreneurs, arose from our desire to ascertain whether individual entrepreneurs would be led, by the profit motive, to adopt investment programmes which were socially appropriate. We were led to inquire whether the private costs of individual firms corresponded to the social opportunity costs of the production on which they were engaged. Differences in the cost and availability of finance were found difficult to account for in these terms, their rationale becoming apparent only when we recognized that, as the estimates of all entrepreneurs could not all be presumed to be objectively correct, some means was required by which the weight to be given to each of them could be determined. It is appropriate to consider here another element of private business costs, the significance of which has to be explained in the same way. It was observed, in Chapter VIII, that the profits which an entrepreneur expected from an investment programme would depend on its

adaptability, and therefore on the strength of his liquidity
position. But although the holding of a reserve of ready
purchasing power will represent a cost to the individual firm, it
corresponds to no social opportunity cost in the ordinary sense
of using up real productive resources which might have yielded
output in alternative employments. How then do the costs of
providing liquidity, or the risks involved in failing to do so,
affect the appropriateness, from society's point of view, of
private investment decisions?

Liquidity is valued by the entrepreneur because it represents
a store of ready purchasing power held in reserve against
future contingencies. By employing it, when required, profits
can be increased or losses warded off. Without it, he would be
obliged either to sell illiquid assets, or to fail to adapt appropriately to circumstances. His liquidity reserves, therefore,
whether in the form of assets or of potential credit, represent
the extent to which he has deliberately refrained from working
up to the limit of his mandate. The losses which could be
imposed upon him if he did not maintain such reserves represent the penalty for undertaking an investment programme
demanding a greater control over resources than that afforded
him by his original mandate, as determined by his total capital
and borrowing power. If these losses result, for example, from
the need to sell unmarketable assets, then they clearly constitute not merely a transfer of ownership, but a real cost to
society as well as a money cost to the entrepreneur, a cost
represented by the consumption of the services of the dealer
who purchased, and would later have to resell, the assets.
If the loss to the seller resulted from the relative indispensability,
rather than the unmarketability of the assets, the matter is
somewhat less simple. *Ex hypothesi*, the value of the asset to
the buyer is less than its value, as estimated by the seller, in
the investment programme. The realization of the asset, in
order to obtain ready cash, represents, therefore, in the opinion
of the seller, an avoidable misallocation of resources. Are we
to conclude that it would be preferable, from society's point
of view, for the entrepreneur to be enabled to borrow the
additional money he requires and to continue his operations as
planned?

This conclusion would be valid only so long as we could safely assume that the entrepreneur's own estimate of his situation was correct, whereas that of other wealth owners in the economy was mistaken. There is no reason, however, that this should be the case. The weight accorded to the entrepreneur's estimates by the economy was determined by his original mandate, the limits of which he now wishes to exceed. While a further extension of this mandate, in the form of an additional loan, might seem, to the entrepreneur, as making all the difference between success and failure, it might appear to the potential lender merely as throwing good money after bad. It is desirable, therefore, that there should be some sanction imposed on entrepreneurs who exceed the extent of their mandate. This sanction is represented, in competitive economies, by the threat of realization losses or by the abnormally high costs of distress borrowing; but they would have their counterpart in any economy in which there is fragmentation of knowledge and difference of opinion. An individual manager, in a collectivist system, may find that he unexpectedly needs more resources than were allocated to him in the plan, and it will be for some superior person in the hierarchy to decide whether or not he may have them. In the competitive economy, the ultimate tribunal is composed of particular owners of wealth who feel able to form an opinion on the matter. It is clearly impossible to decide, *a priori*, whether, in any particular case, they will act correctly, but we may be able to form some estimate of the probability that they will do so from a consideration of the efficiency of the selective forces which operate within the economy.

Let us now recall the precise relevance of these considerations to the matter in hand. Our aim was to investigate the effect of uncertainty on the likely degree of correspondence, in a competitive economy, between private and social profitability. We first established that, in conditions of uncertainty, the optimum investment programme was one which, by providing appropriately for a range of possible circumstances, minimized the chances of serious misallocation. It then appeared that, provided the force of competition was reasonably strong, entrepreneurs motived by the desire to maximize the expected value of profits, would be led to adopt investment programmes which were optimal in this sense. But we had to recognize the existence of private business expenses, represented by differential borrowing charges and by the costs of maintaining the required liquidity position, which had no immediately obvious counterpart in terms of real social costs, in terms that is of the consumption of productive factors with alternative marginal products elsewhere. At first sight, these particular costs, which owe their existence to the fact of uncertainty, seemed to upset the correspondence between private and social profitability; in fact, however, they could be shown to perform an essential function—that of determining the extent of the control over resources entrusted to each entrepreneur.

XI

RISK AND WELFARE, II:
CONSOLIDATION AND PUBLIC OWNERSHIP

1. WE have so far considered the social appropriateness of private investment decisions on the assumption that these are taken in order to maximize the expected value of total returns, irrespective of their uncertainty. In Chapter IX, however, arguments were advanced which seemed to show that most people, at any rate as consumers, would justifiably discriminate against income expectations according to the degree of their uncertainty; the foregoing analysis is therefore something of a first approximation requiring subsequent qualification. We must now inquire, therefore, how this discrimination against uncertain returns will influence the pattern of investment and how this influence is to be appraised from the social point of view.

It should be remembered that the arguments advanced in Chapter IX to prove the rationality of preferring a certain to an uncertain income were limited in scope; they applied only to the ultimate recipients of income who desired it for their own consumption purposes. We are therefore not justified in assuming, without further argument, that such discrimination will be exercised by all those who take investment decisions, many of whom will not stand to lose or gain, at least directly, from their outcome. Although it may be reasonable to interpret the decisions of a farmer, or the owner-manager of a small business, as motived by the desire to maximize utility rather than income, and, therefore, as influenced by an aversion to uncertainty, it is not at all obvious that this can also be done in the case of the directors of large limited companies. The effect of the consumer's dislike of an uncertain income will be registered, in many investment decisions, only indirectly and to an attenuated extent. The incomes of directors will in general be fixed, perhaps for a period of years, but they will generally be influenced, in the longer run, by the gains and losses earned by the company. More important perhaps will be the influence of shareholders, either actual or prospective, who will be known to favour more certain returns and without whose support the directors cannot for long operate. It by no means follows, however, that firms will exercise a degree of discrimination against uncertainty which will be approximately comparable with that exercised by the single consumer; its magnitude will depend on additional factors which have as yet not been considered.

Before we can proceed to an explanation and an appraisal, from the welfare standpoint, of the effect on investment programmes of discrimination against uncertain returns, there is an important preliminary issue to be considered. In the previous discussion about the nature of the optimum investment programme, we took as the ultimate criterion the class of possible arrangements, known as Pareto optima, which are such as make everyone as well off as he can be, without impairing the position of others. I shall continue to assume that economic improvement can be made so long as it is possible for the gainers from the change to more than compensate those who lose from it; but it will be necessary to recognize two distinct ways in which people can be made better, or worse, off. If the analysis of the previous chapter is correct, then it follows that the utility prospects of a consumer can be increased either by an increase in the expected value of his income or by a reduction in its uncertainty. Thus reduction in the uncertainty of personal income expectations must be regarded as one of the objectives of economic policy; we cannot maintain that consumers show a preference for income certainty and then proceed to ignore this fact in our appraisal of their welfare.

On the basis of these criteria, there would appear to be a very general prima facie case against the efficiency of the competitive economy. It could be maintained, granting a number of assumptions the validity of which we shall consider presently, first, that the income expectations of everyone in the society could be made less uncertain, even without the reallocation of resources, merely through a redistribution of gains and losses, and, secondly that incomes could be made both greater and less uncertain, if reallocation of resources as well as redistribution of incomes were permitted. Uncertainties, it is generally supposed, can be reduced by grouping; the uncertainty of the aggregate yield from all the investments in the economy, taken together, ought, therefore, to be less than that of the average individual investment. Is it not, therefore, conceivable in principle, that, by breaking the link between the outcomes of particular investment decisions and the incomes of those associated with them, we could redistribute total income so as to give to everyone an individual income expectation no smaller and yet less uncertain than previously? And can one not further argue that, if investment decisions were freed from the influence of discrimination against the uncertainty of their yield, and resources reallocated on the basis merely of expected return,[1] then the actual value of the national income would be raised, so that everyone could be made better off than before, in both the senses which we considered? Does the system of private enterprise, through its inability to secure an adequate amount of risk-bearing, unnecessarily retard economic growth?[2]

2. In the bald and simplest form in which I have presented it, the argument is scarcely convincing, and it contains in fact, together with an important core of truth, much that is false or misleading. Nevertheless, I believe that careful examination of it will advance our inquiry. It will be useful to begin by asking why, if there are in fact substantial advantages to be gained from the pooling and redistribution of the income from all investments, the movement towards consolidation has not, in private enterprise economies, been pushed the whole way. It is true, of course, that the principle has been realized, in practice, to some extent; many large firms spread their investments over a variety of fields and it is usual for owners of wealth

---

[1] Expected return, it will be remembered, has to be interpreted rather carefully. If investment decisions are taken by a public authority, it is not sufficient simply to equate the best estimates of price and long run marginal cost; the welfare consequence of errors in prediction, in one direction or another, have to be taken into account.

[2] It is worth stressing that investments may be regarded as uncertain merely because they can only pay for themselves over a long period. The more remote the expectation of receipts the more heavily will they be discounted for uncertainty. The discrimination under discussion may therefore be exercised chiefly against long-term projects.

to hold a mixed portfolio of securities. But it cannot be maintained that grouping of this kind has been carried to what would appear, at least superficially, to be its useful limit—to the point, that is, where the number of different investments combined is so large as to minimize the uncertainty of their aggregate expected income. What, therefore, are the resistances by which the movement is checked?

Paradoxically, both the factors which initiate the movement towards consolidation, and those which halt its progress, can be attributed to different aspects of the same phenomenon— the imperfection of knowledge. The grouping of investment decisions is made advantageous by the fact that the estimates on which they are based is uncertain; its advantages are reduced, however, by the fact that not all individuals are able to make these estimates, and that the estimates which are made may differ. Investments are undertaken in the expectation of profit, but the very possibility of profit, in excess of some minimum return on capital, may owe its existence to the fact that the opportunities which afford it are not known equally to all. The projects which the entrepreneur is obliged to seek out, therefore, must not only be those of which he is able, without too much uncertainty, to estimate the yield; they must also be those which are not generally known, or easily exploitable, by others. The profits which he can hope to earn will depend, therefore, on the degree to which he has special knowledge and experience, a special position in the market and a quality of imagination and foresight greater than the average. As his special knowledge or advantages will inevitably be confined to certain particular spheres and capable of extension only through the expenditure of time and effort, the number of independent ventures offering profits greater than normal about which he is able to form reliable estimates will, therefore, be small.

This principle obviously applies to the ordinary private investor who wishes to reduce the uncertainty of his expected income by diversifying his holdings. He may already possess, or, at a certain cost in time and effort, may be able to acquire, some detailed information about the prospects of particular companies; but the number of these will inevitably be limited.

The more numerous and varied the shares which he wishes to include in his portfolio, the greater will be the extent to which his estimates of their yield will be based on superficial knowledge or on general reputation. But if his estimates of the yield to be expected from a particular holding are based on superficial knowledge, they will be uncertain, and, if they are based on a widespread reputation, they are likely to be low. It is possible, of course, to make use of the specialized advice of a broker, but his knowledge, like that of the investor, will either be deep but narrow, or wide but superficial. Neither can the dilemma be wholly avoided by placing wealth in an investment trust which itself has diversified holdings, if only for the fact that, to the extent that the trust is widely known to be successful, the yield on its shares will be low.

3. I have argued that consolidation can ensure a total yield which is higher or less uncertain only if the size and certainty of the individual yields of the component investments is not impaired in the process. The reason which I have given for expecting such an impairment, and for expecting it to increase progressively with the number and variety of the investments grouped, was simply the limited knowledge and capacity of a single mind. But cannot this difficulty be overcome, it may be argued, by institutional arrangements designed to pool the information, the special advantages and the capital of several people? Much of contemporary business does achieve precisely this result; the large joint stock company, in particular, commonly undertakes a number of investments which may be spread over a wide range of but tenuously related fields. The existence of important scale economies, and the need for a large capital to exploit them, is an additional, and may be in fact the principal reason for industrial groupings, but the gains from risk-spreading are a justification in their own right. Provided that the quality of the component investments can be sustained, it is difficult to see why the benefits from consolidation should not continue to be available until the whole economy is encompassed; as yet, however, the movement towards amalgamation has not proceeded to its ultimate limit and no single firm would appear to be on the way to bringing all industry under its control. It follows, therefore, that counteracting forces must be at work.

In order that a firm should willingly enter into amalgamation with others, its owners would have to be assured that their prospects would be improved as a result. They would, there-fore, wish to compare, in terms both of size and certainty, the expected income from their own concern, acting independently, with the income which they would expect to receive after amalgamation, this latter depending on the amount both of the profits of the united enterprise and of their own particular share of them. Now, in the first place, it may be very difficult for any particular entrepreneur to estimate what the total profits of the group would be. From his point of view, as distinct from the objective realities, the future income from his own concern will generally be less uncertain than that which he expects to be earned by others, for the former is determined by circumstances of which he has more direct and detailed knowledge. It follows, therefore, that his estimate of the aggregate income of the firms after amalgamation will be subject to considerable uncertainty, even if he is prepared to grant that amalgamation would not impair the quality of the investment decisions and the general level of efficiency. A further result of the uncertainty may be the inability of firms to agree upon a proper distribution of the resultant total profit. The past profits of the firms, it is true, are known to all of them but it is their likely future profits which are relevant, and these are not capable of unique, objective assessment. Evidence of disagreement on this particular issue is supplied by the example of contested take-over bids, the unwilling directors believing that the future earnings of the company, remaining independent, would exceed the compensation offered by the firm which desires to acquire its assets. Needless to say, there may be factors other than disagreement about profit shares which prevent fusion, just as there are motives other than the desire to reduce risks, for desiring it.

4. These considerations have an important bearing on a familiar problem in the theory of competition and of the firm. It has long been recognized that technical conditions of

production do not provide a reason why the unit costs of the firm should ever increase with its size, although they do give reasons why, at least up to a point, unit costs should fall. Economists therefore felt obliged to find other reasons why the process of concentration did not proceed, in actual competitive economies, to its ultimate limits.[1] Some sought the explanation chiefly on the side of demand, others on the side of costs. According to Professor Hicks, 'There must indeed be something to stop the indefinite expansion of the firm; but it can just as well be stopped by the limitation of the market as by rising marginal costs, though of course both of these may be in operation simultaneously'.[2] The limited nature of the market for any particular product, however, does not offer a sufficient reason why the firm should cease to grow, for expansion should still be possible in other directions; economies of scale might thereby be sacrificed, at least to some extent, but gains from risk-spreading would continue. Those explanations which seek on the other hand to show that the long-run marginal cost curve does in fact rise, usually rely on the existence of so-called managerial diseconomies of scale, which cause the administrative, as contrasted with the production costs of the firm to increase by more than in proportion to its size.

Whatever the validity of the doctrine of managerial diseconomies of scale, it is very difficult not to attribute its invocation to a desire to preserve a certain theoretical structure, within which the equilibrium of the firm has to be associated with the equation of marginal costs and marginal revenue as ordinarily computed. The relationship between efficiency and scale is a question upon which I believe that the analysis of this and previous chapters can throw some light, and I shall endeavour to consider it presently. My present contention is that the existence of limits to the growth of the individual firm is capable of an alternative and much more convincing

---

[1] The literature dealing with this issue is very extensive. See, for example, the following:

N. A. Kaldor, 'The Equilibrium of the Firm', *Economic Journal* XLIV (1934), pp. 60–76.

E. H. Chamberlin, 'Proportionality, Divisibility and Economics of Scale', *Quarterly Journal of Economics*, LVII (1947–8), pp. 229–62.

[2] J. R. Hicks, *Value and Capital*, second edition, p. 84.

explanation; the apparent necessity of finding some reason why long-run marginal costs should ultimately rise is created not by the phenomena themselves, but by the nature of the theoretical schema through which we have chosen to study them. We, as theorists, viewing the competitive system from the outside, have to recognize that there are undisputed benefits to be obtained from increases in the scale of the firm, whether they take the form of lower production and selling costs or the form of risk-spreading; in so far as they result from the second of these factors, at any rate, there would seem to be no reason why these benefits should ever come to be exhausted. But although amalgamation should, therefore, never cease to be profitable, the fact remains that, in actual competitive economies, it takes place only to a limited extent. It seems natural to inquire, therefore, whether there exists an irrational unwillingness to merge, which overcomes the desire for profit maximization, or whether there are other factors, causing an ultimate rise in the marginal cost curve, which the economist has neglected.

In order to resolve this paradox, it is essential to avoid the confusion, noted previously in different contexts, between the angle of vision of the observer—the analysing economist—outside the system, and the angle of vision of the entrepreneur within it, between the general nature of objective reality, as postulated by the former, and the particular and limited information on which the decisions of the latter must always depend. In order that an entrepreneur should judge it profitable to enter into amalgamation, it is not sufficient that he should be aware of the truth of the general principle of large-scale economies; it is necessary, as we observed above, that he should be assured that his income after some particular amalgamation would be larger, or less uncertain, than it would have been had he kept his independence. If he is to judge this, we concluded, he would have to be able to assess not only his own future prospects, about which he should know a good deal, but also the future profitability of the activities on which the other firms are engaged, about which he might be much less able to form as confident an opinion. Very frequently, the uncertainties surrounding such calculations will be overborne in his mind by the obvious importance of the likely economies to be achieved; but where these are small, and confined chiefly to the possibility of risk-spreading, these uncertainties may present a formidable barrier to amalgamation.

Let us now recall the relevance of these considerations to the central argument of the chapter. We were examining the contention that, in a competitive economy, insufficient resources would be devoted to directions where the expected yield, although high, was uncertain. The motive for discrimination against uncertain returns could, it seemed, be weakened, if not eliminated, by a process of consolidation which would break the link between investment decisions and the incomes of those associated with them. We decided first to inquire, therefore, why consolidation, if it did offer unlimited benefits, nevertheless took place only to a limited extent, and we found this to be explained by the fact that knowledge of investment opportunities was in the form of uncertain estimates dispersed among many minds. All that was shown, however, is that full consolidation might not come about spontaneously; it does not follow that such consolidation is therefore socially undesirable, or that it could not be brought about by social action deliberately directed to this end.

5. It appeared that the root cause of discrimination against investments with uncertain yields was the operation, albeit in a diluted form, of the principle of *individual liability*, according to which the authority to take decisions was associated with the obligation to bear at least part of their financial consequences; this principle is in turn a corollary of the institution of private property, which is itself the very hallmark of the competitive economy. It would appear therefore, if only prima facie, that by abolishing this institution, so that the consequences of an investment decision became a public rather than a private liability, this motive for discrimination could be suppressed, resources could then be allocated more rationally, and the increased yield could be distributed in accordance with whatever canons of equity were currently accepted. In this way, principles of organization would be applied to the whole economy which were already in force within the large corporation.

We are obliged to ask, therefore, whether there would be any offsetting diseconomies or disadvantages resulting from such a change. The reader will not expect anything in the nature of a conclusive answer to this formidable question; we shall have to be content to find out whether the proceeding analysis can cast some light on it.

It will be useful to begin by reminding ourselves of what is, and what is not implied by the general principle on which the argument for consolidation is ultimately grounded. It is a fundamental assumption of probability theory that if the *a priori* probability of an 'experiment' having a certain 'result' is *p* (this being a fraction of unity), then the proportion of a class of such experiments showing this result will approach *p* more closely the larger the number in the class. If the probability is of a statistical character, the principle is still applied; though it may be difficult to predict, with any degree of confidence, whether a particular man will die at fifty, it is still possible, as our insurance companies have long since been aware, to estimate, with tolerable accuracy, what proportion of a large class will die at this age. The probability estimates with which we have been concerned cannot be easily regarded as of either of these two types, being the product of some kind of subjective assessment, but it is assumed that they can be treated in the same, or at least an analogous, way. The successive estimates of one person, or the estimates of different persons, it is presumed, will be subject to uncorrelated errors which may be expected to cancel out the larger the number of estimates which are combined. Now we clearly cannot proceed from this to argue that a certain magnitude, such as the aggregate yield from a group of investments, could be predicted with certainty, if only the prediction were to rest on component estimates which were sufficiently numerous, for these estimates might all be subject to common and systematic errors. The degree of confidence which it is legitimate to place in the estimate arrived at by grouping, will depend on the average degree of confidence which can be placed in the component estimates, and on the likelihood that the errors in them will be uncorrelated. Here again it is important to distinguish between the objective reality as conceived by someone outside the system and the subjective views of it entertained by those within it. In order to estimate the change in the total yield from investible resources which would result from a redistribution designed to equate the expected value of their marginal returns in different directions, irrespective of uncertainty, we should like to have individual probability estimates which were, in some sense, objectively correct, and which therefore indicated the degree of belief which it was rational to associate with each possible outcome on the total evidence available; there exist, however, only the subjective estimates of those people within the system, who cannot be assumed to be infallible and whose evidence may be incomplete. It is these estimates which must form the basis for any of our judgements; we are not obliged to assume, however, that their quality is independent of the institutional arrangements which determine who is to take them; on the contrary, we are obliged to consider whether, as a result of the change designed to remove discrimination against uncertainty, there is any prima facie reason to believe that the estimates will deteriorate or will be subject to any kind of systematic error. In other words, in order to make objective judgements, we are obliged to consider not only the probability estimates of entrepreneurs, but also the probability that these estimates will be soundly based, this being regarded as functionally dependent on the nature of the institutional arrangements prevailing.

6. The discrimination we have been discussing owes its existence to the principle of individual liability; so also, however, do the systems of selection and of motivation characteristic of the competitive economy. The profits or losses resulting from an investment decision will, given individual liability, affect the future mandate of the entrepreneur who made it; at the same time, it will affect the amount available to him for consumption purposes. These two influences relate to selection and to incentive respectively, but in so far as entrepreneurs may have an interest in extending their own mandate, quite apart from any associated financial gains, it is difficult sharply to distinguish between them. They will both obviously affect the quality of the estimates upon which investment decisions are based; the selective forces will influence the distribution of capital among entrepreneurs, while the financial incentives give them a motive to make careful and unbiased estimates of expected yield.

It is clear, therefore, that if the principle of individual liability were to be abolished, in order to remove the motive for discrimination against uncertainty, then some other way would have to be found of performing the functions which it discharges. In any practicably workable economy, authority will have to be delegated, or decentralized, at least to some extent, if only because of the natural limits to the number of decisions which can be taken by one man or one directorate. There will, therefore, always be the need for a system of efficient selection which will determine the scope of individual mandates. Selection might be no longer automatic, but planned; inevitably, however, it would be influenced by actual performance, towards which the respective contributions of luck and judgement would be very difficult to assess. If, as is likely, managers gained satisfaction from an increase in their mandate, but suffered even greater dissatisfaction from its reduction, this would in itself constitute a motive for discrimination against risky ventures. If personal income were itself correlated with the size of the mandate, then the original motive for discrimination would of course straight away be reintroduced. On the assumption, therefore, that the setting up of a collectivist economy would not abolish the desire of human beings for money and for power, it would seem that consolidation could not be indefinitely extended without some loss of efficiency, resulting either from the absence of a proper system of selection and incentive, on the one hand, or from the reintroduction of motives for discrimination against uncertain returns on the other.

7. There is yet a further way in which the institutional arrangements required to consolidate investments would affect the nature of the particular estimates of profitability upon which they were based. The mandate which is afforded to entrepreneurs in a competitive economy by the possession of wealth and credit, permits them to allocate resources in whatever way they choose, subject to whatever legal restraints are in operation; they are free, in other words, to do anything that is not forbidden. In a collectivist economy, the mandates given to individual managers take the form of delegated authority, which will be of a relatively specific character as determined by the general plan for the whole economy. The competitive economy is essentially acephalous; it contains no ultimate authority by which all significant economic decisions must be endorsed; different opinions may persist unresolved and may give rise to the simultaneous adoption of contradictory policies. In the collectivist system, on the other hand, all decisions will, in principle, be consonant with the master plan and with each other; differences of opinion will, of course, exist, but, being subject to ultimate arbitration, they will not normally find direct expressions in actual investment decisions. Now this distinction has some bearing on the gains, in terms of the reduction of uncertainty, which are to be expected from the pooling of different investments. Our belief that the aggregate yield from a number of investment projects will be more predictable than the component yields, rests on the assumption that the estimates of different entrepreneurs are subject to errors, which, being uncorrelated, will cancel out. To the extent that these estimates cease to be independent, however, and become subject to revision by some higher authority, the errors to which they are liable are more likely to be correlated. Other things being equal, therefore, less gain is to be expected simply from consolidation in itself, on the assumption that the process of revision does not improve the quality of the individual estimates either through the reduction of market uncertainty obtained from planned co-ordination, or because of the presumably superior capacities of the higher authorities.

By being represented, however, within this somewhat sterilizing formal framework, the argument for individual autonomy is robbed of much of its scope and force. The principle to which our discussion has naturally led us, appears, in this special context, as concerned with the gains to be expected, in yield and in certainty, from the consolidation of investment decisions; on a wider interpretation, however, it is the very essence of the utilitarian justification for the liberal society. Realization of the inevitable imperfection of human knowledge, by inducing an appropriate sense of humility, should lead us to welcome diversity both in action and in opinion.[1] By setting out on a plurality of paths, we may hope to discover those along which best to proceed; the failure of some policies and the success of others, and the gradual accumulation of knowledge and experience enable society to select the most appropriate premises for action.

Competitive private enterprise, though not in itself ensuring diversity, does create a climate favourable to it. The institution of private property, by giving to particular individuals or organizations the authority to devote resources to any lawful purpose, is a strong bulwark of non-conformity; by setting up automatically a large number of centres of independent initiative, it furthers freedom and variety in action, without which freedom and variety in thought and discussion lose much of their significance. Central economic direction, on the other hand, though it need not eliminate diversity, does present it with a hostile environment. The central authority might, it is true, deliberately set out to favour diversity of decisions by its subordinate agencies, but there is no strong presumption that it will in fact do so; while every man will admit to his fallibility, few of them, as Mill observed, think it necessary to take precautions against it. It might be argued that liberty was of importance in thought and discussion, in scientific inquiry and artistic creation, but unnecessary or undesirable in economic affairs; it is far from obvious, however, why individuality and diversity should be of value in the former spheres and yet have no contribution to make in the production of goods and services—even although we have to admit that the need for deliberate co-ordination and direction is much greater in this field. In addition, it is by no means clear that all ultimate

[1] 'That mankind are not infallible; that their truths, for the most part, are only half-truths; that unity of opinion, unless resulting from the fullest and freest comparison of opposite opinions, is not desirable, and diversity not an evil, but a good, until mankind are much more capable than at present of recognising all sides of the truth, are principles applicable to men's modes of action, not less than to their opinions.' John Stuart Mill's essay 'On Liberty', from which this quotation is taken, contains what is probably the most famous, and what is perhaps in some ways the best, statement of these arguments.

responsibility for resource allocation can be given to a central authority without loss of autonomy and individuality in spheres other than that of economic activity in the narrow sense.

Economic progress depends, as much as on any other factor, on the energy, inventiveness and creative imagination of particular men, attributes which are more likely to be developed and maintained by opportunities for independent action and by the relatively untrammelled exercise of power.[1] The long-run consequences of excessive centralization, through its influence on the dispositions of men, may be more serious in the long, than in the short run. The fact that these considerations elude precise analysis and can scarcely find a place in formal economic models is no reason for doubting their importance.

8. The purpose of this chapter was to examine the prima facie case that the total yield from investment could be increased if resources were allocated so as to equate the expected

---

[1] '. . . a state which dwarfs its men, in order that they may be more docile instruments in its hands even for beneficial purposes—will find that with small men no great thing can really be accomplished; and that the perfection of machinery, to which it has sacrificed everything, will in the end avail it nothing, for want of the vital power which, in order that the machine may work more smoothly, it has preferred to banish.' (J. S. Mill, op. cit.)

It is interesting to compare this observation with those made, a century later, in a study sponsored by the Institute of Economics of the Hungarian Academy of Sciences. (Janos Kornai, op. cit.) 'A socialist society must be based on the activity and initiative of the workers. It must promote the development of the personalities of people; it must educate persons in top positions to be capable of independent creative action, of shouldering responsibilities, and of courageous thought. But the development of people in these directions is hampered by the excessive use of instructions. If instructions were confined to a few important matters, this would exert a useful educational influence; it would accustom people to discipline and to respect for the common good. But a proliferation of instructions inevitably throttles independent action and initiative on the part of individuals. It threatens to transform economic administrators from being active agents of progress into being mere passive tools governed by instructions. An instruction is a command which brooks no argument. Plainly, the readiness of the managements of enterprises to criticize is diminished by the inordinate proliferation of instructions.

'A characteristic social type has emerged in this situation—the top manager who is reluctant to make decisions independently, that is, in the absence of instructions or the approval of central authorities. It is not that he is a cowardly type, as it were, from the outset. Rather, he has become accustomed to doing everything in accordance with instructions.'

value of marginal yields regardless of their uncertainty. The conclusion reached was that the consolidation of investments, and the suppression of individual liability, even if they put an end to discrimination, would impair entrepreneurial performance and prejudice variety of decision. A collectivist economy, it would seem, is obliged, no less than the economy of private enterprise, to seek the best compromise. It is worth while to pause and consider just how far, in the competitive economy of the present day, this compromise has been carried. The principle of individual liability is, in practice, subjected to a great deal of dilution. In the first place, many important investment decisions are taken within the public sector, on authority which, in the ultimate analysis, is delegated by the sovereign assembly, and with consequences which are borne by the public at large. Some of these decisions are associated with much uncertainty, either because of the nature of the scientific knowledge on which they are based—as in the case of the development of atomic power—or simply because their expected yield would have to be recovered over an unusually long future period. If this uncertainty is very great, it may be that the decisions could not be taken unless liability for their consequences were generalized as widely as possible. Even within the private sector, liability may in part be borne by the state. In industries as diverse as aircraft construction and farming, the state is expected, in the United Kingdom, to bear part of the losses which would result from unsuccessful investment; without its support, it is feared that socially appropriate decisions would not be taken because of the degree of risk which they entail.

Even in the absence of state intervention, the liability for the outcome of investment decisions, within the private sector, is diffused in a great variety of ways. The obligation to bear any losses is enforced, in the ultimate analysis, by the laws of the state, but has been tempered, in Britain since 1855, by the introduction of the principle of limited liability, which results in a devolution of some of the responsibility for risk bearing to creditors. Moreover, as we have seen, large multi-product firms derive their income from a number of different, and relatively independent activities; representing, as they do, islands of collectivism within the competitive economy, they incur all the problems of planned selection and of incentive which we attributed to the collectivist economy itself. The income of these companies, itself made less uncertain by the grouping of investment decisions, forms, in general, only part of the incomes of the persons to whom it accrues, being yielded by shares which go to make up a diversified portfolio. The link, therefore, between the outcome of an investment decision and the incomes of those associated with it, though not entirely broken, is made weaker and more indirect. In this way, a compromise is reached, though not necessarily by deliberate decision, between the need to reduce the discrimination against uncertain yields, on the one hand, and the desirability of retaining some measure of competitive selection and direct financial incentive, on the other.

The criticism may be made that the analysis of this chapter, or indeed of the book as a whole, fails to indicate unequivocably what particular economic arrangements or system can be regarded as ideal. The analysis implies that the planned co-ordination of investment decisions may be necessary in some circumstances and not in others, and that centralization may result in losses as well as in gains. For this I make no apology. We can hope to find which arrangements are optimal only by taking account continuously of different circumstances and by weighing up different requirements, the variety and conflicting nature of which exclude the possibility of a tidy, clear-cut solution. Without some measures of planning and co-operation, whether public or private, harmony between competitive or complementary investment decisions may not be achieved, market uncertainty may not be brought within tolerable limits and the risks of investment may present too great a deterrent to individual firms. Without some degree of competition, on the other hand, it may be difficult for monopolistic exploitation to be checked, for the authority to allocate resources to pass to those most fitted to exercise it, for diversity to be preserved and for the springs of individual energy and initiative, on which all economic progress must ultimately depend, to be kept unchoked.

Very rarely, indeed, will these requirements be wholly compatible; policy has therefore to be based on an appraisal, in particular circumstances, of their quantitative significance and on striking a just balance between them. A successful outcome will depend, very largely, on political wisdom and administrative skill, it being the function of economic analysis to unravel the complex network of considerations on which choice should depend. It has been suggested, in this book, that parts of our theoretical apparatus are ill-suited to this task, that our model of competitive equilibrium in particular has served to mask or to misrepresent the requirements of successful adjustment, and that the consideration which we give to the availability of information — and the need for it — should be fuller and more systematic than it has been hitherto.

Annex I

THE ORGANIZATION OF INDUSTRY[1]

1. I WAS once in the habit of telling pupils that firms might be envisaged as islands of planned co-ordination in a sea of market relations. This now seems to me a highly misleading account of the way in which industry is in fact organized. The underlying idea, of course, was of the existence of two ways in which economic activity could be co-ordinated, the one, conscious planning, holding sway within firms, the other, the price mechanism, operating spontaneously on the relations between firms and between firms and their customers. The theory of the firm, I argued, had as its central core an elaboration of the logic of this conscious planning; the theory of markets analysed the working of the price mechanism under a variety of alternative structural arrangements.

I imagine that this account of things might be acceptable, as a harmless first approximation, to a large number of economists. And yet there are two aspects of it that should trouble us. In the first place it raises a question, properly central to any theory of economic organization, which it does not answer; and, secondly, it ignores the existence of a whole species of industrial activity which, on the face of it, is relevant to the manner in which co-ordination is achieved. Let us deal with each of these matters in turn.

Our simple picture of the capitalist economy was in terms of a division of labour between the firm and the market, between co-ordination that is planned and co-ordination that is spontaneous. But what then is the principle of this division? What kinds of co-operation have to be secured through conscious direction within firms and what can be left to the working of the invisible hand? One might reasonably maintain that this was a

[1] I am grateful to Mr. J. F. Wright, Mr. L. Hannah, and Mr. J. A. Kay, each of whom gave helpful comments on a draft of this article which first appeared in *The Economic Journal*, Vol. 82, September 1972, pp. 883–96.

key question—perhaps the key question—in the theory of industrial organization, the most important matter that the Divine Maker of market economies on the first day of creation would have to decide. And yet, as I hope soon to show, it is a matter upon which our standard theories, which merely assume but do not explain a division between firm and market, throw little light.

Let me now turn to the species of industrial activity that our simple story, based as it is on a dichotomy between firm and market, leaves out of account. What I have in mind is the dense network of co-operation and affiliation by which firms are interrelated. Our theoretical firms are indeed islands, being characteristically well-defined autonomous units buying and selling at arm's length in markets. Such co-operation as takes place between them is normally studied as a manifestation of the desire to restrict competition and features in chapters about price agreements and market sharing. But if the student closes his textbook and takes up a business history, or the financial pages of a newspaper, or a report of the Monopolies Commission, he will be presented with a very different picture. Firm A, he may find, is a joint subsidiary of firms B and C, has technical agreements with D and E, subcontracts work to F, is in marketing association with G—and so on. So complex and ramified are these arrangements, indeed, that the skills of a genealogist rather than an economist might often seem appropriate for their disentanglement.[1] But does all this matter?

[1] The sceptical reader might care to look up a few cases in the reports of the Monopolies Commission. The following example is found in the report on cigarette filter-tips. Cigarette Components Ltd. made filter-tips for Imperial Tobacco and Gallaher using machines hired from these companies. It has foreign subsidiaries, some wholly and some partially owned. It was both licensee and licenser of various patents, one of which was held by the Celfil Trust, registered in Liechtenstein, with regard to the ultimate control of which Cigarette Components told the Monopolies Commission they could only surmise. Nevertheless, this patent was of key importance in that the Celfil licensees, of which Cigarette Components was only one, were bound by price and market-sharing arrangement. Cigarette Components was itself owned by Bunzl Ltd., in which Imperial Tobacco had a small shareholding. The raw material for the tips is cellulose acetate tow, which was made by Ectona Fibres Ltd., a company in which Bunzl had a 40% interest and a subsidiary of Eastman Kodak 60%. Agreements had been made providing that, should Bunzl lose control of Cigarette Components, then Eastman could buy out their shares in Ectona . . . etc., etc.

Theories necessarily abstract and it is always easy to point to things they leave out of account. I hope to show that the excluded phenomena in this case are of importance and that by looking at industrial reality in terms of a sharp dichotomy between firm and market we obtain a distorted view of how the system works. Before doing so, however, I wish to dwell a little longer on the several forms that co-operation and affiliation may take; although the arrangements to be described are no doubt well known to the reader, explicit mention may nevertheless help to draw attention to their variety and extent.

2. Perhaps the simplest form of inter-firm co-operation is that of a trading relationship between two or more parties which is stable enough to make demand expectations more reliable and thereby to facilitate production planning. The relationship may acquire its stability merely from goodwill or from more formal arrangements such as long-term contracts or shareholding. Thus, for example, the Metal Box Company used to obtain a discount from its tin-plate suppliers in return for undertaking to buy a certain proportion of its requirements from them, and the same company owned 25 per cent of the share capital of the firm supplying it with paints and lacquers. In the same way Imperial Tobacco owned shares in British Sidac, which made cellophane wrapping, and in Bunzl, which supplied filter-tips. Occasionally shareholdings of this kind may be simply investments held for their direct financial yield, but more generally they give stability to relationships through which the activities of the parties are co-ordinated both quantitatively and qualitatively. Not only is it made easier to adjust the quantity of, say, lacquer to the quantity of cans which it is used to coat but the specification and development of the lacquers can be made appropriate to the use to be made of them. And in the synthetic fibre industry likewise, linkages between firms at the various stages—polymer manufacture, yarn spinning and finishing, textile weaving—help bring about the co-ordinated development of products and processes. The habit of working with models which assume a fixed list of goods may have the unfortunate result of causing us to think of co-ordination merely in terms of the balancing of quantities of inputs and outputs and thus leave the need for qualitative co-ordination out of account.

Co-operation may frequently take place within the framework provided by subcontracting. An indication of the importance of this arrangement is provided by the fact that about a quarter of the output of the Swedish engineering industry is made up of subcontracted components, while for Japan the corresponding figure is about a third and in that country's automobile industry almost a half. Subcontracting on an international basis, moreover, is said to be becoming more widespread and now a dense network of arrangements links the industries of different countries.[1] Now the fact that work has been subcontracted does not by itself imply the existence of much co-operation between the parties to the arrangement. The plumbing work on a building contract may be subcontracted on the basis of competitive tenders for the individual job. Frequently, however, the relationship between the parties acquires a degree of stability which is important for two reasons. It is necessary, in the first place, to induce subcontractors to assume the risks inherent in a rather narrow specialization in skills and equipment; and, secondly, it permits continuing co-operation between those concerned in the development of specifications, processes, and designs.

Co-operation also takes place between firms that rely on each other for manufacture or marketing and its fullest manifestation is perhaps to be found in the operations of companies such as Marks and Spencer and British Home Stores. Nominally, these firms would be classified as retail chains, but in reality they are the engineers or architects of complex and extended patterns of co-ordinated activity. Not only do Marks and Spencer tell their suppliers how much they wish to buy from them, and thus promote a quantitative adjustment of supply to demand, they concern themselves equally with the specification and development of both processes and products. They decide, for example, the design of a garment, specify the cloth to be used, and control the processes even to laying down the types of needle to be used in knitting and sewing. In the same way they co-operate with Ranks and Spillers in order to work out the best kind of flour for their cakes and do not neglect to specify the number of cherries

---

[1] See the *Economic Bulletin for Europe*, Vol. 21, No. 1.

and walnuts to go into them. Marks and Spencer have laboratories in which, for example, there is development work on uses of nylon, polyester, and acrylic fibres. Yet all this orchestration of development, manufacture, and marketing takes place without any shareholding by Marks and Spencer in its suppliers and without even long-term contracts.

Mention should be made, finally, of co-operative arrangements specifically contrived to pool or to transfer technology. Surely the field of technical agreements between enterprises is one of the underdeveloped areas of economics. These agreements are commonly based on the licensing or pooling of patents but they provide in a quite general manner for the provision or exchange of know-how through the transfer of information, drawings, tools, and personnel. At the same time they are often associated with the acceptance by the parties to them of a variety of restrictions on their commercial freedom—that is to say, with price agreements, market sharing, and the like.

This brief description of the varieties of inter-firm co-operation purports to do no more than exemplify the phenomenon. But how is such co-operation to be defined? And how in particular are we to distinguish between co-operation on the one hand and market transactions on the other? The essence of co-operative arrangements such as those we have reviewed would seem to be the fact that the parties to them accept some degree of obligation—and therefore give some degree of assurance—with respect to their future conduct. But there is certainly room for infinite variation in the scope of such assurances and in the degree of formality with which they are expressed. The blanket manufacturer who takes a large order from Marks and Spencer commits himself by taking the appropriate investment and organizational decisions; and he does so in the expectation that this company will continue to put business in his way. In this instance, the purchasing company gives no formal assurance but its past behaviour provides suppliers with reason to expect that they can normally rely on getting further orders on acceptable terms. The qualification 'normally' is, of course, important, and the supplier is aware that the continuation of orders is conditional on a sustained demand for blankets, satisfaction with the quality of his manufacture, and so on. In a case such as this any formal specification of the terms and conditions of the assurance given by the supplier would scarcely be practicable and the function of goodwill and reputation is to render it unnecessary.

Where buyer and seller accept no obligation with respect to their future conduct, however loose and implicit the obligation might be, then co-operation does not take place and we can refer to a pure market transaction. Here there is no continuing association, no give and take, but an isolated act of purchase and sale such, for example, as takes place on an organized market for financial securities. The pure market transaction is therefore a limiting case, the ingredient of co-operation being very commonly present, in some degree, in the relationship between buyer and seller. Thus although I shall have occasion to refer to co-operation and market transactions as distinct and alternative modes of co-ordinating economic activity, we must not imagine that reality exhibits a sharp line of distinction; what confronts us is a continuum passing from transactions, such as those on organized commodity markets, where the co-operative element is minimal, through intermediate areas in which there are linkages of traditional connexion and goodwill, and finally to those complex and interlocking clusters, groups, and alliances which represent co-operation fully and formally developed. And just as the presence of co-operation is a matter of degree, so also is the sovereignty that any nominally independent firm is able to exercise on a *de facto* basis, for the substance of autonomy may often have been given up to a customer or a licensor. A good alliance, Bismarck affirmed, should have a horse and a rider, and, whether or not one agrees with him, there is little doubt that in the relations between firms as well as nation states, the condition is often met.

3. It is time to revert to the main line of our argument. I had suggested that theories of the firm and of markets normally provide no explanation of the principle of the division of labour between firms and markets and of the roles within a capitalist economy of planned and spontaneous co-ordination. And I also maintained that these theories did not account for the existence

of inter-firm co-operation and affiliation. It is upon the first of these two deficiencies that I now wish to concentrate.

Probably the simplest answer to the question of the division of labour between firm and market would be to say that firms make products and market forces determine how much of each product is made. But such an answer is quite useless. If 'products' are thought of as items of final expenditure such as cars or socks, then it is clear that very many different firms are concerned with the various stages of their production, not only in the sense that firms buy in components and semi-manufactures from other firms but also in that there may be a separation of manufacture and marketing (as in the case of Marks and Spencer and its suppliers) or of development and manufacture (as in the case of licensers and licensees). If, alternatively, we simply define 'products' as what firms do, then the statement that firms make products is a tautology which, however convenient, cannot be the basis of any account of the division of labour between firm and market.

It is worth observing that we learn nothing about this division of labour from the formal theory of the firm. And this is perhaps not surprising as the theory, in its bare bones, is little more than an application of the logic of choice to a particular set of problems. It may be that the theory indeed makes it more difficult to answer our question in that, in order the better to exhibit this logic of choice, it is formulated on the assumption of 'given production functions' which represent the maximum output obtainable from different input combinations. However useful this representation of productive possibilities, it leaves one important class of ingredients out of account. It abstracts totally from the roles of organization, knowledge, experience, and skills, and thereby makes it the more difficult to bring these back into the theoretical foreground in the way needed to construct a theory of industrial organization. Of course I realize that production functions presume a certain level of managerial and material technology. The point is not that production is thus dependent on the state of the arts but that it has to be undertaken (as Mrs. Penrose has so very well explained)[1] by

---

[1] E. T. Penrose, *The Theory of the Growth of the Firm* (Oxford, 1959).

human organizations embodying specifically appropriate experience and skill. It is this circumstance that formal production theory tends to put out of focus, and justifiably, no doubt, given the character of the optimization problems that it is designed to handle; nevertheless, it seems to me that we cannot hope to construct an adequate theory of industrial organization and in particular to answer our question about the division of labour between firm and market unless the elements of organization, knowledge, experience, and skills are brought back to the foreground of our vision.

It is convenient to think of industry as carrying out an indefinitely large number of *activities*, activities related to the discovery and estimation of future wants, to research, development, and design, to the execution and co-ordination of processes of physical transformation, the marketing of goods, and so on. And we have to recognize that these activities have to be carried out by organizations with appropriate *capabilities*, or, in other words, with appropriate knowledge, experience, and skills. The capability of an organization may depend upon command of some particular material technology, such as cellulose chemistry, electronics, or civil engineering, or may derive from skills in marketing or knowledge of and reputation in a particular market. Activities which require the same capability for their undertaking I shall call *similar activities*. The notion of capability is no doubt somewhat vague, but no more so perhaps than that of, say, liquidity and, I believe, no less useful. What concerns us here is the fact that organizations will tend to specialize in activities for which their capabilities offer some comparative advantage; these activities will, in other words, generally be similar in the sense in which I have defined the term although they may nevertheless lead the firm into a variety of markets and a variety of product lines. Under capitalism, this degree of specialization will come about through competition but it seems to me likely to be adopted under any alternative system for reasons of manifest convenience. Mrs. Penrose has provided us with excellent accounts of how companies grow in directions set by their capabilites and how these capabilities themselves slowly expand and alter.[1] Dupont, for example,

[1] Ibid.

moved from a basis in nitro-cellulose explosives to cellulose lacquers, artificial leather, plastics, rayon, and cellophane, and from a basis in coal tar dyestuffs into a wide range of synthetic organic chemicals, nylon, and synthetic rubber. Similarly, Marks and Spencer, having acquired marketing and organizational techniques in relation to clothing, were led to apply them to foodstuffs.

There is therefore a strong tendency for the activities grouped within a firm to be similar, but this need not always be so. In the history of any business random factors will have left an influence, and the incentive to take up a particular activity will sometimes be provided, not by the prior prossession of an appropriate capability, but by the opportunity of a cheap acquisition, through a family or business connexion or because of management's belief that the profitability of investment in some direction was being generally underestimated. There is no need to deny, moreover, that a variety of potential gains are provided by grouping activities irrespective of their character; risks can be spread, the general managerial capability of the firm can be kept fully employed, and the allocation of finance can be planned from the centre. None of this is in contradiction with the principle that it will pay most firms for most of the time to expand into areas of activity for which their particular capabilities lend them comparative advantage. A firm's activities may also, on occasions, be more similar than they superficially appear. If a firm acquired companies irrespective of the character of their activities we should term it conglomerate; but if the motive for the purchases were the belief that the companies were being badly managed, the hope being to restore them to health before reselling them at a profit, the management would be exercising a particular capability.

4. I have argued that organizations tend to specialize in activities which, in our special sense of the term, are similar. But the organization of industry has also to adapt itself to the fact that activities may be *complementary*. I shall say that activities are complementary when they represent different phases of a process of production and require in some way or another to be co-ordinated. But it is important that this notion of complemen-

tarity be understood to describe, for instance, not only the relationship between the manufacture of cars and their components, but also the relationship of each of these to the corresponding activities of research and development and of marketing. Now it is clear that similarity and complementarity, as I have defined them, are quite distinct; clutch linings are complementary to clutches and to cars but, in that they are best made by firms with a capability in asbestos fabrication, they are similar to drain-pipes and heat-proof suits. Similarly, the production of porcelain insulators is complementary to that of electrical switchgear but similar to other ceramic manufacture. And while the activity of retailing toothbrushes is complementary to their manufacture, it is similar to the activity of retailing soap. This notion of complementarity will require closer definition at a later stage, but it will be convenient first to introduce one further (and final) set of conceptual distinctions.

It is clear that complementary activities have to be co-ordinated both quantitatively and qualitatively. Polymer production has to be matched, for example, with spinning capacity, in terms of both output volume and product characteristics, and investment in heavy electrical equipment has likewise to be appropriate, in scale and type, to the planned construction of power stations. Now this co-ordination can be effected in three ways; by *direction*, by *co-operation*, or through *market transactions*. Direction is employed when the activities are subject to a single control and fitted into one coherent plan. Thus where activities are to be co-ordinated by direction it is appropriate that they should be *consolidated* in the sense of being undertaken jointly by one organization. Co-ordination is achieved through co-operation when two or more independent organizations agree to match their related plans in advance. The institutional counterparts to this form of co-ordination are the complex patterns of co-operation and affiliation which theoretical formulations too often tend to ignore. And, finally, co-ordination may come about spontaneously through market transactions, without benefit of either direction or co-operation or indeed any purposeful intent, as an indirect consequence of successive interacting decisions taken in response to changing profit opportunities. Let us now make use of this somewhat crude categorization to reinterpret the questions with which we started.

5. What is the appropriate division of labour, we should now ask, between consolidation, co-operation, and market transactions?

If we were able to assume that the scale on which an activity was undertaken did not affect its efficiency, and further that no special capabilities were ever required by the firm undertaking it, then there would be no limit to the extent to which co-ordination could be affected by direction within one organization. If production could be set up according to 'given' production functions with constant returns, no firm need ever buy from, or sell to, or co-operate with any other. Each of them would merely buy inputs, such as land and labour, and sell directly to consumers—which, indeed, is what in our model-building they are very often assumed to do. But, of course, activities do exhibit scale economies and do require specialized organizational capabilities for their undertaking, the result being that self-sufficiency of this kind is unattainable. The scope for co-operation by direction within firms is narrowly circumscribed, in other words, by the existence of scale economies and the fact that complementary activities need not be similar. The larger the organization the greater the number of capabilities with which one may conceive it to be endowed and the greater the number of complementary activities that can, in principle, be made subject to co-ordination through direction; but even if a national economy were to be run as a single business, it would prove expedient to trade with the rest of the world. Some co-ordination, that is to say, must be left either to co-operation or to market transactions and it is to the respective roles of each of these that our attention must now turn.

Building and brick-making are dissimilar activities and each is undertaken by large numbers of enterprises. Ideally, the output of bricks ought to be matched to the volume of complementary construction that makes use of them and it is through market transactions that we expect this to come about. Brick-makers, in taking investment and output decisions, estimate future market trends; and errors in these estimates are regis-

tered in stock movements and price changes which can lead to
corrective actions. As we all know, these adjustments may work
imperfectly and I have myself argued (in Chapter III) that the
model which we often use to represent this type of market is
unsatisfactory. But this is a matter with which we cannot now
concern ouselves. What is important, for our present purposes,
is to note that impersonal co-ordination through market forces
is relied upon where there is reason to expect aggregate demands to be more stable (and hence predictable) than their
component elements. If co-ordination were to be sought
through co-operation, then individual brick-makers would seek
to match their investment and output plans *ex ante* with
individual builders. Broadly speaking, this does not happen,
although traditional links between buyers and sellers, such as
are found in most markets, do introduce an element of this kind.
Individual brick manufacturers rely, for the most part, on
having enough customers to ensure some cancelling out of
random fluctuations in their several demands. And where sales
to final consumers are concerned, this reliance on the law of
large numbers becomes all but universal. Thus we rely on
markets when there is no attempt to match complementary
activities *ex ante* by deliberately co-ordinating the corresponding plans; salvation is then sought, not through reciprocal
undertakings, but on that stability with which aggregates, by
the law of large numbers, are providentially endowed.

Let us now consider the need to co-ordinate the production of
cans with tin-plate or lacquers, of a particular car with a
particular brake and a particular brake lining, of a type of
glucose with the particular beer in which it is to be used, or a
cigarette with the appropriate filter-tip. Here we require to
match not the aggregate output of a general-purpose input with
the aggregate output for which it is needed, but of particular
activities which, for want of a better word, we might call *closely
complementary*. The co-ordination, both quantitative and qualitative, needed in these cases requires the co-operation of those
concerned; and it is for this reason that the motor car companies
are in intimate association with component makers, that Metal
Box interests itself in its lacquer suppliers, Imperial Tobacco
with Bunzl, and so on. Co-ordination in these cases has to be

promoted either through the consolidation of the activities within organizations with the necessary spread of capabilities, or through close co-operation, or by means of institutional arrangements which, by virtue of limited shareholdings and other forms of affiliation, come somewhere in between.

Here then we have the prime reason for the existence of the complex networks of co-operation and association, the existence of which we noted earlier. They exist because of the need to co-ordinate closely complementary but dissimilar activities. This co-ordination cannot be left entirely to direction within firms because the activities are dissimilar, and cannot be left to market forces in that it requires not the balancing of the aggregate supply of something with the aggregate demand for it but rather the matching, both qualitative and quantitative, of individual enterprise plans.

6. It is perhaps easiest to envisage co-ordination in terms of the matching, in quantity and specification, of intermediate output with final output, but I have chosen to refer to activities rather than goods in order to show that the scope is wider. The co-operation between Marks and Spencer and its suppliers is based most obviously on a division of labour between production and marketing; but we have seen that it amounts to much more than this in that Marks and Spencer performs a variety of services in the field of product development, product specification, and process control that may be beyond the capability of the supplying firms. And one may observe that inter-firm co-operation is concerned very often with the transfer, exchange, or pooling of technology. Thus a subcontractor commonly complements his own capabilities with assistance and advice from the firm he supplies. New products also frequently require the co-operation of firms with different capabilities, and it was for this reason that ICI originally co-operated with Courtaulds in the development of nylon spinning and now co-operates with British Sidac in developing polypropylene film.

It is indeed appropriate to observe that the organization of industry has to adapt itself to the need for co-ordination of a rather special kind, for co-ordination, that is to say, between the development of technology and its exploitation. A full analysis of this important subject cannot be attempted here but it is relevant to consider those aspects of it that relate to our principal themes. What then are the respective roles, in relation to this kind of co-ordination, of direction, co-operation, and market transactions? Obviously there are reasons why it may be convenient to co-ordinate the activities of development and manufacture through their consolidation within a single organization. Manufacturing activity is technology-producing as well as technology-dependent; in the process of building aircraft or turbo-alternators difficulties are encountered and overcome and the stock of knowledge and experience is thereby increased. But there are also good reasons why a firm might not be content to seek the full exploitation of its development work through its own manufacturing activity. The company that develops a new product may itself lack sufficient capacity to manufacture it on the scale needed to meet the demand and may not have time enough to build up the required additional organization and material facilities. It could, of course, seek to acquire appropriate capacity by buying firms that already possessed it, but this policy might prove unattractive if it entailed taking over all the other interests to which these firms were committed. The innovating firm might judge that its comparative advantage lay in developing new products and be reluctant, therefore, to employ its best managerial talents in increasing the output of old ones. It would be aware, moreover, that not only manufacturing but marketing capability would be needed and might properly consider that it neither possessed nor could readily acquire this, especially in foreign countries. All these considerations may lead firms to seek some indirect exploitation of a product development. And, in the case of the new process, the incentive might be even stronger in that there might be a wide variety of fields of production in which the process could be used.

The indirect exploitation of new technology could be sought, in terms of our nomenclature, either through market transactions or through co-operation with other firms. But technology is a very special commodity and the market for it a very special market. It is not always easy, in the first place, to stop knowledge becoming a free good. The required scarcity may have to be created artificially through a legal device, the patent system, which establishes exclusive rights in the use or the disposal of new knowledge. Markets may then develop in licences of right. But these are very special markets in that the commercial freedom of those operating within them is necessarily restricted. For suppose that A were to sell to B for a fixed sum a licence to make a new product, and sell the product himself. In this case the long- and short-run marginal costs of production of the good would, for both parties, be below unit costs (because of the fixed cost incurred by A in the development work and by B as a lump sum paid for the licence) so that unrestrained competition would drive prices to unremunerative levels. It might at first seem that this danger could be avoided if licences were charged for as a royalty on sales, which, unlike a fixed sum, would enter into variable costs. But the licensee might still require assurance that the licenser, unburdened by this cost element, would not subsequently set a price disadvantageous to him or even license to others on more favourable terms. These dangers could be avoided if the parties were to bind themselves by price or market-sharing agreements or simply by the prudent adoption of the policy of live and let live. But, in one way or another, it seems likely that competition would in some degree have been diminished.[1]

[1] Professor Arrow reaches a different conclusion. The matter is considered in his article 'Economic Welfare and the Allocation of Resources for Invention', in *The Rate and Direction of Inventive Activity*, ed. National Bureau of Economic Research (Princeton, NJ, 1962). Professor Arrow maintains that 'an incentive to invent can exist even under perfect competition in the product markets though not, of course, in the "market" for the information containing the invention' and that 'provided only that suitable royalty payments can be demanded, an inventor can profit without disturbing the competitive nature of the industry'.

The issue is simplest in the case of a cost-saving invention. Professor Arrow considers a product made under constant costs both before and after the invention and shows how the inventor can charge a royalty that makes it just worth while for firms making the product to acquire a licence. On the face of it one might then conclude that the licenser would have no need to bind himself not to reduce price below the level that provided licensees with a normal profit or to relicense for a lesser royalty, for, if he were to do either of these things, existing licensees would make losses, stop producing, and therefore discontinue royalty payments. But this conclusion is valid only under the highly special assumption of there being no fixed costs. For firms will in general continue in production so long as price does not fall below variable costs. Thus the licenser

It would appear, therefore, on the basis of these considerations, that where the creation and exploitation of technology is
co-ordinated through market transactions—transactions in
licences—there will already be some measure of co-operation
between the parties. The co-operation may, of course, amount
to little more than is required not to rock, or at any rate not to
sink, the boat. But there are reasons why it will generally go
beyond this. Technology cannot always be transferred simply

---

could find it in his interest, having sold as many licenses as he could at the higher
royalty, to license others at a lower royalty, or to enter the market himself. He
would thus extend the market for the product and increase his earnings
provided, of course, that the price was kept above variable costs and therefore
high enough to induce the original (and by then no doubt aggrieved) licensees to
stay in business. It is true, of course, that *in the long run* fixed plant would wear
out and firms deprived of their quasi-rents would cease producing, but the fact
that an opportunity for exploitation is merely temporary does not warrant our
assuming that it will not be seized. In general the licenser would stand to gain by
'cheating' the licensees in the manner described and the latter would therefore
want some measure of assurance (which need not be formal) that he would not
do so. There would be a market for licences, that is to say, only if the commercial
freedom of the licenser were in in this way reduced.

It may be that Professor Arrow would not consider this to represent a
significant restriction of competition; and indeed the important practical issue
concerns the manner and degree in which the parties accept limitations on their
freedom of action. I have suggested that the licenser would be in a position,
having licensed other firms, subsequently to deprive them of expected profits. A
firm will therefore seek a licence only if it believes that this will not happen, but
it may consider that sufficient assurance is provided by the fact that the licenser,
in his own long-run interest, will not wish to acquire the reputation for such
sharp practice. Much the same situation obtains in the context of the relationship between a larger purchaser and a small supplier. Marks and Spencer,
having offered attractive enough terms to induce the blanket manufacturer to
devote a large proportion of his capacity to meet its needs, might subsequently
press for a price reduction that left him with a poor return. The hapless
supplier, in the short run at any rate, might have no option but to give way. But
although the purchaser could thus act, it could scarcely be in his own long-run
interest to acquire the reputation for doing so.

The upshot would therefore seem to be this. A market for licences can
function only if the parties to the transactions accept some restraints, but, in
certain circumstances, no more restraint might be required than enlightened
self-interest could be depended upon by itself to ensure. In practice, of course,
licensing arrangements are commonly associated with much more—and often
more formal—restraint of trade, the extent of which may or may not be greater
than is necessary for the transfer of technology to take place.

by selling the right to use a process. It is rarely reducible to mere information to be passed on but consists also of experience and skills. In terms of Professor Ryle's celebrated distinction, much of it is 'knowledge how' rather than 'knowledge that'. Thus when one firm agrees to provide technology to another it will, in the general case, supply not only licences but also continuing technical assistance, drawings, designs, and tools. At this stage the relation between the firms becomes clearly co-operative and although, at its inception, there may be a giver and a receiver, subsequent development may lead to a more equal exchange of assistance and the pooling of patents. Arrangements of this kind form an important part of the networks of co-operation and affiliation to which I have made such frequent reference.

7. This article began by referring to a vision of the economy in which firms featured as islands of planned co-ordination in a sea of market relations. The deficiencies of this representation of things will by now be clear. Firms are not islands but are linked together in patterns of co-operation and affiliation. Planned co-ordination does not stop at the frontiers of the individual firm but can be effected through co-operation between firms. The dichotomy between firm and market, between directed and spontaneous co-ordination, is misleading; it ignores the institutional fact of inter-firm co-operation and assumes away the distinct method of co-ordination that this can provide.

The analysis I presented made use of the notion of activities, these being understood to denote not only manufacturing processes but to relate equally to research, development, and marketing. We noted that activities had to be undertaken by organizations with appropriate capabilities. Activities that made demands on the same capabilities were said to be similar; those that had to be matched, in level or specification, were said to be complementary. Firms would find it expedient, for the most part, to concentrate on similar activities. Where activities were both similar and complementary they could be co-ordinated by direction within an individual business. Generally, however, this would not be the case and the activities to be co-ordinated, being dissimilar, would be the responsibility of different firms. Co-ordination would then have to be brought about either through co-operation, firms agreeing to match their plans *ex ante*, or through the processes of adjustment set in train by the market mechanism. And the circumstances appropriate to each of these alternatives were briefly discussed.

Let me end with two further observations. I have sought to stress the co-operative element in business relations, but by no means take the view that where there is co-operation, competition is no more. Marks and Spencer can drop a supplier; a subcontractor can seek another principal; technical agreements have a stated term and the conditions on which they may be renegotiated will depend on how the strengths of the parties change and develop; the licensee of today may become (as the Americans have found in Japan) the competitor of tomorrow. Firms form partners for the dance but, when the music stops, they can change them. In these circumstances competition is still at work even if it has changed its mode of operation.

Theories of industrial organization, it seems to me, should not try to do too much. Arguments designed to prove the inevitability of this or that particular form of organization are hard to reconcile, not only with the differences between the capitalist and socialist worlds, but also with the differences that exist within each of these. We do not find the same organization of industry in Yugoslavia and the Soviet Union, or in the United States and Japan. We ought to think in terms of the substitutability of industrial structures in the same way as Professor Gerschenkron has suggested in relation to the prerequisites for economic development. It will be clear, in some situations, that co-ordination has to be accomplished by direction, by co-operation, or through market transactions, but there will be many others in which the choice will be difficult but not very important. In Great Britain, for example, the artificial textile industry is vertically integrated and the manufacturers maintain that this facilitates co-ordination of production and development. In the United States, on the other hand, antitrust legislation has checked vertical integration, but the same co-ordination is achieved through close co-operation between individual firms at each stage. It is important, moreover, not to draw too sharp lines of distinction between the techniques of co-ordination themselves. Co-operation may come close to direction when one of the parties is clearly predominant; and some degree of *ex ante* matching of plans is to be found in all markets in which firms place orders in advance. This points, however, not to the invalidity of our triple distinction but merely to the need to apply it with discretion.[1]

---

[1] In his article 'The Nature of the Firm', *Economica*, 1937, pp. 386–405, R. H. Coase explains the boundary between firm and market in terms of the relative cost, at the margin, of the kinds of co-ordination they respectively provide. The explanation that I have provided is not inconsistent with his but might be taken as giving content to the notion of this relative cost by specifying the factors that affect it. My own approach differs also in that I distinguish explicitly between inter-firm co-operation and market transactions as modes of co-ordination.

PLANNING VERSUS COMPETITION[1]

SCOPE AND METHOD

WHAT are the proper roles, in economic organization, of planning and of competition? In what circumstances should economic activities be fitted together deliberately through a coherent set of instructions given by a central authority? And when should this co-ordination be left to the spontaneous interaction of independent, decentralized decisions? Is planning essentially an alternative to competition or can it be employed, in an indicative form, not to replace but somehow to illuminate, guide, and thereby improve the operation of market forces? These questions, it need hardly be said, admit of no definite answer, objectively valid irrespective of time and place. Nevertheless, they are real questions of obvious practical importance, so that it is worth while trying to find some answers to them, however partial and provisional these may be.

I wish to make only two preliminary observations, one about scope, the other about method. The scope of this paper is very wide. But its subject is competition versus planning, not capitalism versus socialism; the questions which I raised at the outset pose themselves in countries which have no private property in the means of production but seek to decentralize decision-taking. In so far as method is concerned, I seek justification in terms of what Sir Roy Harrod has called, rather grandly, the need for Continuing Conceptual Refurbishment. I try to take a fresh look at the first principles. Progress in economics does not depend only upon rigorous analysis, observation, and measurement; it requires also that effort of imagination that enables us partially to escape from conventional categories of thought. Being realistic is not merely a question of testing hypotheses,

[1] From *Soviet Studies*, Vol. XXII, No. 3 (January 1971), pp. 433–47. Reprinted by permission of the editor of *Soviet Studies*.

important though this is; it also requires sustained and strenuous effort to consider whether our inherited stock of theoretical constructions do not distort our vision of the plain facts of economic life.

THE TASK OF ECONOMIC ORGANIZATION

Let us begin at the beginning and ask what it is that we want competition or planning to accomplish. The answer might be that their function is to secure an efficient allocation of resources. To say this, however, although obviously correct, may be misleading. For we normally concentrate, in economic theory, on the pure logic of resource allocation and, in order to exhibit this logic, early, we assume that both ends and means are given. Thus we assume, in the so-called theory of consumers' behaviour, that income, prices, and tastes are given and concern ourselves exclusively with the logic of choice. And when we turn to the economy as a whole and seek to establish conditions for efficient allocation in Pareto's sense, we follow the same procedure; we adopt the vantage point of someone standing outside the system with full knowledge of all the relevant preferences, resources, and productive techniques. This approach is justified in that it enables us to focus our attention on the pure principles of economizing; but it is important, when we turn to consider the working of economic organization, to keep well in mind the obvious fact that in reality no one is provided with a bird's-eye view. Allocative decisions are in fact taken, and in the nature of things have to be taken, on the basis of individual beliefs and opinions, usually uncertain and sometimes contradictory. It is not merely that our knowledge is probabilistic in character; the point is that it is fragmented, in the form of imperfectly consistent estimates held by different people. The function of economic organization is therefore to make the best use of this knowledge, and, in appraising the relative effectiveness of different systems, we have to think in terms not only of allocative logic but of search and discovery.

Let us suppose that a body of men land on a desert island on which, in a variety of places, buried treasure is to be found. If the men have with them a map showing the location of treasure throughout the island, then a plan of campaign can readily be drawn up. The appropriate organization is that of central planning, each man being given a particular job to go. Of course there will be problems of incentives, of distribution, and so on, but the propriety of centralized decision-taking can scarcely be in doubt. But let us now suppose that there is no map, or at least no map in existence that can be presumed accurate. Each man may have bits and pieces of information that he considers relative to the location of the treasure, but no more. There is now room for choice between alternative forms of organization. The centralized solution would be to invite the men to pool their information and opinions and endeavour therefrom to construct a map of the most likely location of the treasure; a plan of campaign could then be drawn up and jobs allocated. The purely decentralized solution would be to allow each man to go forth and dig where he liked. Now these alternative approaches differ in two ways. Under central planning, the activities of different men will be co-ordinated by means of a set of integrated instructions which, ideally, will produce an optimum pattern of search—or allocation of resources—with respect to the evidence and opinion embodied in the map. Under *laissez-faire*, on the other hand, such co-ordination as does take place will be the unintended result of each man taking account of what the others are doing; if, for example, men start to crowd in one corner of the island, then some will no doubt be induced to seek their fortunes in other areas where, if the evidence of treasure is less strong, the competition is weaker. Clearly, therefore, planning and competition represent alternative techniques of co-ordination; less obvious, perhaps, is that they differ also in the way in which they make use of knowledge. Under central planning, evidence and opinion will be consolidated in order to construct the map on which the programme of search is to be based. Under *laissez-faire*, however, each and every opinion will affect the pattern of search provided that whoever holds it is in possession of a pick and shovel. Now it does not seem to be possible, unless the circumstances are further specified, to say whether the consolidation of knowledge will improve the pattern of search; it is easy to see that something will be gained, as bits of the jigsaw are fitted together, but easy to see also that something may be lost if heterodox opinions are sacrificed in the name of consistency, and new findings, if they appear to threaten the presumptions of the plan, are quietly put aside. All that one can say at this stage is that the relative merits of planning and competition are not solely a matter of the way in which they co-ordinate interrelated activities; they depend also on whether, in a particular set of circumstances, it is desirable to endeavour to weld a variety of estimates and opinions into some kind of coherent whole.

I hope that the relevance of this naïve analogy is reasonably clear. In normative economics, when considering how best to adapt means to ends, we assume that we have knowledge of the available resources, opportunities, and objectives in order to concentrate on the logic of the problem. In positive economics, on the other hand, when we come to consider how particular systems would work, this assumption has to be abandoned. Maps are not provided; economic organization has to find some way of constructing maps or of doing without them. In a centrally planned system, the authorities take steps to prepare a map; after discussions with the subordinate bodies in the hierarchy, with the various industrial commissions or their equivalents, they specify a feasible and desired future composition of output and then proceed to give appropriate instructions designed to ensure that it is produced. Consistency is thereby produced not necessarily, of course, with resources, technical possibilities, and needs as they objectively exist, but with one central agreed or imposed conception of what these are. In practice, of course, planning systems will differ in the detail in which the future pattern of output is set down, but the essence of the matter is that resources are allocated according to some central view of objectives and opportunities built up through some organized consolidation of the information in the hands of the central and subordinate bodies.

In competitive systems, firms do what they like in pursuit of profit and a large part of economic analysis is devoted to discussing whether this will cause the right things to be produced in the right amounts. The price mechanism is supposed to do the trick: if too much of a good is produced, the price will sink below costs; if too little, it will remain above them; in either

event the profit motive, combined with free mobility and
competition, should bring the required adjustment. For the
flawless operation of this mechanism—subject to qualifications
about externalities, etc.—most economists put forward an institutional blueprint, perfect competition, while acknowledging
with regret that scale economics may make it impossible to
secure its full realization in practice. Now I have maintained, in
Chapters 1 and 2, that perfect competition, even if realizable,
could never do what is claimed of it.[1] The essence of the matter
can be put quite briefly, but there is no room here for the full
supporting argument. Under perfect competition, it would be
quite impossible for any firm to know how much of a good to
produce. According to the usual story, entrepreneurs are guided
by prices; each of them sets an output that equates the price of
the good he sells to its marginal cost. Now it is clear that current
prices cannot be the appropriate signals; they reflect the appropriateness of past output decisions but are not directly relevant
to decisions about what to produce for the future. Presumably,
therefore, firms are supposed to equate marginal costs to future
prices. But how then is a producer able to predict future prices,
depending as they do both on the demands of consumers and on
the supply plans of all his competitors? This the textbooks do
not tell us; the most we are likely to be told is that producers are
assumed to know what the relevant future prices are. But a little
reflection suffices to show that even this is not enough to ensure
that firms know what to do and that, as a result of their actions,
the equilibrium configuration of output is obtained. For let us
imagine that the system is out of equilibrium but that the true
equilibrium prices are somehow announced to all producers as
from on high. How would the possession of this information
enable the individual firm to know which goods to produce, or
cease producing, and in what quantities? If the future price of a
good were known to be greater than the current cost of making
it, then a profit opportunity may be said to exist; but if there is
an unlimited number of firms equally able and ready to respond
to the opportunity no individual firm will know whether to do

---

[1] The same matter is dealt with, though less fully, in my article 'Equilibrium,
Expectations and Information', *Economic Journal*, Vol. LXIX (1959), pp.
223-37.

so. A profit opportunity which is available equally for everyone is in fact available to no one at all.

My own view, therefore, is that there would be no tendency under conditions of perfect competition for the equilibrium associated with it ever to be attained. My fear is that the brief argument just provided will not persuade anyone who has not already accepted this view now to accept it. In any case a large number of economists—perhaps even an increasing number—continue to maintain (even although they are unable to prove) that perfect competition would produce the outputs and prices associated with its so-called equilibrium position. But it is particularly interesting to note that the founding fathers of the doctrine—or at least Walras and Edgeworth—had their doubts; they were aware of the informational deficiencies of perfect competition and sought to offer some remedy. Both suggested hypothetical systems of recontracting designed to ensure that the plans of producers and consumers were welded into a consistent set. Offers to supply a particular good were made, it will be recalled, first on a provisional basis, and did not become firm commitments until, after repeated revisions, plans to buy were seen to be consistent with plans to produce and sell. We shall consider later the way in which these proposals prefigure the organized dialogues of indicative planning. The question now before us is whether such a network of forward contracts, quite apart from administrative cost and complexity, does in fact provide a theoretical answer to the problem of co-ordination that the price mechanism, in perfect competition, cannot by itself resolve. I maintain that it does not. The obstacle to creating a complete and consistent network of contracts, in the last analysis, is simply the imperfection of our knowledge. Consumers do not wish to contract for their future purchases because they cannot foretell what their future needs and opportunities will be; and producers do not generally wish to commit themselves to forward purchases of inputs because they cannot predict the productive possibilities that will be open to them. By supposing that the network of contracts could ever be complete and closed, we assume away that essential imperfection of knowledge with which economic organization has somehow to cope.

How competitive systems work

But where do we go from here? I have rejected the traditional model of the working of a decentralized economic system, perfect competition; the introduction of a complementary apparatus of forward contracts, I have further argued, merely evades the problems created by the imperfection of knowledge. But free enterprise systems, as even their keenest critics would admit, do in fact work, at least imperfectly; central planning might work better, but one could not maintain that we have chaos without it. Let us therefore endeavour to set out how the market system does work, for until this is clear we are not likely to be able to judge how far, and in what ways, central planning can usefully supplement or replace it.

If we are to explain how the economic world goes round—at least, the capitalist world—we have, I believe, to attend to three circumstances. First, there takes place within it a great deal of what, for want of a better term, I shall call piecemeal planning. Secondly, much reliance is put on the fact that aggregates are often more predictable than are, on average, their several components. And, thirdly, there have evolved market structures and codes of business behaviour which facilitate foresight and thereby permit enterprise planning. We shall now deal with each of these circumstances in turn.

(a) *Piecemeal Planning*

Walras taught us, in his general equilibrium analysis, that all economic activities are interdependent; but although this inter-dependence is universal, some activities are more interdependent than others. Consider the relationship between intermediate and final output. General-purpose inputs, such as steel and fork-lift trucks, will normally be bought on a market; the individual user will not choose to place contracts much in advance of his future requirements, and the individual seller will hope to secure some stability and predictability in the demand for his output by having a number of different accounts on his books. But in the case of specific-purpose inputs bought by only one firm or very few firms, other arrangements will generally prevail. Piecemeal planning will generally be the best means of dealing with close complementarity, both quantitative and qualitative, between output plans. It has to secure quantitative co-ordination, in the sense of making the rate of output of a final good appropriate to the rate of output of the required inputs; thus refining capacity has to be in balance with crude oil supplies. It has also to secure qualitative co-ordination where, for example, the development of a nylon polymer has to be hand in hand with the development of the processes used to spin it. Joint production planning and joint product development can be secured by a variety of techniques ranging from loose inter-company understanding to full vertical integration. A highly informal but highly effective form of piecemeal planning is conducted by Marks and Spencer. Although it concerns itself with the product development, the output, and even the investment decisions of its suppliers, yet its relationship with them is based merely on mutual trust and goodwill. The operations of a major international oil company provide an example of extensive and highly developed piecemeal planning through vertical integration. The plain fact is that so-called market economies do not rely entirely on market mechanisms; their structure permits, and has in fact been adapted to permit, a great deal of piecemeal planning. It is in terms of the need for such planning, rather than in terms of conventional scale economies, that much industrial morphology has to be interpreted.

(b) *The Law of Large Numbers*

But, if planning is all around us, it is far from complete. A great bulk of output, final and intermediate, is, as we say, for the market. Producers of intermediate goods commonly deal with a large number of buyers and the producers of consumer goods almost always do. In such cases, refuge from uncertainty is sought not in planning but in what has been called the unstrict law of large numbers. Brick manufacturers do not try to forecast the demand for bricks by adding up the several demands that the many builders and contractors with which they deal say are likely to put upon them. They study the trends in aggregates. They rely on the cancelling out of random elements to which the demands of individual customers are subject. Of course, we should not rush to the conclusion that for a firm of a given size the larger the number of its independent accounts the better. In the first place, the gain from grouping does not rise in proportion to the number of accounts grouped but—if sampling theory can be followed in this context—to the square root of their number. And, secondly, the firm's forecasts will generally be part synthetic, part analytical; they will supplement the projection of aggregate trends with particular information about the likely demands of particular customers or groups of customers and the larger the number of accounts the greater the cost of acquiring this information is likely to be.

In her critique of French planning Mrs. Lutz[1] puts great stress on this unstrict law of large numbers and refers to a German school of writers who make it the corner-stone of their account of how foresight and co-ordination is made possible in market economies. Certainly the principle seems to me important, but I do not think that it can bear the full weight of explanation. It is certainly true that the aggregation of the component demands for a particular product makes for predictability, but if this is to result in predictability in the demand for the output of particular firms, then the structure of the markets in which they are operating has to be appropriate. Here, it seems to me, is the third essential requirement for the working of decentralized systems; market structure and business behaviour must be such as permit firms to plan current output and investment decisions; they must facilitate enterprise planning. Perhaps this too, like much else I have said, may seem obvious and certainly ought to be. In fact, however, the point is almost completely ignored in almost all the literature, and I have had very little success in drawing attention to it.

(c) *Market Structures*

Let us suppose that we are asked not to explain how markets work but to design them. We may imagine that we have been invited to advise the government of an East European economy, currently organized by detailed central direction, on how best to introduce some decentralized decision-taking. Let us suppose

[1] Vera Lutz, *Central Planning for the Market Economy* (London, 1969).

that we are concerned with an industry (producing a homogeneous commodity) in which enterprises are to be given freedom of decision with respect both to current output and to investment. We are asked to design an appropriate market structure and prescribe the rules to which the enterprises are to be made subject. Those who really believed in this theory of perfect competition might recommend along these lines: set up as many independent enterprises as the relevant scale economies permit, give them equal access to finance, instruct them to seek maximum profits, and forbid them to limit the competition in any way. If this recipe were adopted, its proponents would urge, we would get as close as possible to the ideal self-regulating system with prices constantly varying to ensure the optimal adjustment of supply to demand. Were these recommendations to be accepted, then the enterprise managers would, I fear, be in despair. Even if they could form a capable estimate of the likely total demand for the product, they would have no idea how much they each and individually ought to plan to produce. We must hope, therefore, that these recommendations would be rejected.

But what then ought we to recommend? We could of course suggest that the authorities divide up the market between the several enterprises according to geographical area or some stated percentage share. This, at any rate, unlike the previous recommendation, could give to each enterprise something they could usefully try to predict; and the success or failure of their individual predictions would be made manifest. But most of the merits of decentralization would be lost; neither costs nor profits would be subject to competitive pressures, and it would be absurd not to arrange for the accidental surpluses that might develop in some part of the market to be used to offset scarcities in others. Let us then consider a further set of recommendations which, for ease of exposition, I shall put in somewhat simple-minded form. Let the price of the homogeneous commodity be fixed on the basis of some estimate of normal unit costs. Allot customers between the several enterprises in such a way that each of them has a regular supplier from whom he is normally obliged to buy. But lay it down that, should a buyer find his regular supplier unable to meet his full demands, then he will be transferred, in some pre-arranged fashion, to an enterprise with additional supply available.

How would these arrangements work? First we note that each supplier has now something he can aim at. His first job is to predict the demand from his regular clientele and plan to meet it. He can do this without the fear that, if other suppliers over-produce, he will no longer have a profitable outlet for his goods. Secondly, we should note that each supplier has a strong incentive not to underestimate his regular demand, for, if he does so, he will lose custom on a quasi-permanent basis to those who have the capacity to meet demands in excess of those from their regular customers. Thirdly, suppliers have an incentive not to overestimate demand, for, if they do so, they themselves will bear the losses occasioned by excess capacity. And finally, suppliers have an incentive to consider whether their rivals are likely to have underestimated demand, for, if this is so, there is an opportunity to wrest custom from them.

A market of this type, it seems to me, would have clear advantages over the perfectly competitive, flexible-price type of market that often represents the textbook ideal. Not only does it facilitate foresight; it ensures that errors of forecasting are borne by those who make them. In a flexible-price system, the sins of the few may be borne by the many; for over-investment, by causing a collapse of prices, will penalize all suppliers.

It is not difficult to discern the strong family resemblance between these recommended arrangements and competitive markets that actually exist in the manufacturing sector of free enterprise economies. These markets, to use the Hicksian terminology, are normally of the fix-price rather than the flexible-price variety; they are so usually because of oligopoly, sometimes because of inter-firm agreements, sometimes because of governmental controls. Firms do generally have regular clienteles, either because of transport costs, or product differentiation, or goodwill, or for some other reason. If they cannot meet the demand of the regular customers, they lose them. If they install too much capacity, they suffer loss, but prices do not normally fall to the level of marginal costs. Of course, there is the danger, which engages the exclusive and almost obsessional attention of many economists, that prices may be kept too high in relation to unit costs. Inter-firm rivalry or the threat of entry may, and I am inclined to believe usually do, prevent this; but, if they do not, the public authorities can intervene.

But let us return to our hypothetical East European economy. The task given to us was that of designing a framework for workable competition in the supply of a homogeneous product. But it is natural to ask whether, in this context, the gains from decentralized decision-taking are really worth while. It is true that we have introduced competition in forecasting, but it is arguable that a central bureau, by collating all the available evidence, might make a better forecast than could any individual enterprise. Might it not therefore be better to maintain centralized control, fix an industry output target, and give to the enterprises individual output targets derived from it? After all, it would still be possible to stimulate competition in cost reduction simply by fixing a uniform price and rewarding enterprises with the highest profits.

It seems to me that, so long as we take the case of a homogeneous product, or near-homogeneous product, the argument for decentralization is not strong. I for one would not wish to denationalize the coal-mines. It is when we turn to the general case of product differentiation and, more especially, of continuous product development, that the merits of competition of decentralized forecasting and investment decisions come into their own. So long as there is uncertainty merely with regard to the future total demand for a homogeneous product then it seems not unreasonable to pool all the individual opinions and distil some kind of average view therefrom; central planning, in other words, may be appropriate. But, where there exists uncertainty in its more general form, I can see little merit and much danger in endeavouring to agree or impose some central view about what lines of development, in product or process, ought to be pursued or about what product varieties will best meet the needs of consumers. In considering how we might design a workable market structure, I took the case of a homogeneous product, for it is in that context that the forecasting problem, created by the interdependence of individual producers' plans, presents itself most sharply. I wished to show

how it was possible to reconcile competition with the requirements for informed output planning even in this extreme case.
But our imaginary East European reformers might have been
better advised not to select homogeneous product markets as the
first place in which to introduce decentralized decision-taking.
For not only do product differentiation and development make
it more important to have competition, they make it possible to
dispense with the special hypothetical arrangements according
to which customers were allotted among suppliers. Provided
that we have short-run price stability as indeed we generally do
in manufacturing business, then firms will generally be able to
proceed from estimates of the total demand for their product
class to estimates of the sales which they themselves will be able
to make; but they will be obliged to recognize, in this general
case, that they may lose custom not only if they are unable to
supply but also if they cannot offer a price–product combination
as attractive as that offered by rivals.[1]

I set out, in this section of the paper, to say something about
the way in which market economies cope with the problem of
allocating resources under conditions of imperfect competition.
Of course, this summary account is quite inadequate; nothing
has been said, for example, about prices, but then their role in
promoting efficient allocation is well known. My aim was to
make these points: first, that critical interdependencies both
quantitative and qualitative are dealt with by private, piecemeal
planning; secondly, that in the absence of such deliberate co-
ordination enterprise planning and prediction depends very
largely on what has been called the unstrict law of large
numbers; thirdly, that an essential condition for this prediction
and planning is the existence of market structures and codes of
business behaviour different from those to which economists
usually give their warmest approval; and, fourthly, that the
merits of competition are strongest where products are hetero-
geneous and subject to constant development.

---

[1] How strange it is that economists have often set up, as a paradigm of
decentralized decision-taking, the hypothetical system—perfect competition—
in which not only the workability but also the advantages of decentralization
would be most in doubt.

INDICATIVE PLANNING

It is perfectly apparent, from the preceding discussion, that planning and competition are in one sense compatible; they can and do coexist peaceably, on the basis of a division of labour, within the same economy. But I maintained at the outset, nevertheless, that planning and competition were essentially alternative ways of organizing economic activity with different roles to play. For the remainder of this paper I wish to consider whether there is a kind of planning, indicative planning, which can be adopted in conjunction with competition to co-ordinate the same set of economic activities. Can indicative planning be used, not to replace decentralized decision-taking, but to make it better informed?

Indicative planning, as practised in France and Britain, is a procedure by which the government works out, after consultation with private industry, a set of more or less disaggregated output targets for the various commodity groups within the national product. These targets are said to be consistent and usually, in some sense or other, to be agreed; they do not correspond, however, to binding obligations imposed on individual firms. What can be said, in the light of the analysis of this paper, about the logic and utility of these arrangements?

In terms of our analogy of the treasure hunt, indicative planning would correspond to an arrangement which brought the men together to compose a map but then left them free to seek their fortunes as they each saw fit. On the face of it, this would not appear to be a very effective procedure, for the searchers would have neither much incentive to disclose their true opinions about the location of the treasure nor any clear indication, once the map was constructed, of what they each and individually ought to do. Nevertheless, this combination of centralized forecasting and decentralized decision has sometimes been represented as the peculiar virtue of the system; the copious French literature on the subject abounds with references to the way in which indicative planning illuminates but does not dictate enterprise decisions, often moving on to references about the reconciliation of order with freedom, harmony with diversity, organization with initiative, and so on and so

forth, in a manner that seems to belie the reputation of the
French language for clear and precise expression.

I recall reading that the origins of indicative planning might
be sought in the work of Quesnay, whose Tableau Économique
represents the earliest attempt in the field; be that as it may, it
seems to me that, in so far as the logic of the process is
concerned, Walras is the true forerunner. The process of
consultation by which a set of consistent interrelated output
plans is said to be built up under indicative planning reminds us
forcibly of the hypothetical system of recontracting, which both
Walras and Edgeworth said could, theoretically, provide a
direct route to equilibrium. If indicative planning is taken to be
such a process, then the objections made against the Walrasian
conception apply here also. Given that knowledge is imperfect,
admitting of both uncertainty and differences of opinion, then
individual expectations and plans cannot thus be knitted
together into one single consistent set. It may indeed be that the
remote origins of indicative planning, based as it is on a
supposed consensus, ought to be sought not in Walras, nor even
in Quesnay, but in Rousseau's influential if obscure notion of
the General Will.

But perhaps the analogy with recontracting should not be
pushed thus far. In the first place, the output targets in the plan
are not associated with contracts to buy or to deliver; they
represent some agreed expectation about what future outputs
are likely to be. Secondly, the disaggregation in the plan is not
carried through right down to output targets for each individual
firm's product lines; the figures relate to the outputs of branches
or industries usually large and and highly diversified. Given
these qualifications, the logic of indicative planning is less easily
assailed, if only, I fear, because it becomes more difficult to
discover what it is.

The target output figures set out in the plan are normally
obtained by a combination of two methods. One method is to
estimate the future rate of growth of the national product and
proceed from there to deduce the rate of growth of the component elements. Let us call this the analytical approach. The
other method is to call for estimated output figures from
industries; sometimes the firms or associations approached are

asked to give two estimates, one corresponding to what they themselves expect to happen, the other to what they think would be appropriate to the particular rate of growth of output postulated in the plan. Let us call this the synthetic approach.

On the face of it, one might not wish to put much faith in industry output figures reached by the analytic method, if only for the reason that this method proceeds from what is more predictable, namely aggregates, to what is less predictable, namely components thereof. In so far as the larger sub-aggregates are concerned, such as consumption, investment, government expenditure, and so on, the procedure makes some sense, if only because these totals are subject to governmental policy influence. But when we come to deduce industry outputs, far less the output of particular products, the approach becomes highly questionable. One reads not uncommonly that rates of output growth for individual products could be deduced from the rate of growth of national product, provided one could calculate the appropriate income elasticities of demand. If one conceives these in terms of the relationship between changes in aggregate output and particular outputs as manifested at the end of the planning period, *ex post*, then of course the statement is tautologous; but if income elasticities are taken to refer to the change in the demand for an individual product consequent on a certain change in national income other things being equal, then of course the statement is not true. Income changes represent only one of the many factors which influence the demand for particular products or product groups; they often appear more important than they are simply because we are working in terms of models which abstract from the elements of changing requirements, changing products, changing processes and costs, and so on.

But let us wave aside these difficulties and suppose that industry output forecasts are produced and that, for the sake of argument, each and every firm becomes convinced that they are correct. What then? I cannot believe that an accurate forecast of the output of, say, the mechanical engineering industry, in the classification features in the British Plan of 1965, would have been of much use to an individual manufacturer of compressors, or diesel engines, or cranes, or pumps. No doubt forecasts would be somewhat more useful if they were further disaggregated, but even a forecast for cranes as such would not much help the individual manufacturer to estimate the demand for his particular type of dockyard crane, or steelworks crane, or moving overhead crane, diesel-powered crane, small electric crane, and so on. And there is the further crucial point that, the more detailed the disaggregation, the less credible the analytic procedure becomes.

But forecasts, it may be said, are also synthetic. In general, moreover, they are agreed with the industries concerned. This latter claim, in my own experience, does not amount to much. The large firms or trade associations consulted are usually prepared to agree to a very wide range of industry output forecasts, not merely because they wish to please, but simply because the relationship between the likely size of the future output of their own product and the size of the so-called industry output figure is so very tenuous. The remedy then lies, it may be urged, in further and further disaggregation, down, if necessary, to the level of the outputs of each individual firm. But here we go out by the door through which we came. If indicative planning is taken to mean the knitting together of each and every output plan, then it does indeed come close to the Walrasian conception of a complete network of forward contracts. It presumes a consensus that simply does not exist, for no amount of organized dialogue, it seems to me, can hope to weld the expectations of each and every entrepreneur into a consistent plan.

If this analysis is correct, then there exists no coherent logical basis even in a closed economy for indicative planning; whether the process yields indirect benefits, such as creating confidence and inducing managements to look ahead, is a matter I do not propose to discuss. My own view is that the government should not attempt to set detailed output targets in the manner of the French and British plans, but there is good reason why it should endeavour to estimate the growth of total output and to influence the way in which it divides between investment, exports, government expenditure, and the like. And I believe that the publication of its opinions and intentions on these matters will be of some use to some firms. It is evident, moreover, that governments will be much concerned with piecemeal planning; they will engage in it directly within the public sector or in partnership with the private sector and they may wish to supervise or even to stimulate the arrangements made by private firms. For many it seems natural that all the islands of piecemeal planning should gradually come together, that the sea of market relations should recede and that which was an archipelago become a continent. I believe that this is a mistaken view. My argument has been that there are subsets of economic activities so rigidly related that it is desirable to plan their co-ordination on the basis of some consensus of expectation and belief. Equally, there are wider areas within which the interdependence of individual activities is much looser; decentralized decision-taking, co-ordinated through the market, is here appropriate. Rather than endeavour to impose a consensus, it is better to let individual decisions be taken on the basis of a variety of opinions on what an uncertain future may hold in store.

Index